CW00549287

Language People

And the whole earth was of one language and of one speech . . . And they said to one another, Go to, let us build us a city and a tower whose top may reach unto heaven; and let us make us a name, lest we be scattered abroad upon the face of the whole earth. And the Lord came down to see the city and the tower which the children of men builded. And the Lord said, Behold, the people is one, and they have all one language; and this they begin to do: and now nothing will be restrained from them which they have imagined to do. Go to, let us go down, and there confound their language, that they may not understand one another's speech. So the Lord scattered them abroad from thence upon the face of all the earth: and they left off to build the city. Therefore is the name of it Babel; because the Lord did there confound the language of all the earth.

Genesis, XI.

And when the day of Pentecost was fully come, they were all with one accord in one place . . . And they were all filled with the Holy Ghost, and began to speak with other tongues . . . and they were all amazed and were in doubt, saying one to another, What meaneth this? But Peter . . . lifted up his voice and said unto them. Ye men of Judea, and all ye that dwell at Jerusalem, be this known unto you, and hearken to my words: For these are not drunken, as ye suppose, seeing it is but the third hour of the day. But this is that which was spoken by the prophet Joel: And it shall come to pass in the last days, saith God, I will pour out of my spirit upon all flesh: and your sons and your daughters shall prophesy, and your young men shall see visions and your old men shall dream dreams.

Acts of the Apostles, II.

Other titles recently published under the SRHE/OU Press imprint:

Michael Allen: *The Goals of Universities*
William Birch: *The Challenge to Higher Education*
Heather Eggins: *Restructuring Higher Education*
Colin Evans: *Language People*
Gunnar Handal and Per Lauvas: *Promoting Reflective Teaching*
Vivien Hodgson *et al*: *Beyond Distance Teaching, Towards Open Learning*
Peter Linklater: *Education and the World of Work*
Graeme Moodie: *Standards and Criteria in Higher Education*
John Pratt and Suzanne Silverman: *Responding to Constraint*
Marjorie E. Reeves: *The Crisis in Higher Education*
John T. E. Richardson: *Student Learning*
Derek Robbins: *The Rise of Independent Study*
Gordon Taylor *et al*: *Literacy by Degrees*
Alan Woodley *et al*: *Choosing to Learn*

Language People

The experience of teaching and learning Modern Languages in British Universities

Colin Evans

The Society for Research into Higher Education
& Open University Press

Open University Press
Open University Educational Enterprises Limited
12 Cofferidge Close
Stony Stratford
Milton Keynes MK11 1BY

and
242 Cherry Street
Philadelphia, PA 19106, USA

First Published 1988

British Library Cataloguing in Publication Data

Evans, Colin
Language people: the experience of teaching and learning modern languages in British universities.
1. Great Britain. Higher education institutions. Curriculum subjects. Modern languages
I. Title
418'.007'1141

ISBN 0-335-09501-1

Library of Congress Cataloging-in-Publication Data

Evans, Colin (Colin H.)
Language people.

Bibliography: p.
Includes index.
1. Languages, Modern – Study and teaching (Higher) – Great Britain. 2. Languages, Modern – Study and teaching (Higher) – Social aspects – Great Britain.
I. Title
PB38.G7E94 1988 440'.7'1141 88-12422
ISBN 0-335-09501-1

Typeset by Rowland Phototypesetting Limited
Bury St Edmunds, Suffolk
Printed in Great Britain by St Edmundsbury Press Limited
Bury St Edmunds, Suffolk

Contents

Part 2: Staff

Part 3: The Staff–Student Relation

Part 4: The Discipline

Acknowledgements

My main debt of gratitude is to my respondents, staff and students. Their vivid accounts of their experience and their precise articulation of their understanding of that experience constitute the best part of this book. I appreciated their trust and my greatest hope is that they should, as language people, feel adequately represented by *Language People*. I saw them and see them as co-workers in a continuous process of collaborative enquiry of which this book is a stage. I am particularly grateful to my colleagues in the French department at Cardiff. My absence during the academic year 1984/85 meant extra commitments for them which they undertook willingly. Colleagues at Salford and Southampton also accepted an investigative stranger into their midst and made me feel welcome.

I was fortunate in Cardiff to be able to discuss my work with some highly experienced sociologists and psychologists. I found no reluctance or condescension, only an enthusiastic wish to encourage and help. My sincere thanks to Martin Albrow, Mike Apter, Sara Delamont, David Fontana, John Liggett, Dave Owens. Tony Becher at Sussex and Liam Hudson at Brunel also offered much-needed support, both in personal communication and by showing in their own work that what I was trying to do was not completely impossible. Janet Mattinson and her colleagues at the Institute of Marital Studies read portions of the book and gave support, as did other friends and colleagues from different parts of the academic world: Peter Agulnik, Tony Callen, Cynthia Holme, Allen Martin, Nano McCaughan, Norman Schwenk, Barbara Seidlhofer. The Library Staff at Cardiff were most helpful. Intellectually, the book owes most, perhaps, to the group relations tradition and I owe most to the people who made that tradition meaningful for me in a higher education context through DUET, the Development of University English Teaching project. I am thinking particularly of John Broadbent and Barry Palmer. Barry Palmer read the entire manuscript and provided the perfect combination of overall encouragement and detailed criticism. The fact that he was doing the latter on his new word-processor does not detract from his generosity. Sabina Thompson had the job of processing and re-processing my whirling words. I appreciated her collaboration. Finally, to express fully my debt to my wife Carol would require another book: there is nothing in this one which has not been shared with her, though her main contribution has been to make sure I remember that there are more important things in life than writing books. To her and to my son Nicky who, in his own way, offers me the same reminder, I dedicate *Language People*.

I am grateful to Jossey-Bass and to William Perry for permission to reproduce the figures on pages 62 and 64.

The research was carried out with the help of a grant of £3,900 from the ESRC for which I was very grateful on practical grounds and also because it showed that it is possible, even in hard times, to get (modest) funding and support for cross-disciplinary, qualitative research like this.

Introduction

1 Why?

This book is an attempt to describe and understand a particular range of experience. As with many books, the initial motivation comes from a desire to clarify the author's experience. In school, I chose Arts rather than Science; at University, I chose French rather than English; as a postgraduate, I specialized in the Nineteenth century and eventually wrote a biography of Taine; in 1963, I applied for a post in a University French department and was appointed to the job I still have. The subject, the job, have not been my whole life, but they have been an important aspect of it and the wish to stand back and reflect is a wish to understand this aspect and its connection with the rest, a wish to see the pattern, vital parts of which are subject-choice and career.

My own experience is personal and specific, but aspects of it are shared by all those – pupils, students, teachers, academics – who, over the years, have made the same subject-choice, who are, in one way or another, 'language people'. So, while the book may start from curiosity about my own choices and my own experience, it is not an autobiography but rather an exploration of the lived experience of a group of people, of whom I am one: disparate people linked by this one factor – the choice of a particular (and peculiar) subject.

The belief which informs the book is that the effort to understand the experience of a group and to articulate it has value for the person making the effort, for the group itself and for those outside the group who wish to or are required to relate to it in some way. In this latter category come young people who are deciding which group to join, and also members of other groups who need to work with people from different disciplines in the larger groupings of Higher Education or the professions.

I have become aware that group-portraits like the one I am attempting are rare. Tony Becher, one of the few researchers to venture into the area, began his article 'Towards a definition of disciplinary cultures' (1981) by stating: 'A preliminary search of the literature yielded little in the way of directly useful precedent or precept for the study'. Burton Clark, in a contribution to the SRHE Leverhulme enquiry (Shattock, 1983) which usefully summarizes his major work on Higher Education (Clark, 1983b), claims that 'wise investigators . . .

are now off studying the separate cultures of the individual disciplines', since, he says, this is the way to understand higher education. I hope this is true, but I have yet to see the results of their investigations, in Britain at least.

My hope is that my attempt will stimulate others to describe the experience of different subjects – Mathematics, Geology, Physics – so that we may eventually have what might be called an ethnography of the disciplines. I would like to think that this book might contribute to reducing what Campbell (1969) calls the 'ethnocentrism of the disciplines'. 'Reductionism', as analysed by the contributors to Peacocke's book (1985), is a powerful force in British intellectual life and any effort which tends in the opposite direction, towards communication, synthesis or even, as Goodlad suggests, *celebration* (Peacocke, p. 161), is worth making. But I shall be satisfied if this book provides members of the discipline of modern languages – pupils, students, teachers, academics, administrators – with an opportunity to reflect on their own experience of the discipline and to develop an enhanced awareness of themselves as members of this particular group at this particular time of rapid change.

2 How?

> Never quantities, always shapes, forms and relations. (Bateson, *Mind and Nature*, 1979, p. 8)

The aim, then, is to describe and understand the experience of a particular group of people. What is the best way to achieve it?

As far as previous research is concerned, the answer seems to be that one devises a questionnaire and one administers it to as many members of the group as possible. One then uses statistical techniques in order to discover 'factors' which, when named ('integrative', 'instrumental'), can be used to describe the group. Gardner and Lambert (*Attitudes and Motivation in Second Language Learning*, 1972) describe as follows the technique they applied to school children:

> In conducting a factor analysis, the investigator first obtains the matrix of relationships among variables, i.e., the correlation matrix, and then performs a fixed set of operations on this matrix to produce a new matrix (the factor matrix) which contains as many rows (variables) as the correlation matrix, but fewer columns . . . In this book two different types of matrices are obtained, a centroid factor matrix and a principal axis factor matrix . . . Typically, these matrices are then subjected to one further arithmetical analysis known as a 'rotation' and the resulting matrix is referred to as a rotated factor matrix.

Naiman and his colleagues in *The Good Language Learner* (1976), used, in addition to questionnaires, achievement tests, cognitive style tests, personality tests, class-room observation and face-to-face interviews.

There are no studies specifically of modern language teachers, but authors like Gerstl and Hutton (1966), Evans (1967), Halsey and Trow (1971),

Lazarfeld (1977) all use the questionnaire method to study academics in general.

One feature of this quantitative method is that it requires large sums of money (though exactly how much is never specified). Even if I had not had doubts about its suitability for the objectives of my research and about my capacity to work in that way, the cost would have ruled out this methodology. Given my resources and my capacities, the answer to the question 'How?' has to be some form of qualitative method.

The dominance of the quantitative method has been questioned in the Social Sciences for many years. C. Wright Mills wrote *The Sociological Imagination* (1959) as an attack on 'abstract empiricism'. Parlett (1970) called the survey method 'a paradigm for plants not people'. Reinharz (1979) describes her apostasy. In France, the sociologist, Bertaux (1981) describes his discovery of the 'life history' approach. Liam Hudson, whose work was one of the triggers for this book, concludes *Frames of Mind* (1968) thus:

> In 1962 I was still subjecting boys to tests of the various psychological qualities and measuring their performance much as I might have measured feet or femora. Gradually this has changed. I have become more interested in the experiential life of individuals . . . (p. 90).

Even Naiman *et al.*, in the study referred to above, acknowledge that their fifteen minute interviews were more revealing than all their tests.

In the 1960s, authors like Becker (1961, 1968) developed ways of studying groups of people (students, in particular) through participant observation and, in general, ethnography as a method has achieved academic respectability through specific, illuminating studies like that of Delamont (1976) and, more importantly given the academic value-system, through theoretical and methodological statements like those of Spradley (1979, 1980), Hammersley and Atkinson (1983), Burgess (1984), Goetz and Le Comte (1984) and Woods (1986). Main-stream journals have devoted special issues to qualitative methods (e.g. *Sociology of Education*, 57, 4: October 1984) and, at the radical end of the spectrum, *Human Enquiry* (1981), edited by Reason and Rowan, makes a strong case for 'new paradigm research', 'action research', 'collaborative enquiry'. 'Educational researchers', says Goodlad, in a postscript to Peacocke (1985) 'are becoming aware of the danger (indeed futility) of "scientistic" accounts of education processes which miss vital factors in pursuit of some Holy Grail of "objectivity"' (p. 163).

In short, I do not feel that in the current Social Science climate, I have to defend qualitative methods, or even enter the epistemological debate (fascinating though this is and highly relevant to the integrative function of modern linguists in the academic world). I hope it will be enough to describe the actual methods I used in this enquiry.

The basic method is the interview, as described by Hammersley and Atkinson (1983) and as practised by Marris in his pioneering book *The Experience of Higher Education* (1964). I devised a schedule which I modified in the light of the early interviews. I covered all the questions in most cases, but the order was often determined by the respondent. Each of my interviews lasted between an hour and three hours and was recorded. I was conscious of doing 'action research', in the broad sense of a two-way teaching–learning process: I learned certain things but so did my informants, who appreciated the opportunity to think aloud and who often commented that this was a satisfying and infrequent experience; interviews in Universities are associated with testing, and interaction is characterized more by competitive turn-taking than by sympathetic, collaborative listening. Sanford (1982) quotes William Perry who carried out interview research at Harvard: 'At the end of his study . . . he asked the Harvard students . . . for their suggestions on how to improve education at the University. Almost all of them said "Have interviews like these".'

My situation was unusual, of course, in that, unlike Perry or Becker, I was also interviewing my peers: the average ethnographer is typically interviewing cocktail waitresses, deep-sea fishermen or business tycoons, people with whom he is not going to have a subsequent relationship.

Interviewing one's peers is not entirely unheard of, however. Jennifer Platt has written an article 'On interviewing one's peers' (1981) and, while demonstrating that all the orthodox accounts of interviews exclude situations where interviewer and interviewee are of equal status and are known to each other, she shows that peer interviews, though difficult, have advantages which outweigh the traditionally acknowledged disadvantages (difficulties of distancing oneself, of seeing one's own assumptions as strange, observer bias, etc.). In particular, one's peers do not 'provide raw data to be interpreted by someone else'; they 'provide objective information to be taken more or less at face value'. An informant is 'a distinct person with something unique to contribute, not just a randomly sampled and replaceable member of a crowd'. An African anthropologist, researching among his own people, had this to say, describing his 'insider' research:

> Because I was one of them, and not a 'foreign intruder', the fear and suspicion which always lurk in the minds of subjects and informants during social research in general were almost absent. They had confidence in me because they knew I could not 'sell them'. Many a time informants were met who admitted 'This is a thing we normally don't divulge to outsiders, but since it is you, we shall give you all the necessary help'. (Quoted in Burgess (1984))

I think this also describes my experience. My field-work was done not in a foreign field but in one which I have tilled for over twenty years. The result is certainly different from what an outsider would have discovered but not, I think, automatically less informative and true.

Apart from this peer aspect, my use of the semi-structured interview as a tool is quite orthodox. What is innovative is my use of the group and inter-group interview. The model for this is the Grubb Institute's work on overseas students, *Freedom to Study* (1978), but even the Grubb researchers did not actually bring different groups together. Indeed, there is no research I know of which looks at staff and students in their relatedness.

The reason for this aspect of the methodology is my awareness that it is not possible to understand a group solely in terms of individuals since groups are not aggregates of individuals. The inter-group work is an attempt to deal experientially with the complexities of the relatedness of groups and individuals. This book is not about some abstract entity called Modern Languages; it is about human beings, who can be grouped, or who group themselves, in a variety of identity-bestowing ways, one of which is by discipline. My wish is to do justice to the individuals *and* to the group, and this entails recognizing the fantasy elements which are the most crucial factor in groups, which exist through shared assumptions and values. The staff–student seminar and the gender-workshop were attempts to study these aspects by getting groups to explore their perceptions of themselves, their perceptions of other groups, and their perceptions of others' perceptions of them. Part Three describes this enquiry, but the whole book is influenced by this kind of thinking. As Sartre put it, memorably and pithily: 'Valéry is a petty bourgeois intellectual but not every petty bourgeois intellectual is Valéry' (1964). John Smith is a modern linguist, but not every modern linguist is John Smith. We have somehow to deal with the 'hierarchy of mediations' (Sartre, again) which link John Smith and modern languages, modern languages and the University, the University and society and we have to do this not statistically but dynamically, for the world does not pose for us.

In addition to the interviews and the inter-group workshops, I have obtained whatever statistics seemed relevant. I accept Parlett's (1970) admonition that 'there should be no pig-headed reaction against quantitative data' (p. 442). The Universities Statistical Record holds a wealth of information which is all the more valuable for not being selective.

The one general epistemological point I wish to make is about representativity. The numbers I worked with were relatively small (though quite large for this type of research). I interviewed almost fifty students and roughly the same number of staff. They came basically from three universities: Cardiff, Southampton and Salford, though I interviewed individuals from Cambridge, London and Sussex. There is clearly no question of a statistically representative sample. But such representativity is only relevant where simple decisions (such as voting) are involved. When the aim is to describe and understand a complex, shifting reality in some depth, when one is working with the sheer messiness of human reality, it has to be recognized that the apparently 'unrepresentative' individual is expressing something vital and that what is certain and verifiable is likely to be superficial and simplistic.

It may seem that I am labouring this point, but I have found that my modern language colleagues are the first to ask 'How *typical* is this?' although in their own work with literature or history they would never equate truth with the 'typical' in this way.

The problem of qualitative research is, it seems to me, a problem of writing. The respondents must be allowed to speak, since their words are what gives the book life and the power to convince. This is why I have taken the unusual step of giving each of my respondents a number, so that each quotation is clearly attributed to an individual. The chart in the Appendix enables the reader to discover the basic facts about each while protecting their anonymity.

If, on the whole, qualitative research is more readable than quantitative research it is because of this immediate access to the voices of real people and the authentic experience. Roizen and Jepson's *Degrees for Jobs*, (1985) enables us actually to hear employers saying what they are looking for in students. Whatever we make of it, we know that one employer at least *actually said that*.

But if the respondents speak all the time we simply hear a cacaphony (*Degrees for Jobs* doesn't always avoid this pit-fall). The reader needs some help towards polyphony. The *writer's* voice has to be heard and the experience has to be grounded in theory and concept. This balance of voices is the writer's problem and there are no off-the-shelf solutions.

It may be we need reception-theory to concern itself with social science as well as literary texts. I am sure that the use readers make of books, the assent they give to their conclusions, is only loosely connected with 'proof' (whereas the myth is that it is entirely connected) 'The roots of rationality are not themselves rational, but more a matter of intuitive commitment, of passion' (Hudson, 1968, p. 69). In other words, the notion that books about people can decribe a complex reality in such a way that all normal people will say 'Yes, that is how it is' is a pipe-dream. The truth is that, exactly as with literary texts, the meaning is made by the reader, who brings his or her own experience to the act of reading, so that the meaning and the usefulness is to be found neither in the text and the statistical tables nor in the reader, but in the meeting space between. That is where bells are rung – or not, as the case may be.

Part 1

Students

There are 13 196[1] students of modern languages in British Universities and I interviewed 50 of them. It is true that I have been working closely with Modern Languages students for twenty years and that I also interviewed 50 other university teachers who shared with me their knowledge and experience of undergraduates. Nevertheless, as I hope I made clear in the introduction, the validity of what I say does not depend on numbers but on my necessarily subjective efforts to understand the whole through close attention to individuals.

'The first part of the interview is about how you got into modern languages and the second part is about what it is like now you are in it'. This is how I prefaced the interviews, and this part of the book is organized in the same way. The first chapter is concerned with how students chose the subject, the second with their experience in it and the third is a reflection.

1

Choice

Devine, si tu peux, et choisis, si tu oses. (Corneille)

1 School

Berger has shown (1979) how peasant communities are characterized by very limited choice. But, for large numbers of children in urban environments, choice may also be an illusion. Ryrie and his colleagues, in their study of Scottish 13–14 year olds, (1979), state bluntly: '"Occupational choice" in any way that involves a variety of options or freedom of choice may in reality be available only to a certain proportion of young people' (p. 7).

However, the young people who figure in this book are an élite and a proportion of a proportion. Indeed, from the age of 13, their lives were punctuated by choices and by the exercise of responsibility as they picked (and chose) their way through the school system. Teachers and parents may have advised but Ryrie, after interviewing pupils, concluded that they 'felt the responsibility for the choosing to be largely their own' (p. 53).

To have experience of choice is one thing. To be articulate about that experience is another. I could have said, 'Please tell me about fundamental, existential choices you made between 12 and 16 and the way in which your adolescent search for identity and fear of emptiness was bound up with your institutional and societal involvement with the school system as well as with your growing need to detach yourself from your mother and father, while nevertheless remaining attached and while finding suitable role models and groups for potential socialization', but it might have had an undesirable effect on the subsequent interview. Reflection on life choices is not easy for any of us, and, as you might expect, the most insightful thoughts on subject choice come from Faculty who have had time to think about their lives: these thoughts are reported in Part 2.

Educational research seems to have very little insight to offer despite the fact that British schools demand earlier and more drastic choices than most countries. There is work on career choice (such as Ginzberg *et al.* 1951; Super 1980) but much of this is American and, although choosing a subject has obvious implications for careers, it is not the same thing, since career orientation is only one of the operating criteria.

I have already referred to the research of Ryrie and his colleagues in Scotland.

They use a sensible mix of quantitative and qualitative methods and are aware of the limitations of self-reporting from 13-year-olds – the tendency (for example) to underreport motives which are known to be frowned upon by teachers (such as choosing an option in order to be with your friends (p. 58)) and the tendency to rationalize ('It is one of the fallacies of some social research that it assumes that respondents have clear, conscious and logically consistent reasons for their attitudes, intentions or actions. Young people in particular frequently produce "reasons" to satisfy an interviewer when they have not in fact given the matter conscious and rational thought' (p. 93)).

Hurman (1978) used the productive technique of asking pupils to keep diaries while they were making their choices. Numerous extracts are given and make fascinating reading, particularly with regard to French where the 'escalator effect' (my phrase, not Hurman's) is demonstrated clearly. Children are reluctant to give up French and people discourage them from giving it up because the previous work would be 'wasted': 'I have put French down on my form because when I was in my middle school I did four years on this subject, and if I had droped this, it would of been a waste of time Ever learning it' (p. 93). This says something, I think, about the way the goals of foreign language learning are clearer than the goals of any other subjects. This may have a depressing or a stimulating effect (many students are excited because they see themselves near the ultimate goal of native fluency) but, either way, it is a major factor: pupils see the language learning process as a marathon in which those who collapse get no medals.

However, Hurman's research gets bogged down in detail and suffers badly from 'methodological inhibition'. There is a dearth of hypotheses, ideas which might link subject choice with personality and identity. Neither Ryrie nor Hurman has anything to say about choices at 16 plus.[2]

The results of this work are, then, fairly predictable but still worth stating:

1. Teachers are almost exclusively concerned with ability, which means ability to pass public examinations: 'It is mainly marks, to be honest. Often they (i.e., teachers) don't bother with career intentions' (quoted in Ryrie, p. 74).
2. There is a hierarchy of subjects, with the academic subjects at the top. The band 1 pupils are discouraged from taking practical or creative subjects (ibid., p. 47). In other words the question of fitting personality to subject or vice versa is obscured for band 1 pupils by the fact that only cognitive aspects of the personality are considered relevant.
3. Pupils are influenced by teachers' views and, in the case of very good pupils, may be the object of 'canvassing' or 'touting' (ibid., p. 77).
4. Pupils' criteria are: liking the subject; finding the subject useful for a job; being good at it (ibid., p. 54).

I am handicapped here by the fact that I have no first-hand interview material with school pupils (the nearest I have come to it is GCE oral examining and standardizing which is a very peculiar form of ethnography). However, there are advantages in talking to students and staff who have the benefit of hindsight and, in any case, considering the dearth of data and reflection on older pupils and on the specific choice of modern languages, what follows, however tentative and limited, represents an initial step towards understanding.

There are differences between the motivation of the various groups of students I studied (Salford, Cardiff, Southampton) but they do not seem sufficiently salient to focus on, so this section covers all my sample of students. I will deal with the differences when I discuss the process of choosing higher education courses.

For most of these students there was no real question of choice at 14 years. They were academically able and French was compulsory. The choice concerned a second language, and whether they took a second language or not depended on all sorts of variables, such as the school's option system. Many took up second languages much later.

The striking thing about them is the high proportion who had some kind of language background: they learned French in a primary school experiment; their parents or grandparents were not English-speaking (Hindi, Polish, Italian, Turkish . . .); their parents had lived and worked abroad; or else they had been brought up in an area of Britain which was bilingual (Wales) or where there was a marked dialect (Shropshire). It could even be a Spanish holiday beach: one student of Spanish (51) remembered being delighted at the age of 6 at discovering this foreign language; he went around happily saying 'gracias' to sunbathers. It is as if these individuals had unconsciously learned how to learn; they knew what language was, that is to say that it is a code and that there are many codes. This gave them a head-start over others who had to try to unlearn a deep-seated false notion that there is no code, that words and things are somehow the same or that there is only one code, their own.

However, I occasionally had the sense that for some individuals their family language background had been a mixed blessing. It was as if they had been deceived into thinking that modern languages were right for them simply because they spoke Polish at home or had been sent to the Lycée Français by parents who believed languages were an asset. Later, in their uncertainty about what to do, they opted for this subject where they did indeed have a head start, but that is exactly what it was; their hearts were never in it. In spite of having learned foreign languages they were not good linguists. They may have lacked what many students without this background have, a good ear, an ability to mimic, a good verbal memory, an outgoing personality, a readiness to take risks.

For most of the students (unlike the Scottish school-children) enjoyment was the key. In a school world which was highly instrumental, languages were 'fun', 'easy', 'less hard work'. I had vivid descriptions of language lessons involving the singing of songs and the playing of sketches, but the 'fun' was not limited to obviously playful activities; the amassing of vocabulary was 'fun', 'the old thrill of learning new words' (81). There was the sense of growing mastery; speaking French was 'romantic' (in the First Form!). While teachers were important (much more so than for the Scottish pupils), especially, but not exclusively, when young, attractive and enthusiastic, liking for the subject could survive mediocre teaching:

> She said 'Now, I am a big milk jug and I am going to pour all my knowledge into you little milk jugs'. She was horrific . . . I knew what was wrong, I liked French. I didn't like her. (70)

Visits to foreign parts during their teens played a role but usually, it seemed to me, they were a reinforcement rather than a decisive element in pupils' choices. However, my requests for an account of students 'best experience abroad' frequently elicited descriptions of idyllic teen-age visits to families which had entailed dramatic moves up the social scale into previously unknown luxury. No other school subject has this sesame effect.

The question of other subjects is complicated and is connected with the question of the *content*. You cannot *only* be a linguist: but what can you be? What goes with language-study?

All the students I interviewed were clear from early on in their school careers that they were not scientists.

> I was hopeless at science. (55, 66)

> My father wanted me to be a scientist: 'good jobs happen to scientists'. But I couldn't grasp the basic principles. (69)

> I hated biology. (60)

But they were frequently good at mathematics:

> My Maths were good, I could have gone on to Oxford or Cambridge to do Maths, but I just found it boring and stupid and not challenging. I found French more challenging. (61)

and frequently bad at English:

> English was always my third subject. I was thinking of doing Maths for A level. (95)

> O level English was my worst grade. (97)

> I am a novice at English literature. (93)

> English was a mistake. (84)

> I failed English Literature O level. (98)

Inevitably, by the mere fact of asking questions, recording answers and reporting them as I have done, the process of choice is made to appear more rational than it actually is; Ryrie's caveat quoted above is relevant to students as well. Therefore it is important to repeat what one student said as she was leaving the interview:

> I have been honest. People say 'I had a burning wish to do modern languages'. To me it was the rat race, the cover-up, just getting on with it . . . it was coming up through the system, it was a natural progression. (97)

Others made similar comments:

> There was nothing else I wanted to do. (88)
>
> I decided I wanted a degree to get on, and French seemed the one I might be best at . . . there wasn't an awful lot of things I could do. (52)

The 'irrational' aspect may be taken to include the effect on pupils' subject-choice of social pressures. In modern languages, this is manifested dramatically by the perceived feminine nature of the subject. Weinreich-Haste (1981) asked school-children to rate academic subjects on a masculine/feminine scale: French (jointly with English) was perceived as the most 'feminine' by school-girls, and schoolboys saw it as even more feminine than English (p. 221). While there are distinctions to be made between languages (Hurman discovered that in one school German was twice as popular with boys as with girls) nevertheless, in purely numerical terms, the proportion of boys studying languages decreases sharply throughout the educational process. Powell's report, *Boys, girls and languages in school* (1986), charts this process. He points out that it is analogous to the problem of girls abandoning science but much less well documented (and the object of much less concern). His statistical survey shows that there are nearly four girls to every one boy pursuing an Advanced level language course and even at 16+ (O level and CSE) the ratio is 3:2, rising to 3:1 in some languages (pp. 30, 34). He deplores this gender stereotyping and one can certainly agree that everyone loses out when choices are made not on the basis of aptitude and affinity but as a result of a superficial need to conform. However, this is to underestimate the power of young people's need to construct an identity precisely through conformity to group norms and stereotypes. To be good at French for a girl is to reinforce a feminine gender identity whereas for a boy it is to weaken a masculine gender identity (the same applies *mutatis mutandis* to girls in science). The very fact (noted by Powell, p. 74) that parents let girls study what they enjoy, while boys are required to think in terms of career, reinforces the feminine nature of the subject. The system is a self-perpetuating spiral, since, of course, those who are good at something gain approval from significant individuals or groups and thus get better at it. As Burstall (1974) says (p. 234). 'Achievement variables have a more powerfully determining effect on later behaviour than attitudinal variables'. In other words, nothing succeeds like success – so that girls get better, boys get worse and the feminization accelerates. The result is that to describe the experience of modern languages students is largely to describe the experience of young women and this is something that needs constantly to be kept in mind.

2 University

The next life choice, occurring at the somewhat riper age of 17 or 18, has to do with higher education. The 'best' of the sixth formers will spend a great deal of time and energy choosing a course in higher education and, in Britain, the range of choice is very wide indeed.

This may be the moment to make a point about *all* students, irrespective of discipline. They are the cream of the cream, the product of the finest sieve, the runners left after the last hurdle. Whatever else they are, they are the product of the cream-making, sieving, hurdle-jumping process. A discussion of this process would be out of place here, though this book, by looking at the successes of the system, may be seen as a contribution, from an unfamiliar angle, to the discussion of the sociology of the school (Young, 1972; Illich, 1973; Bourdieu and Passeron, 1979).

I think there would be general agreement that 'success' entails as a *sine qua non*:

ability to pass examinations, which in turn means:

a) cognitive abilities, logical thinking, and information-processing
b) diligence, tolerance of boredom, postponement of pleasure
c) respect for authority and institutional rules
d) acceptance of fragmentation (the breaking up of the day into disconnected 'periods' and the breaking up of knowledge into 'subjects', both in contrast to the primary school
e) acceptance of a split between 'academic' activities and practical/creative ones.

So, whatever the discipline, not only are the incapable and the incurious screened out, but the odds are also against undisciplined, imaginative, creative individuals. Higher education is saved a great deal of anguish in this way (as can be seen by the small number of individuals who save their dropping out for higher education) but we pay a price in terms of blandness and absence of challenge. What we are missing can be judged from the few mature age students, from certain foreign students, from accounts of the post-war ex-servicemen students, and also from students who were selected by the Oxbridge procedure which does not use A-levels and which lays more stress on creativity and originality, looking for potential rather than previous achievement. It is significant, though, that this system is being phased out in favour of A-levels. A senior academic at Cambridge informed me that, in his opinion, it produced 'zany' students.[3] In short, I am simply saying by way of introduction that students are more likely to be, in Parlett's (1970) terms, Sylbs (syllabus-bound) than Sylphs (syllabus-free). It is highly unlikely, say, that a student will have a complete indifference to examination results, when the whole process of his or her education, the whole 'collateral learning' (Dewey, 1974) or 'hidden curriculum' (Snyder, 1971) will have been about the importance of examination results. When we discuss modern language students or a subset of modern language students, we need to bear this wider social and educational context in mind.

What then determines sixth-formers' choices of subjects, courses, institutions? Everyone in higher education would dearly like to know, because students are the currency by which these institutions are judged rich or poor: the mean A-level scores, the ratio of applications to places are the key statistics, the equivalents of the FT index.

As with all life choices, it's a messy business. Ideally, students would be fully aware of their needs, aspirations or capacities, they would have access to a complete (computerized) list of courses and combinations of courses for all institutions, including information on the quality of the library, the quality of the staff, their qualifications, personalities, ages, value-systems, teaching styles, research interests . . . they would have access to back-stage or under-stage information, would know that Professor Bonaventure, with whom they would like to study, is thinking of accepting a Chair in Melbourne, or is alcoholic (or both), that, of the forty fascinating options listed, only five are available 'for reasons beyond our control', that the University of Y has just appointed a young woman who is an amazingly inspiring teacher . . . Reality is different.

Students have very vague ideas about what their aspirations are, often have no idea of a career, for example; not only do they not know who they are, but in part they are going to University to find out. They may have clearer ideas about their capacities after their A level results, but clarity does not necessarily mean accuracy or appropriateness. There is no computerized list of courses and our incredible system means that students are studying prospectuses while also preparing for their A-level examinations. And of course the prospectuses are 'front-stage' material. Students frequently informed me of major misreadings of prospectuses; some had clearly been ignorant of courses which would have suited them. As for the quality of the staff, how could students make rational decisions? They make their visits and judge mainly on the criterion of friendliness. If they perceive the staff as being cold, supercilious and generally unwelcoming, they will ignore everything else and reject the place. Conversely, if the staff are perceived as being particularly friendly and interested (as is the case, for example, at Salford) in case of doubt they will treat this as the most important criterion.

> I went to X, on Open Day, and one of the lecturers said 'If you have any doubts about coming here, just don't come because there are plenty of people as good as you who will willingly take your place', so I ruled that out straightaway. (64)

> When I went to Y, I was very disappointed. I thought they thought students were way down on the list of priorities which really annoyed me. (60)

They will judge institutions on 'reputation' which is an euphemism for shared fantasy based on minimal and superannuated evidence, augmented by commercial guides and occasional Sunday supplement articles. 'Cambridge is actively dismissive of language skills; speaking French badly is fashionable there', I was told. The Professor of French swore to me that that was a slander and always had been.

And of course students are not solely concerned with academic matters. Like everyone else, they take into consideration where they are going to live for three or four years: one student I interviewed only considered institutions situated in places that had First Division football teams (66); another carefully balanced the wish to leave her home town with a wish not to be too far from her boyfriend (the relationship broke up three months after she started her course, but by then the die was cast); another turned down a place in Bradford because of the Yorkshire Ripper (the next day the police announced his capture but by then she had accepted a place elsewhere). North/South plays a big role: there were students in Southampton who would never have dreamed of journeying North, students in Salford who took one look at Cambridge and said 'not for me'. Others say 'not for me' without even taking one look, believing that Cardiff is black with coal (which it is not) or damper than most places (which it is) and Salford perched on the edge of the A6 (which it is) or hostile to Southerners (which it is not). There is nothing an institution can do about geographical site: it cannot transport itself to the banks of the Cam or to the Sussex coast, nor (though such an urge would be quixotic) away from those places. It cannot even do very much about the myths. It can do something about its courses, but the process of building a reputation is slow, and by the time it exists it may no longer be deserved.

To sum up, the process of choosing a University degree course is an exercise in decision-taking in the context of inadequate data. But, since most decision-taking in the real world is like this, it could be argued that this is the real educational value of the exercise and the privilege these young people have. The only way to become good at taking life decisions is to take life decisions. Learning to choose is a major part of the 'hidden curriculum'.

What happens, I think, is that students *eliminate* institutions on what might be called non-academic grounds (location etc.) but then *select* from what remains on a combination of academic and non-academic criteria. They choose a place but the course counts. Students frequently want to study a new language from scratch. They want (more and more) to combine two languages, or a language and another arts subject, or a language and a vocational subject. When they are still undecided (as they often are), they are attracted to courses which give them the possibility of making major changes of direction after their first year (the University of Wales has a three-subject Part One; at Cambridge it is possible to switch from one tripos to another). They are attracted by options; they are not at all concerned, as far as I can judge, by teaching methods, even less by Faculty research. They are concerned about how seriously language work, particularly oral work, is taken.

There is, however, one academic consideration which can override non-academic concerns and cause middle-class girls from Little Chalfont or Somerset to settle in Salford: this is the distinction between courses where to study languages means to study literature and courses where it does not. Other distinctions, Oxbridge/Redbrick/Plateglass will be important but the literature/language distinction is the one where they make a statement about a discipline and about their place in it. UGC data indicate that the discipline of Modern Languages is in fact unique in the way course-content can over-ride the reputation of institutions in the minds of students.

My initial sample of institutions and courses – 'non-literary' in Salford and the Cardiff BSc in European Community Studies (ECS), 'literary' in Southampton and the Cardiff BA – was, of course, based on this crucial distinction.

(a) The non-literary choice

The 'non-literary' students had decided in the sixth form that they were primarily linguists – the decision to take two languages being an indication of this – and were therefore qualified to apply for courses that required two A-level languages (all the Salford students had two languages, the few Cardiff BSc students who had only one at A level took a second language in their first year). The other A level subject was a make-weight and this seemed especially the case with English. Economics is much more frequent than with the 'literary' group. In addition one student did take Economic History and others mentioned that they would have taken Economics had it been available in their school. So already at A level there is a clear division between those who are Arts students and those who are something else. I have some data which bear out my impression that sixth formers are now combining languages more frequently with Social Science subjects than with English.[4] English is an important indicator. While the student who failed it at O level is unusual, the following are fairly typical:

> I was never very good at English. English literature was my worst subject. Literature doesn't interest me at all and I am not very good at expressing myself. I remember doing comprehension, you had to say what a poem meant. It completely passed me by. I would just guess and be wrong. (83)

These students are also likely to express a lack of interest in reading:

> I am not really interested in doing a lot of reading. (88)

> I don't read a lot, I can get the information I need from other sources. (98)

Others (who were likely to have taken English) say they enjoyed reading but objected to the way literature was taught. They may have been subjected to a pedantic line-by-line approach; they may have objected to a dogmatic method which left no space for independent thought and response, but the most common attitude is an objection to redefining as work an activity which was previously construed as pleasure or, more specifically, to analysing experience.

> I didn't like the literature side very much. I enjoyed reading, I didn't like being forced to read books. (86)

> English literature, we would go through it line by line, and that killed it dead. (96)

> Literature I enjoyed to A level, but I just didn't see there was much point in it. It is quite nice to read a book, but I couldn't see where it led to, it doesn't really help your general knowledge or your understanding of the world. You can read historical books to get the history, sociology and anthropology books to get cultural aspects. (87)

These students do see a use for literary texts – they are instruments for language improvement:

> I just picked up *L'Etranger* and *La Peste* to improve my French for essays. (83)

Both opted for non-literary courses because of a combination of disaffection with literary studies and a wish to do a course which was vocational. They saw the ECS course and the Salford course as being vocational in ways that traditional literary degrees were not: Salford, because it promised high-level skills in two, possibly three, languages; Cardiff, because vocational subjects like Law are involved. Students are not, it should be emphasized, concerned merely with avoiding unemployment: it obviously varies with the abilities of the student, but many of them are very ambitious and aspire to very senior, well-paid jobs:

> I am not doing languages for any motive which makes me want to look at language *per se*. I want to be able to speak and write other languages as a tool for my future career. I want to be able to look, with my qualifications as a graduate and my experience, for a very good job . . . one which will enable me to use the languages I have obtained and also a job which wouldn't be in the public service, but in a market which is fairly young. Which is initially fairly highly paid. I would also like to have a great degree of job satisfaction. A degree has value in terms of one's acceptance by other people and especially by one's employers, for future promotion. (98)

They can be quite scathing about Arts students

> I don't feel I belong with the arty-farty people. They are doing a degree for a degree's sake. I feel it should lead to something. (83)

In general these are students who are hard-nosed, ambitious, practical and down to earth:

> You've got to think about your career from the word go. I am course representative and it is because it will look good on my CV . . . There are people on my course who wouldn't go to East Germany because it might ruin their chances of getting a job in the diplomatic service. (97)

They want courses that will give them language skills; but a language school, however effective, will not give them what they want, which is status (the same thing applies to business schools). They see the distinction between training and education clearly, but the education part is often (but not always) perceived instrumentally rather than in terms of personal growth:

> Oxbridge was the thing. But I said this was not for me. No way. I said I don't want to do a straight French/German degree. I wanted something which would help me get a job afterwards. Something slightly more vocational. On the other hand I didn't want to do the straight business studies-management. I wanted something which combined the two things. (82)

There is a basic distinction to be made between those students who continue to study school subjects in higher education and those who make some kind of a break. While 'Physics' in school is not 'Physics' in University, nevertheless the word represents a real continuity: 'Physics' can stand for all those subjects which can only be pursued in higher education if they have been studied at A level. At the other end of the continuum is Philosophy; the student who chooses to do Philosophy is taking a leap. In between, are all the subjects which may have been studied at school, but which are usually started from scratch – Economics, Sociology, Psychology, and the vocational subjects like Law. My hypothesis is that readiness to branch out into new terrain as evidenced by choice of higher education subject indicates something about the personality of students: one would guess that the student choosing to study Philosophy would be more curious and independent than the student choosing to go on with Physics – or French. This does not take account of students who are passionately interested in Physics and want more of it, nor of students who have found nothing to interest them and for whom something as indeterminate as Philosophy is a last resort. I am suggesting simply that students who are prepared to continue doing more or less what is familiar to them are likely to be fairly cautious, conservative people.

The 'non-literary' students have made a break. They have certainly opted for non-traditional institutions, institutions which were probably unknown to their teachers when they did their degrees (at that time they may have been Colleges of Advanced Technology (C.A.T.s)); they may well have had to make a stand and defend what may have seemed an aberrant choice. They know what they wanted and what they wanted was not traditional or orthodox. They are not committing themselves to new subjects to the extent that a student of Philosophy or Sociology is, but they know that they will have some involvement with disciplines they have not studied in school.

(b) The literary choice

The students choosing a traditional arts degree in a traditional university are not deviating in this way. The path is very well signposted, very well trodden and traditional A-level courses – the vast majority – are at the moment designed as preparation for this particular journey. This applies mainly to students doing single honours in one language or joint honours in two languages: it does not apply to the brave souls combining French and Mathematics or French and Philosophy – but these are a small minority. Most are playing safe:

> [when choosing to go on with French] I felt a bit cowardly really, because I felt, I have never done any politics or anything like that, but talking to people who last year took up economics and found it very hard [I thought] my background was language and literature, so at least if I had had a year of doing literature I would be better at it. (56)

> I thought it would be better to do something I knew I was good at, rather than take the risk of starting something completely different. I played safe. (66)

They are playing safe in one sense: they know that they will be studying in familiar ways. But in another sense, they are accepting more risk than the non-literary students in that they recognize that, while the degrees may be a bit more practical and vocational than other arts degrees, they are still not vocational in any real sense. On balance, I think it takes more confidence, in other words more tolerance of uncertainty and ambiguity, to do an arts degree than to do a non-traditional degree which, rightly or wrongly, is perceived as being more job-orientated.

There are two types of arts students. Some have no idea what they want to do in the future and are using the time to find out:

> I've no definite idea of what I want to do, that is one reason why I did University, because I didn't know what job I wanted to do. (66)

> When I think you have to make decisions about your career at the age of 15, I find it horrifying. French has provided me with a very happy stop-gap. (59)

(This student discovered in his final year that he wanted to be a doctor and has raised a large loan to pay for his studies:

> I was poking around until something clicked, and Medicine clicked. [I said] 'I'll hang around doing French, enjoying the language, reading and see what happens', and Medicine happened. (59))

Others however are more positively excluding all thought of career and vocation:

> I don't want to think about career prospects. That is not why I am here. I am here to get something from the experience. (68)

Particularly interesting are those students who have come to languages after a disastrous assay at a vocational course, usually Law. It seems as if families with a very strong professional involvement in law or accountancy bring considerable pressure to bear on their children (particularly their sons) to choose vocational subjects. I have no data on the experience of those who yield, but I met a number of modern languages students who first yielded, then rebelled. They tell us a lot, not only about the modern language students but about arts students in general who seem to be consciously postponing the time when their identity will be a professional identity:

> I took the advice of others, rather than following my own instincts that time. I went for something I was told was going to be practical rather than doing what I do now, not caring about the practical side of it and doing what I am interested in. I went up this blind alley for 2 years . . . The fact that it was law comes from the family background – my grandfather is a

> doctor, my father is an accountant. A professional background. It is a conflict between the two sides, and one side won out temporarily and now the other one is in control . . . Law is so vocational. You wouldn't go into languages for a career. I felt like an alien from outerspace in the law department. The way they teach it, it is geared to the vocation. The transition from getting a degree to becoming a solicitor is such a smooth one. You just have to put your name on a piece of paper and you are on your way. There is hardly any decision involved. (58)

Another student (a woman this time) who did a year's law as a result of parental pressure (her father had started a law degree but had not completed it) abandoned it because she felt intellectually not up to it and imaginatively thwarted:

> [in law] there was no scope for imagination or what you felt about things, or if you did, you had to back it up with so many cases and ideas from other people. I could never say 'this is what I think because . . .'. (52)

Finally her parents told her, 'Do what you enjoy'.

In summary then, these students are much more volatile and uncertain than the non-literary group. Their decision to do an arts degree is in many ways a postponement of a decision – a reluctance to answer the question 'who am I?' in any clear-cut way, or to commit themselves. I am reminded of an inter-group workshop I once ran for Austrian students of English at the University of Vienna: the method of working was that the participants were to form themselves into groups and each group would go off into one of the various rooms which were available. The whole of the first session took place in the corridor in front of all the open doors as these students put off committing themselves to one room and to one group.

2

Experience

This conflict cannot be solved by an either/or but only by a kind of two-way thinking: doing one thing while not losing sight of the other. (Jung, *The Undiscovered Self*, 1957)

Inevitably, one explores dissatisfactions, conflicts, tensions – because here students are doing their own questioning of the discipline, but it should be said at the outset that on the whole these students are not dissatisfied with their courses; they are not challenging the way their degrees are structured, threatening to leave unless things are changed. *Au contraire* and, some might say, *hélas!*

1 Courses

(a) Cardiff. European Community Studies

> This integrated programme of study leads to an honours degree in modern languages and social studies, containing a central core of study of the European Community. Students are able to study one or two modern European languages in the context of the contemporary political, economic, legal and social structure of Western Europe. (Prospectus)

The Cardiff BSc degree in European Community Studies, which began in 1979, can, like other non-traditional language degrees, be defined negatively as non-literary; but, positively, it is a unique development, distinct from degrees in 'Area Studies' and 'European Studies', in that it has a specific focus – the European Community – and in that it is totally inter-disciplinary: the elements of law, economics, sociology, geography, social administration, politics are taught by staff from those departments. While some social science courses are given for language students only, and while staff from the language departments offer politics or history options, in most cases students follow the same courses as non-linguists – economists, sociologists, etc.

Students take two languages and their time is in theory divided equally between language work and social science. This split is exactly what they experience and for them the integration which the degree aspires to is only imperfectly realized. They have the sense of 'doing two degrees', of being torn; they have classes in two buildings; they feel they do not have a definite 'base'. When asked if they see themselves as linguists or social scientists they almost always replied 'linguists'. The classes they find most useful are the translation classes: 'The emphasis is on the language side of the course'. 'I am a language student'. Some claim to be experts on the Community, or at least to 'know more about it than most people'; others have been ideologically influenced: 'I look on myself as a European'. Although one student said 'I look on myself as an economist', the majority have not been socialized into social science disciplines: they do not see themselves as sociologists or economists. They see what they have done in this area as 'superficial', a 'hodge-podge', a 'smattering', 'bits and bobs', 'nothing in depth' (while also liking the 'variety'), 'I've done Italian law and French law, but what do I know about them? In preference to one of us, they [employers] would take a specialist' (87).

Why is this? The obvious reason is the time taken by language study: they are only spending half the time that a social science student spends on social science and even this may be an exaggeration because many said that the language exercises meant that 'the reading gets dropped'. The extent to which the language departments have adapted their material and methods to these students varies. They feel less split when the language material is clearly 'relevant', but this is not always the case. As far as the social science departments are concerned, their material is rarely in a foreign language. In addition, because the course is, in a sense, problem- or theme-centred (the EEC), the course is also multi-disciplinary in social science terms since it uses a range of disciplinary approaches (law, economics, sociology) to understand the object of study – the Community. In comparison with the student whose approach is disciplinary – say, single honours in Economics – they are doubly split and fragmented. The theory is that the theme or problem, the Community, will provide the unity: the reality seems to be that it does, but only to a limited extent. When we come to look at all this systemically, we will see the difficulties of operating within one mode in a system dedicated to another, of being inter-disciplinary and integrative in a system which is based on strong disciplinary frames.

As far as their social science subjects are concerned, the students are not converts. They see the teaching as based largely on the transmission model with little opportunity or possibility of participation. 'It's straightforward stuff you are being taught; there are no "ifs" and "buts"' (82). What is required of them as far as they can see is regurgitation: 'the social science side is a question of them dictating notes in lectures and us regurgitating the notes in exams' (89).

In the language work, by contrast, they feel freer to experiment, less dependent on authority:

> The variety of the degree inhibits any expression of personal opinion, because you don't know enough. In the language exercises you can express personal opinions. In the social sciences they are looking for factual accuracy and understanding. If you took a stance they turn round and say you don't know enough, they would be able to dispute it. French is a bit hypothetical, you are allowed to express yourself. (87)

This student is showing awareness of a real advantage in working in a foreign language. A positive interpretation goes like this:

> When writing language essays we have been taught to stick our necks out . . . I feel that being taught how to write in favour of something that may be contrary to the lecturer's opinions is a very useful exercise, especially for female students who often fear treading on people's toes and feel ill-at-ease defending their own views in front of 'outsiders'. (87)

The foregrounding of the language may have this liberating effect: however, it may make the whole thing unreal:

> I can't get away from this idea that they are not looking for what you have got to say, they are looking for the language. (86)

On the one hand is the possibility of language being totally transparent: it just happens to be written in French or German; what counts is the social sciences content. On the other hand is the foregrounding of language – accuracy, style and so on. This tension is permanent and a real fear of students is that concern with content can distract from the job of enhancing their language skills:

> My language was better at A-level. Your energy goes into the new subject. You don't have any grammar lessons. Unless you are reading your grammar book every night, you forget. (81)

A striking feature of these students is their submissiveness or 'fear of treading on people's toes' which is coupled with the highly pragmatic attitude to their degree and a readiness to split work and pleasure. The criticisms I quoted earlier ('regurgitation') are genuine and refer to actual feelings of frustration, but not all students object to this aspect and the ones who do are ambivalent, being prepared to collude, to take the easy way.

I asked 'If you had an unusual idea, one which you hadn't seen in a book and which your lecturer hadn't mentioned, would you centre your essay on it, just mention it, or leave it out?' and 'If you disagreed with the lecturer's view would you say so in an essay?'.

The following answers are typical:

> They don't want that. (80)

> They wouldn't like you putting opposing views. (82)

> I would make it a subsidiary part [of the essay] in case I was wrong. I think I'd play safe. It is a lack of confidence in my own ideas. My idea could be totally different to the lecturer's. If I put down my idea and he is not too sure about that . . . but if it's an idea that has been put down in a book and that has been accepted, then he is prepared to accept that . . . it is not very often I come across my own ideas. (88)

> I try and think what the lecturer himself would like. I am just here to get a good mark . . . I know I have always followed X's way of thinking in my

> essay writing, but someone else in the class who writes very good essays doesn't follow X's way of thinking. You can see by the marks. My marks are higher, because I go along with X's way of thinking and X's opinions. I've never written against the grain of a lecturer. (86)

> If I had an idea like that and I based my essay on it and it turned out to be completely wrong that might be my degree up the spout. You've got to bear in mind all the time that you've got to get through the thing. You can't pursue it for your own interest. (82)

> I've chosen sociology type courses purely because I knew the exams were coming up and it would be easier to get good marks in those than in other types of subject. I am not really interested in these subjects and don't enjoy doing them, I just know it will be easier to get good marks in them . . . unfortunately . . . the exams determine what I do . . . (84)

> If I don't enjoy the subjects I am doing at University, I have always got time out of University to do what I want to do. For me, I am here to try to get the best degree mark I can. I study outside to pursue my true interests, well, my other interests. (86)

In other words, the work is tolerated; satisfaction comes from outside or may come later. 'Some things may be boring at the time but you realize you have got to get stuck in and it may be useful afterwards' (82).

In general, this group seems prepared for a life of well-paid, intermittently tedious work in a context where authority is accepted without much question. They will not demand that their work should be deeply satisfying but will get pleasure and emotional satisfaction from elsewhere (particularly from sport – I was struck by how frequently students came for the interview carrying sports equipment). They will make very clear boundaries between work and play. Their creativity is located outside their work. Indeed, one of the reasons for their rejection of literary study, as we saw, was the reluctance to bring a pleasure-object across the work-boundary.

(b) Salford. Modern Languages

BA in Modern Languages

> There has always been a firm conviction that languages, along with the history, politics, institutions and economics of the countries concerned and along with linguistics, could constitute a sphere of investigation which was just as stimulating and exciting – educational in the true sense of the word – as was the concentration upon literature. The members of staff in the department of modern languages remain convinced that this is still the case. (Prospectus)

The Salford students say the same kind of things as the Cardiff ECS students. There is the same demand for strict relevance:

> Stylistics is interesting but not useful. I'm not going to be called upon to do that. (90)

> We are expected to speak and write Castillano Spanish; being given translations from Peru or Mexico to do is not very useful. (98)

There is the same split between work and pleasure or emotional satisfaction:

> The emotional satisfaction is obtained from other sources than the University. (98)

> The course is not my life. (97)

There is the same frustration at the lack of opportunity for discussion

> The subjects we have been studying don't allow for discussion as such. It is thrown down your throats, and you accept it, and you don't answer back . . . The old school of lecturers don't want to be criticized. (93)

But the Salford course is different from the Cardiff one because the emphasis is much more singlemindedly on language: for students choosing a third language as an ancillary subject (and if one classes linguistics as language work) course time devoted to language study is nearly 100%. Even for students choosing all the literature options (and counting linguistics as non-language work, which is probably right) the figure is still 66%; and course-time is not real time: language work – translating and interpreting – tends to take up more than its allotted share. Salford students also have more class hours per week than the Cardiff students (Cardiff = maximum 12; Salford = 18 [21 where an *ab initio* language is concerned]).

Another difference concerns my data-gathering process (and illustrates the truth there is no 'out there' reality, distinct from the process by which it is perceived). In Cardiff, for practical reasons, I was able to interview a much larger proportion of students than in Salford. In Salford the students I saw were much less 'typical'. A member of staff had been asked by the Head of Department to contact students (and staff) on my behalf, so the process of selecting informants was largely out of my hands. The students he selected (and this in itself constitutes useful data about the department) were the most outspoken, with a high proportion of mature age students. One of these said of another, 'You've spoken to Roger.* "Really?" I said to myself, "if the department has any sense it won't sent Roger".' This same student summed up this aspect of the department when she said: 'I am notorious for giving my views . . . you can air your views here without putting your neck on the block' (94).

And 'Roger' himself told me: 'Salford has been receptive to change, people have been interested in what those of us who are awkward have to say'. (91) This explains the different tone of the comments in Salford. It could be that students in Cardiff were inhibited by my staff role, though I don't think so; I think it is more that in Salford I was indeed put in contact with some particularly

* I have, of course, changed all names

articulate ('awkward') informants. At another time the same could have happened in Cardiff.

The dissatisfaction here is less with 'bittiness' than with 'busyness'. The sheer amount of class time, together with the time spent on language exercises makes some of them feel that they are not being educated. A first year student taking the new degree in modern languages and marketing:

> I like the practicality of the course. But because we are given so much work we can't actually do anything else, like read books we want to read in the language, read up more about something . . . I don't read nearly enough. I thought coming to University would give me more time to read what I wanted to read. Read about Politics, read about Philosophy, Psychology. I am really interested but I don't have time to do it. I feel guilty if I am reading a book about Buddhism or whatever. I should be studying or doing a translation. (97)

Roger blames his fellow-students:

> God, the students. I was handicapped by having spent a year working. 85% of the students have come straight from mummy and daddy, and it is a great effort for them not to call the staff Sir and Miss. They want to be spoon-fed, they want to be taught. It is easy enough to think 'disengage brain when entering building' . . .

but also Universities in general:

> I would maintain that the role of the university is to encourage people in every way possible to think for themselves, but unfortunately that doesn't seem to be the case in any university I have come across, or any course. I travel and meet friends in many places. And I just don't find it. I have been applying for jobs with large companies . . . they're looking at a person, not looking at the grades or what you studied. They are looking for the global attitude. They interview hundreds of candidates to get one because at University level, you become so narrow. I got a job because I have managed to retain some overview. (91)

Another respondent blames staff and students for colluding in a 'spoon-feeding' approach:

> What the staff often don't realize is that students have to be told 'look you have to do this'; students are so silly at times. There is a definite feeling that one learns what one has to learn to get through the exam. I too have been lulled into this spoon-feeding business. It is very comforting . . . Students here are spoon-fed far too much. I feel strongly that if a student is confronted with that in the first year, then that is going to set the pattern for wanting to be spoon-fed for four years. An 18-year-old straight from school is used to being spoon-fed. But during the first 18 months they could be gradually weaned, and as well as being given a certain basis to work from, so they don't get frightened and lost, they would be encouraged and pushed towards developing their own faculties. (94)

Language-work is seen as being trivial:

> With so much emphasis on form and so little on content it was very boring, week after week we were translating stupid bloody articles from some newspaper or other of little importance. Lecturers still pick texts which have no relevance to anything really . . . they may be interesting linguistically, but they tend to give texts which are interesting enough so as to be unintelligible and therefore it is a greater challenge to translate it. It's a shame they couldn't do something which is pertinent . . . there is very little content relating to major issues in German History, World War 2 and so on. (91)

There is a hunger for an academic content and a sense that the language work evades all content:

> We were all doing translations and we all came to the conclusion that we had much too much translation work and there is no work you initiate yourself. You don't have to think, you have to apply certain rules to a text . . . I feel thwarted, not being given the opportunity to attempt to express myself in another language. We don't get into anything meaty. Even the subjects that are available . . . noone wants to discuss them in much detail . . . it is fairly easy to do translation. (98)

This student had conceptualized it like this:

> On the whole the course is a course of deconstruction rather than construction. It is taking the language apart rather than creatively doing something to build something. So instead of actively using a language and creating something out of that language, like an essay for example, you would be having a translation. (98)

What emerges from these interviews is that the emphasis on high-level language skills may satisfy most students most of the time, but that there is an underlying sense of missing out on something: they end up thinking that the practical language abilities they undoubtedly have may not be enough.

(c) Arts: Cardiff and Southampton

> The study of modern languages at University involves acquiring a high degree of proficiency in the spoken and written languages, a thorough command of the chosen aspects of the literature written in that language, and an understanding of the history, culture and society of the country concerned. (Prospectus, Southampton)

The BA modern languages courses in Cardiff and Southampton are basically similar both in terms of what they are and what they were. There are differences (more between particular departments than between the two institutions) but on the whole it is true to say that they have both moved quite quickly away from a situation where studying the language meant studying the whole of one national literature from the earliest times up to the present (or at least to 1914), with language work limited to a weekly translation from English into the language. Now language is taken less for granted (in Cardiff the oral examination, for example, counts as a whole paper in the final examination) and the notion of a canon has been almost eroded by the existence of options which enable students to study a whole range of topics – social science topics, historical topics, cinema, art, geography, linguistics, etc., while omitting aspects which would have been considered indispensable less than 10 years ago – and still are considered so in more traditional places.

I heard no complaints about relevance; having chosen an arts course these students see the lack of 'relevance' as a positive virtue or at least as something which they accept. Although the options can produce extremely varied schemes of study, I heard no complaints about 'bittiness', possibly because the disciplinary 'whole' is not perceived so clearly as it is for example in economics so that the 'bits' have a greater reality for the student and also because the pleasure principle is operating quite strongly. These students are literally pleasing themselves.

Like the outspoken Salford students they complain that they aren't able to discuss things enough:

> You don't really have much of a say, you just listen and if you don't agree, you don't have time in that hour to say something. You feel very frustrated that your ideas haven't come up to the fore. (57)

They too tend to blame fellow-students more than the staff. It is quite striking how similar they are to the other students in terms of compliance or passivity. Any notion that, while the non-literary students may be cautious and dependent (perhaps because of their uncertain grasp of the social science subjects), the arts students are challenging and autonomous is not borne out by the interviews. Here is a collection of responses to my questions about what they would do if they had an unusual idea about a text, including the specific question 'Can you be yourself in essays?':

> There are very few people who ever put anything of themselves into an essay. (61)

> Cautious. Its a case of once bitten, twice shy. In the past, I've had one or two ideas, they've been ripped to shreds. When I haven't used criticism for an essay, and talked off the top of my head with ideas that have come to me, they've been called superficial, naive, not relevant or whatever. (59)

> I wouldn't centre the essay on it. The essays we've had have been geared in a specific direction, and it is not open enough to have an original approach. I think there is an element of hedging your bets, of trying to see things from more than one viewpoint, to appreciate that on the one hand, you could see things from such and such a viewpoint, but on the other hand . . . I find essays very difficult, I'm not a genius when it comes to literature. (60)

Their basic position is pragmatic (almost cynical) conformity with the imagined position of the authority figure, specifically the one who will mark the examination papers:

> I don't want to be told to read five or six books from this list. I would concentrate on the subjects set. That is what we are being examined on, after all. (56)

> [I could put my own ideas but] what if he said it was rubbish? . . . I would think, 'I don't agree with him, but, since he is marking my papers, and since I ought to give myself all the chances I can, I will do what he says'. (52)

> To a certain extent you have got to say what they are expecting to hear. It is difficult to disagree with someone who has done a lot of research on the subject. Who am I to dare to differ? In the end I didn't disagree as much as I had planned to, I got cold feet . . . I did an essay on women's lib for [a female lecturer] and she wrote on it, 'I don't agree with your views at all', and I thought then, I wonder if that affected my mark. I didn't feel it did actually, but I sort of feel it might do. I should have been a bit more aware. A woman lecturer obviously has a very hard path to fight in college . . . I should have been aware of that. (54)

> It's all to do with passing exams, that's the trouble. You can't put the degree of originality in the essays that you would like. (63)

Critics can be shadow authorities enabling the deference to be distanced; giving a critic's views seems less compliant than giving the tutor's views:

> I do form my own opinions, but they are usually consolidated by what I read from other people, critics. I wouldn't be sure enough of myself. (56)

Many students simply recognize their limitations and are content to achieve some sort of understanding of the text or of the view of the text expressed by the tutor:

> With difficult authors it's as much as I can do to understand what they're getting at. (63)

But others are very sensitive and articulate about the problems inolved in the act of writing about the text for someone who knows a great deal about it, who has strong views that he or she is prepared to defend and who is in a position to give or withhold approval. Here are some extracts which give an idea of how students struggle with this problem:

> A lot of lecturers say, 'above all, you must say what you believe in' then they ask you questions and you say something, and you find yourself being shot down. So I am very dubious about it. (52)

> If you are in a tutorial and suggest some point the lecturer will say 'that is not strictly speaking so' and you try and argue the point, but instead of

> saying 'well, yes, there is that point of view' they try and convince you that you are wrong. It is not a nasty situation, but you feel as if every time you write something you just have to conform to the right point of view, otherwise what you write will be wrong. You are so worried that you get the right grade that you just conform. (68)

> I got the book in translation and that did help, except that perhaps it didn't, because it gave me ideas about the text which didn't agree with the lecturer's ideas about the text, and therefore it lost me marks. It made me see into it in more depth. For example, how the hero . . . I didn't realize that when I read it in French. We weren't asked to make our own analysis of it, we very much had our lecturer's view of it – a beautiful love story. I didn't see it like that . . . I didn't think my own views would go down too well. I don't know. He said that it moved him to tears at the end, but it didn't move me to tears at all. I took a very cynical view of it. (54)

> I find it so difficult. Someone asks you to give your opinion on a book. I feel so many different things about a book. It seems so stupid to do it in answering this sort of academic question about it. Intellectualizing about something fairly personal. Something you feel rather than think. In the second year, the two literature courses I did were 18th and 19th century. I loved the 19th century books. I liked all the texts, and my exam was the worst I've ever done and my marks the lowest I had. The 18th, I didn't particularly like the texts, but I did really well, because I found it easy to write about. I realized I wouldn't do well because it was subjective. It is very difficult to explain why you react in a certain way to a book when it is on an emotional level. There is no way you can prove it from the text. Most of the people I know read books like they read a text book. I find if I read a book with an essay in mind I end up disliking the book. I just can't do it that way. (64)

They seemed to glimpse that they are in a paradoxical double bind ('Be original and defer to all the critics': 'Speak with your own voice, and with everyone else's'). The most conscientious students find this intolerable:

> It is a false situation. At the beginning of term you get given a reading list . . . I don't know if the lecturers really think you will do it or if they are saying it to salve their own conscience. Because they can't honestly believe you will do it. (56)

> Some lecturers will give you a list of criticisms, say about 12 or 13 criticisms, and that is about a quarter of the course. If you read all those and another seven of another one, and that is just in one half of the year, and then at the end of that you've got to really know that book, because then you forget the book. And at the end of that you have got so much and you've got an exam, and you have got to condense all that work you have done into an hour of the exam. It just seems too much. Sometimes I think I shouldn't read any of the criticisms, rely on the lecturer's notes and keep

> reading the book, but you feel that you have to read all the critics, at least I do, especially when they recommend them. You think there must be something in them. And if you take notes of the writing as well, you have got a great thick wad of notes just to do a few essays or your finals at the end. (57)

> I don't think you ought to make a pretence of doing something you don't want to do. (59)

Another assumption one might make about these students is that, unlike the non-literary students who, as we saw, are in flight from literature, they are unequivocably arts students, avid readers with a great love of literature who just happen to be interested also in foreign literature. This is not the case.

'I have always read a lot', said a First Year student, promisingly, and went on: 'though not books. I've always read magazines – football and cricket magazines'. Here is the same student describing his reading of *Le Père Goriot*:

> I read 10 to 30 sides at a time, making notes of what was happening, to get the essence of the plot. It took me quite a while. I read it during the vacation. 250 pages of solid writing, small type as well, very little gaps. (66)

and a snap-shot of a First Year student taken by a Finalist:

> A first year girl came up to me and she said 'Do you have to read all your texts in French' and I said 'Yes' and she said 'Oh dear'. (59)

In fact students sometimes report that at 'A' level they would read texts in translation, learning quotations in French:

> 'La symphonie pastorale' I read it in English. I learned lots of quotes in French, but we didn't read it in French. We started off in French, and our teacher used to translate every page, but it would take an hour to translate a few pages. So she said bring along a translation. (55)

They do not usually admit to using translations themselves but affirm that other students often do this, especially when the text is difficult or when they are pressed for time.

Even Final Year students rarely claim to be able to read a foreign language book as easily as one in English. Their objections to reading or to literature are surprisingly similar to those of the Salford or Cardiff ECS students:

> What I got fed up with was pulling books apart in minute detail, what every single word means and what he is trying to say . . . I enjoy the reading but you can look into things in too much detail. One of the most important things about a book to me is my reaction to it, straightaway without having to spend hours of seminars and having to read critics and things like that. (61)

In short these students are not avid readers. They do it; they get better at it; but it is never a passion, the work/pleasure boundary is never eliminated.

> Because they [fellow students] have to do literature and a lot of them have found linguistics too complicated, they have trained themselves to like it. If you want to do well you have to. I do love reading books, but not when I have to write an essay. That's what I've hated, you have to read too many books, and everyone says this when they come here. (61)

> I don't read many books in French for pleasure . . . I've read a lot of French books and that's work, and if you are having time off, you want to differentiate between work and play and read English. (59)

> I find it very difficult to sit down for five hours and read a book straight off in any language. (68)

> I find it more pleasurable to get a magazine and read about something I am interested in in another language about a current issue. I can enjoy that. I can't enjoy getting hold of a great literary work and sitting down with it. That is my work. I couldn't do that outside my work . . . I can't sit down and read a book for ages, people talk about getting into your own world when you read, well I can't do that. I can think of books, well I can't actually off-hand, probably remember books I have really enjoyed, that have had an impact on me, but it wouldn't be many. (56)

Their literary tastes are simple:

> The novels I find easiest to read and get most out of are the ones which are coherent. We are doing Nerval at the moment, the least coherent book I have ever read. He was totally loopy when he wrote it anyway, so he isn't sure what he is writing, and I am not sure what I am reading. But Balzac is a really enjoyable story. (68)

and in no way canonical:

> I love things like film, the Songs, because that was about France to me, something uniquely French . . . Baudelaire is not about France in the same way. I am not really an intellectual in that sense of the word at all . . . I felt terribly out of place with the English crowd. Some of them did tend to be very intellectual, found it easy to see images and symbols that I don't see. (54)

The similarities between Salford/ECS students and these arts students are greater than the differences and what the latter share with the former is quite simply an attachment to the language. It would be difficult and probably fruitless to attempt to make comparisons between a degree of commitment (or lack of commitment) to literature on the one hand and to the social sciences or linguistic possibilities on the other. What does seem to be the case is that *all content, both literary and non-literary, is viewed as of secondary interest and importance. What counts is language*, specifically the kinds of language exercises they did in school, translations from the foreign language into English and *vice versa*: 'Prose translation' is the ark of the covenant and when I asked 'in which class situation do you learn most? which class do you enjoy most? which pieces of work do you find most useful and which most satisfying?' 'prose translation' was the most frequent answer I received, with translation from the language next:

> I like prose and the oral. Prose is one of the best ways of being able to express yourself properly. If you do well in that you can apply that in your essays. Prose is a most important exercise. (55)

> Being given something in English, and then being able to say that in a different language. I find it really satisfying to have a certain phrase and to be able to think how would I say that in French, or German, or Italian. Finding out what different words mean. (56)

They frequently compare the business of prose translation to the business of doing jig-saws or cross-word puzzles; 'juggling with a jig-saw' was one memorable phrase. But this was not a dismissive comment and they seem genuinely involved with this activity which is connected with the desire to acquire more language in the incremental sense that one acquires more books or stamps – 'the old thrill of learning new words', 'amassing vocabulary' and with a love of *difference* which is a basic characteristic of modern language students, as we will see when we discuss the relationship with the foreign country.

2 Cases

(a) 'The wrong path'?

The mode of exposition I have adopted and my decision not to highlight year differences among my informants (though the reader can discover these by consulting the appendix) results in a misleadingly static picture. Students change and develop quite dramatically over four years, although psychologists do not seem to have devoted anything like the attention to this developmental stage that they have devoted to earlier ones. To show this development adequately would require a longitudinal study, but it is possible to give a sense of it by looking more closely at individual students and specifically at their changing response to literary study.

Mary is a student from Salford who has just returned from her year abroad, a year which was not very satisfactory – ('a tedious factory job'); her father is a factory drill-setter, her mother a cleaner; she lives at home. At A-level she had an A in English and Bs in French and German. She was interviewed for Cambridge 'but it was not for me'. She was offered a place at a traditional northern University, but found it 'dingy, dull and unfriendly', and chose Salford which was near home, 'very friendly' and which seemed to promise a real skill and eventual employment:

> My strong point is literature. I discovered that. English or foreign, but especially English. It was my best subject but I thought 'so many English graduates are unemployed. You don't come out with a particular skill'.

She describes vividly the process of discovering herself and growing out of modern languages:

> I never thought I was a home bird until I went abroad. That year really brought it home to me that this [Britain] is where I want to be. Until then it was marvellous, the idea of going off to the big adventure . . . French and German were the things that interested me and I enjoyed them. I went abroad in the first year and it was marvellous to try the language out. It was all these ideas you have when you are 16, of being a interpreter . . . they were the exciting subjects, the different subjects, whereas Geography and History . . . I think it was the stupidity of youth or something. I've realized there is nothing special about being a linguist. I couldn't see I didn't have an aptitude for it, because it was overshadowed by this glamour, and as the veils have fallen away, I've seen through it, but for some people the veils will never go . . . I am not a linguist at all, I am someone who has taken the wrong path . . . I will stick it out and do my very best, but I feel I am totally underachieving. I feel I could do so much better in a different subject. (96)

She has opted for as much literary study in her final year as she can, but that is not a great deal (indeed, one of the disadvantages of a degree which is as coherently singleminded as Salford's is that it does not allow for changes and swings as considerable as this) and she finds it unsatisfactory because, for most of her fellow students, it is not a major interest:

> It's been a case of just swotting up for the exam. As long as you know the book for the exam that is all the literature course was intended for . . . most of the people I know saw literature as a chore . . . My only regret is that I was capable of a much higher degree somewhere else . . . I would have succeeded better in a more literary environment, I have a slight aptitude for language but not enough to get a First. (96)

The next student – Pat – did choose a single honours modern languages degree with a traditional amount of literature. At school, languages were her favourite subjects and she had the experience (which is quite frequent) of two radically different teachers – a young direct-method one for German and a much older grammar-based one for French. In literature the books were translated word-by-word. Her interest in language was to a considerable extent fascination with structure. She would, she said, like to learn a new language like Swahili but she would take the grammar book home and study it; 'It is like maths' (which she is good at). She is not good at speaking the language and regrets that the oral counts for 10% in the examination. 'It depends on your personality. If you are a quiet sort of person like me, you are done for'. She found herself 'gormless' in France. On a train in France, given the choice between reading a book and talking to her fellow passengers, she would read a book. The best thing about the year abroad was 'coming home'. She found people unfriendly and her spoken language inadequate. She is hyper-conscientious, works 12 hours a day, reads all the critics, but she has taken to reading her French books in English because of 'frustration' at not getting enough from it in French and from a sense of being overwhelmed by the volume of reading required. But what has happened to her is curious; having almost completed her degree she has developed an interest in literature. It started with an option in Medieval literature (which she read in translation). The group was very small, taught informally by a young woman lecturer who 'doesn't knock you down' who 'builds up your confidence'. But it led to an interest in English literature, and she is now very tentatively thinking about research: 'I enjoy studying a lot more, I wish you could carry on for ever'. She regrets not having done a degree in English and thinks she was mistaken to think that modern languages offered a significantly better chance of a job.

Mary and Pat are atypical, as is the student quoted earlier who is going in for Medicine and who summed up his experience like this:

> After four years, to have to say at the end, that I've been disappointed is a fairly major tragedy, but that's how I see it. It's been an experience, it has taught me to recognize what I don't want. It would be even more tragic if I went into teaching now, I will get so much more out of Medicine now I'm four years older. (59)

Most students do not end up feeling they have made a mistake but, over the four years of the degree, attitudes do change considerably and among some of the non-literary students there is a feeling that they have missed out in some way, that the initial rejection of literary study was somehow immature, the result of a lack of confidence. The student who says of her initial choice

> I didn't fancy the idea of an entire literature course. I thought I wouldn't be able to do it, I thought Salford would be a balance. (94)

now says 'I do like literature very much' and exclaims:

> You can get a degree in Spanish without reading a novel in Spanish in four years. I find that horrific! (94)

Students whose choice of course was highly instrumental now see things differently:

> Your attitude changes as you go through the course. When I first came we all had this image of being a brilliant interpreter at the end of the day, but when I came back from the year abroad I realized I had done it for the same reason I would have done any course, to improve myself, to educate myself. I know I have changed a hell of a lot since I started, so it must have done something. (95)

A postgraduate student:

> I read a lot of English after my degree. I read the whole of the *Jewel in the Crown*. I haven't read anything in French for a while. (70)

My third example – Joan, another arts student – is different. She is from a very modest family and an inward looking community. She telephoned me the evening before our interview to say how nervous she felt about it, but she was there at 9 in the morning and was exceptionally concerned about whether she had helped me enough. She is quiet, shy, withdrawn and not, it seems, good at languages. But, unlike the previous two examples, it is by no means clear what else she is. Here is her account of her year abroad:

> It did put me off at first. 'Doing French, I am going to have to go abroad for a year', I thought and I was really dreading it. But in the first year I thought 'I am going now'. My friend does French and we applied for the same place. She is a bit like me, she likes home. She was very worried about going, we helped each other. It was a lot better then. I don't think I could have gone on my own. That is how it started out, but I didn't waste it and I did really enjoy it. We cooked for ourselves, so we didn't have many French meals except for special occasions when we had wine and different courses and we quite liked it. I did enjoy it, but I am a home bird, I much prefer here. (55)

Her reply to the question 'What was your best experience abroad?' was 'our visit to the Sacré Coeur in Paris'. Compare this with the usual view of the 'typical' modern languages student as given by Mary:

> [ML students] are very independent . . . very outgoing, prepared to go anywhere and do anything, willing to throw everything up and go off. They want to see a lot, do a lot, they are very active people. (96)

or as exemplified by Helen:

> I am more outgoing than most, it has got to be lively, it has got to be fun. [If people are quiet] I will crack a joke . . . I can't stand timidness. There are some very shy lecturers as well. I don't choose their options. (95)

What about students like Joan or like this other example, Margaret?

> I find it quite difficult [using the language in the countries]. I am always being told I am not loud enough. But I can't help it, I just have a quiet voice. I don't want to shout out. I had the idea that you had to be quite extrovert in order to get on with languages . . . it will be much more difficult for me unless I become more confident. I can't say more if they [the confident ones] are going on all the time . . . I would like to say something and I can't, it's all about knowing words. It's embarrassing. (80)

Staff see students like Margaret and Joan as 'weak'. Either they made a mistake coming to University or it was a mistake to admit them, or both. Many would agree with this senior lecturer:

> We do get a certain kind of tail. Poor little souls who have somehow managed to get a B in their A-level. In some cases they do leave in their first year, some stay on and they are going to get thirds and this is sad. (25)

But I found myself developing an admiration for students like this who were confronting their weaknesses with considerable courage. It is the distinction, I suppose, between 'point reached' and 'distance covered'; for a shy young woman from a claustrophobic background to have lived abroad, however cautiously, may be a greater achievement than for a diplomat's son to have dealt with the complexity of the Italian banking system and with the strains of the Paris cocktail circuit. The latter may not have developed at all, while the former, by making the initial choice, gave herself the opportunity of growth.

This whole issue of subject choice, the search for identity and the growth of personality is complex. These two students are not 'typical' but I am not working with a single model, much less with a statistical one. I feel no contradiction in saying 'Most students feel such and such' and 'This totally exceptional individual is significant for our understanding'. These students are exceptional, but they enable us to see what we might have missed; many modern languages students, particularly the non-literary ones, are not good at speaking or even good with words; being good at speaking/listening is not the same thing as being good at reading/writing:

> I am not very good at expressing myself. (83)
>
> Language doesn't come easily to me. It is a real struggle. (99)
>
> I am not really all that good at speaking English. (85)

This aspect of subject choice is not often acknowledged, or it is confused with 'mistakes' like that of Mary's. It is summed up by this comment:

> I am not doing it because I am good at it, but because I am bad at it. (54)

(b) Other disciplines

The approach I am adopting could be called perspectivist. I am trying to see this subject through as many eyes as possible. One particularly illuminating perspective is that of students who are combining a language with another arts subject such as English or Philosophy. I have an example of each, but the important point has to be made that they are very unusual. For most modern languages students these other subjects are not appealing; the exceptional students for whom they are appealing throw some light on the majority of students for whom they are not.

Marco was brought up in the Lebanon. His father is a lawyer who studied modern languages and who is now First Secretary at the International Court of Justice at the Hague. Here is Marco's description of his own development as a reader – from Robin Hood to the novels of Claude Simon:

> I've never really thought about how I read a book . . . if I go back to when I was six, then I would read a bundle of books, the series by C S Lewis, Robin Hood, King Arthur, the Greek heroes. I read those books over and over again. All the tales I heard were based on a conception of nobility, of honesty, of truth and valour . . . So literature became not just a way of

> passing the time, but a means of getting experiences you might not otherwise have had. . . . By the age of 14, I had read every thriller on the shelf of the local bookshop, there was nothing more I could read or buy, and I gradually started to read deeper texts at school, I found that more stimulating. And this year I discovered the Nouveau Roman which I found fascinating because a year ago I would go into bookshops and pick up all the books for the Booker Prize, and sometimes spend the entire afternoon in the bookshop, reading the first chapters. And I would be totally dissatisfied. I didn't know what I wanted, but I felt they were so boring, so traditional, they weren't getting anywhere and then I discovered the Nouveau Roman, totally original, that was fantastic, because it's literature which is itself about different forms of literature. It is a literature which flatters the reader in that it has the reader help create the work, as it were, so it's a creative act . . . Even more so, with someone like Simon who is so poetic. I prefer reading him to other English writers at the moment.

He is also involved in various creative activities – film-making, drama, writing poetry in English and French.

I asked about how his experience of French compared with that of philosophy. Philosophy, he said, was a lot more difficult:

> In a Philosophy tutorial I am treading water, in a French one I am on a lilo . . . In Philosophy the lecturers I see have the attitude 'of course you don't have to come in to your seminars or lectures. We are adults. It is up to us how we conduct our studies'. It is not the same in the French department. The Philosophy department is more relaxed. It has a greater breadth of students, more mature students. In the Philosophy department you can't just come out with a phrase like 'of course existence precedes essence'. It is never that easy in the Philosophy department. In the French department it is that easy. The study of Sartre in the French department has not helped me in the Philosophy department. It is the other way around.

He would love to do an MA or a PhD, but finds the academic environment stifling and the people he knows in industry and films so much more active than academics:

> I take it upon myself in the French department to be a pain in the lecturers' necks . . . they say ridiculous things and the students just take them down and I say 'Hold on, that is a load of rubbish'. (71)

'A rather conceited young man' said one of his tutors, indicating the ambivalence: in one sense he is the ideal student, the fantasy for whom, indeed, many of the courses are designed; in another sense he must indeed be a pain in the neck. It is probably superfluous to comment further except to point out that modern languages as a discipline and even as a department can and does contain students like this as well as students like Joan and Margaret.

The next student – Pauline – is doing French and English. At school she was interested in painting, but she was not allowed to continue with it and, although she is still interested in fine art, she no longer paints:

> I feel very sad. I was always better at creative work. I feel annoyed at myself for letting that go. (65)

This is what she says about the difference between French and English.

> [English and French students] there is a difference in standards, definitely. It is much higher in the English department. There are people who are very good in the French department, but they just don't compare. Academically the English department offers much more. You have got a much more rounded attitude to a text. The top ones are better than the top ones in French. They have original ideas. The English department insists on original ideas, rather than going out to use critics. So the people who are good in the English department are people who can actually deal with literature by themselves quite happily. [In French] there seems to be a very strong tendency to have to refer to an authority, it is a vicious circle. There is not the breadth. The students don't have it and it is not taught in the course. So a single honours student could not approach a text in the way a single honours English student could. I find the French course very, very traditional. The teaching methods are the same, but it is a different approach. The English teachers are much more approachable. I feel freer in the English department. (65)

Finally, by contrast to all the modern languages students, here is a single honours student of English, Peter (101). He himself cautioned me against using subjects as a means of grouping people:

> It is easier to group people in lots of ways than what degree they do.

and it is true that the characteristics one finds in him can be found in modern languages students, strikingly in students like Marco, less obviously in others. The categories are not boxes but Venn diagrams. Nevertheless, attitudes like his are simply not found with this degree of clarity and strength in modern languages students. The first attitude concerns career and vocation:

> Career, that's a funny word. Insurance policy. I hate that concept. Whenever you have got a safety net, you never go for the heights. I hate institutionalization. I am interested in magic as a science, I want to study a lot of eastern religions and philosophy, to work with the aim of self discipline. It is postgraduate study of a kind. But not in an institution. I want to spend as much of my time finding out as much about myself and things that are important to me as I can. I am prepared to forsake salary and things like that for what is important to me.

This is linked to creativity which is seen as excluding and being excluded by a career. A career impedes personal development:

> I have always been interested in performance and creativity. I have never ever envisaged myself in a vocational manner of doing a particular profession. I can only envisage myself in something that is creative. It is so ridiculous to tell a child at 14 these things don't lead to a career. I have a fantasy that the only way in a Utopian future that any country will be able to rise up above another is by its art and its culture.

The function of a University for this student is the facilitation of personal development. He wonders whether he wouldn't have developed more outside the University:

> It has given me something quite negative. I can no longer read for pleasure. On the other hand, I have learned to write a well-argued essay. It is a useful discipline which I use if I want to

and he paints a chilling picture of the way the urge to do personal and original work and to develop oneself can be crushed by the educational system:

> At every stage of education people always say, 'what you do is great and original, but wait till the next stage, because that is when you really get a chance to do that. Although you may be interested in ideas, at this stage we want you to get your O levels, to get your A levels'. Then you get your A levels and it is the same thing. And even at university they say, 'if you are really interested you should do postgraduate work', and I wonder if it is not a never-ending process?

It would be wrong to see him as typical. He certainly sees himself as different from his fellow students – especially the girls:

> You are held back because people are not really interested in getting deeper into the subject, and the girls are just interested in knowing a few quotes and writing to a formula to pass exams. It was a bit restrictive . . . I am generally quite depressed by the ability of most people at university doing English. People don't seem to have a passion for it; in terms of examinations they will probably do better than myself. But when you do open up a discussion they seem to be only aware of set concepts . . . [I ask] 'do you come here for an education or do you come here for a piece of paper?'.

But the other English students I talked to shared these characteristics to a certain extent and were all strikingly different from the modern linguists in terms of their involvement in creative work or performance, in terms of their lack of concern about a career, in terms of their independence of mind, their assumption that their tutors did not want to get their own views or even standard critical views 'regurgitated':

> I am not afraid of taking risks . . . recently I did an essay – every critic said one thing, but I didn't like what they were saying, completely the opposite. The tutor thought it was interesting and though he didn't agree . . . he didn't mind. (103)

And in terms of being natural readers with very fluid work/pleasure boundaries:

> [Reading] if I'm at home, perhaps on my bean-bag near the fire, it gets dark and I haven't realized. I'll get up and realize I should have shut the curtains . . . Initially I was good at the creative side . . . I'd always read all my life, I'd loved reading. The idea of a course where you could read and write seemed good. It involved everything that I had enjoyed doing. Even now, I don't consider reading work. (100)

3 The year abroad

> She is absolutely obsessed by France. She wants to go back and marry a Frenchman. French is brilliant, beautiful. France is paradise on earth. 'This grotty old place' – I can't see it like that, so I go the other way. 'Stupid old frogs' – so there's a running animosity in the house. A lot of her time is spent doing French. She is a lot more worried by translation, she is so busy checking her grammar and pronunciation (she is very hot on pronunciation) that I can't imagine she can ever switch off from that enough to just enjoy. She isn't obsessed with the subject so much as the experience because she had a really good year in France. (Single Honours English Student)

A degree in Modern Languages is a sandwich course and the meat is the year abroad. It is scarcely an exaggeration to say that no other degree, no other subject, offers this opportunity. Not only do modern linguists spend four years over their degrees compared to the three taken by other British students but the nature of this extra year means that their experience of their degree is dramatically different from that of a student of English or History, Psychology or Physics. Only students in vocational subjects like Law, Medicine or Engineering have such an intensely formative experience built into their programme of studies and of these only Medicine in its later stages offers anything like the same human challenge.

The 'year abroad' is a compulsory part of all Modern Languages degrees except at Oxbridge, and even there it is becoming the rule rather than the exception. To choose to do a degree in Modern Languages is to choose, at the age of 18 or 19, to leave a familiar culture and live in a foreign culture, not as a tourist, but as an honorary member of that culture. It is not an option. Only very exceptional circumstances will persuade language departments to waive the foreign residence requirement – and many students give up Modern Languages because they are not prepared to take this step. The majority will have had two years in University before going abroad, but a minority will go in their second year, barely twelve months after they made the Home/University leap. Some will spend the whole year in one country: those doing two languages will settle in one country and, after six months, move to another. Many will maintain the student role, a large proportion will work in schools as assistants, and a smaller proportion will be in work placements, paid employment in factories, offices, banks. Such placements are for students an extremely attractive feature of 'applied' courses and staff devote an extraordinary amount of time and energy finding them and keeping them.[1]

For the student, the year abroad is, in prospect, both attractive and frightening. One feeling or the other can predominate in any student, or at any time. But, whatever the feeling, they all know that 'it is the only way':

> Going abroad does scare me a bit because it is such a big change. But it is the only way. (80)

> There is only one way to learn a language properly. If you want to get to the heart of a language, you go out there. (93)

Even a student who has doubts about the value of the degree has no doubts about the year abroad:

> I may be wasting my time here in University . . . the only reason I will come back is the year abroad . . . I will do it for myself, but I don't think I will get a better job . . . there are opportunities I could go into now, but they may not be there when I come from here. (97)

In retrospect they see it as a crucial developmental event: they may have had idyllic exchange visits or family holidays, but they discover very quickly the difference between being on holiday or on an exchange in a foreign country and actually living and working there. They move from a large homogenous group where their student role is clear to situations where their group-membership is undefined and where their roles and tasks have to be painfully worked out. They move, frequently, to the loneliness of the foreign bed-sitter. They have often left a boy-friend or girl-friend and that can make them wretched. I became aware of the extent of this on a trip I made a few years ago to visit students in France – one student had just spent the equivalent of £50 on a phonecall. Luck plays a great part: if they are assistants, they can end up like Liz who was surrounded by young teachers who acted as friends, guides and mentors, or like Jane, in the depths of Brittany, who had an unheated room with no visitors allowed, in a school which seemed permanently on strike, or like Phillipa, in a town where there were no entertainments, no foreign students, and where no-one recognized her presence. It's sink or swim. Most swim, but there are near-drownings; my question 'What was your worst experience abroad?' produced a crop of horror stories, involving money, police, bureaucracy, lorry drivers, hospitals . . . Helen spent six months in Mexico and six in West Berlin:

> The worst moment was the loneliness. I remember flying into an airport in Texas before going to Mexico. The emptiness, the total going into nothing. (95)

Students go through fire and water:

> The year abroad was a baptism of fire. There was no one to turn to. I was totally on my own in a strange country. (96)

> During the year abroad you grow up. You are thrown in at the deep-end. You discover yourself through the crises. In Spain my whole way of seeing things changed. (51)

The self-realization and self-discovery can take various forms. It can take the form of discovering the degree of attachment to England and home:

> I am very fond of England and don't like leaving it. It was very hard for me to do my year abroad, I wouldn't want to do it again. (86)

or a loss of 'romantic' notions about foreign places:

> I don't have any romantic notions about being abroad . . . I find it interesting to establish the differences between the cultures. (98)

The result is a general increase in confidence:

> I have developed as a person . . . I can see a great difference . . . I am very, very confident now, maybe overconfident. (93)

and a questioning of assumptions. The Salford students who came with sober, instrumental notions of being translators and interpreters and getting good jobs find themselves putting this into question and being tempted by arts-style hedonism, escapism, and 'gallivanting':

> When I came here I wanted a really good job and to get a nice flat in London. I've changed. I have got friends doing that and they are so envious of what I have done. Particularly the year abroad. (92)

> Now I think I feel 'before I settle down I've got a lot more things to do and see'. I want to get my gallivanting done. (90)

In general, there seemed a tendency, as a result of the year abroad, to move away from the instrumental towards the integrative:

> I love my language. It doesn't matter to me whether I earn money by using it. (94)

What is it exactly that they have learned during this year abroad? They have learned the language, the real language. In most cases, they have acquired real, demonstrable language skills, and the heady self-confidence which comes from that kind of learning, like swimming a length for the first time, riding a bicycle, staying on a wind-surfer. They feel superior to the 'bloody British':

> This summer I worked with an English company in France. I was one of the few who could talk to people, get the French to do things, whereas the others were just stuck there. Ignorant bloody British. If you are so ignorant and arrogant not to want to learn French then they didn't want to talk to you at all. (83)

They have learned self-reliance; they can stand up for themselves and they can be alone:

> I said to myself 'If I can take this I can take anything'. (52)

They have learned to learn:

> You mustn't worry, you have to jump in. I didn't understand a word of Spanish at first, I spent a week with my ears stuck against a radio letting Spanish hit me. (51)

Intellectually too, they often discover that they have made a breakthrough:

> This year I find it easier to write. I can see things . . . in English books as well. It is almost as if something has become unblocked quite suddenly. (52)

But the crucial learning, crucial both for them as individuals and for the society that ultimately pays for them to learn, is learning about *difference*:

> The way different people think . . . I found the whole thing was so different, their attitude to life so different, different moral standards. I think it's good. I don't like it when you go to another country and find it's very similar . . . I don't like it when people play down the differences and try to merge everything into one culture. (56)

It is true that by the act of moving, say, from Chalfont to Salford, some students have already begun this process:

> I think I have changed, because I went to a Grammar School in Buckinghamshire which is a very conservative area, and everyone gets jobs in London and their parents have company cars. Then I came to Salford and you really do see what is happening to the industrial areas, they've gone to pieces. You see how the other half live, how families live, how my parents treated me and how parents treat children here. And the year abroad makes you become even more aware, because you see the advantages students have in England over students in France and Spain. We are rolling in money compared with students there. They are totally dependent on their parents, so most come from well-off backgrounds. (90)
>
> Coming from Somerset, Salford is quite a shock. (92)

But the Southampton students, for example, had not had this experience, and, in any case, the extent of the difference is considerably greater abroad, the demands more radical:

> The Italians are so different, and if they want something they will go out and get it. I've been taught that you ask for it politely. You realize that unless you do what they do, shout, nothing will come of it. I would have thought she [landlady] would have been more perceptive. Perceptiveness in Italy doesn't count. They are not subtle. You have to sit down and say 'I am not prepared to carry on like this'. We tend to think that if people shout at you it is really serious, and you go around treading really softly. In Italy that is not the case, when it is done it is done, so you have to learn you can shout as well. (87)

The awareness that 'they do things differently over there' is the cultural equivalent of the earlier linguistic discovery that languages are codes. Cultures are seen to be codes as well; there is no 'right' threshold for the experience of anger; the decibel count in a home counties restaurant is no more proper than that of a Roman trattoria. Each individual has to make a personal response to cultural difference. What do I feel about the public circumcision of 500 babies in Marrakesh? or suppositories? or bull-fighting?

It is possible to deny that difference:

> Once you got into the pattern, living in Nantes or Pisa wasn't very different from living here. (89)

> Lille is just like Salford. (86)

It is possible to judge negatively and defensively as in this article written for a student newspaper by a Southampton student:

> Spend a few weeks here and you begin to dream of hedgerows and new-mown grass, experiencing strange cravings for vegetation which may only be partially assuaged by frequent dashes into Marks & Spencer to gaze hungrily at the Yucca palms . . . I can't say I get much of a kick out of living in perpetual fear, afraid to glance at passers by in case they happen to belong to the vast omnipresent immigrant population – slimy North Africans whose insolent stares both threaten and degrade . . . Like its inhabitants, the North of France at this time of year is miserable and wet. It's certainly hard work, this business of developing your personality through contact with the unknown, and Christmas seems a long way off. Roll on next May – one month down, seven to go. (*Wessex News*, 22-11-84)

It is possible to be an indifferent, quizzical, spectator–anthropologist:

> I was with a very right-wing family though I am a socialist. It was interesting to observe them. I tried to understand. It taught me to concentrate and listen. Language forces receptivity because you are not in a position to dominate. (72)

Finally, it is possible to love the difference, and, although I heard statements illustrating all the positions, this is by far the most common:

> France became home. I felt more at home there, I got on particularly well with the culture and philosophy. It didn't seem odd there to go to the cinema and want to talk about the film afterwards [as it does] here in Britain. Talk in Britain is on a superficial level. People are less ready to discuss emotions . . . (70)

The most striking difference to be positively valued in this way is indeed emotional freedom. It can be French people driving expressively:

> They are such a crazy nation . . . we were stuck in a traffic jam, and they just started driving on the grass verge on either side, because they were fed up with queuing. Their immediate response was 'why the hell should you

be stuck there when there is plenty of space on either side of the road?'. (70)

It can even be hostility openly expressed rather than hypocritically concealed as tolerance: one male student who wears eye make-up approved of the disapproval of the Parisians because it was honest. It can be the general acceptance of the display of emotion: the same student found it very liberating to be able to show emotion between men in France and Italy:

> In Britain it is just about accepted for women to show their emotions to men or to other women, if men show their emotions to women it is just about alright, but to show their emotions towards another man is really dodgy. It is so nice to see a friend in France that you haven't seen for a couple of days and to give him a kiss. Over here you do that and everybody stops and looks at you in the street. It is a lot more distant, a lot colder. (61).

In general students found people abroad more ready to express emotion and they responded positively to this difference, identifying with it and adjusting their own way of being permanently as a result of it. They see the British as *a* way, not *the* way:

> I remember the first time I went there. In the common room there were two teachers having this discussion, and they were really shouting at each other, and thumping their fists on the table, and screaming. I thought, 'oh, they are going to start fighting, what am I going to do?' In fact they were perfectly alright, they seemed to be able to say exactly what they thought. People would have arguments and shout, but it didn't mean that they lost their friends. I think that is typically English . . . you don't say 'no you are wrong'. (52)

> There is something about the Latin temperament that I really enjoy. They are an emotional bunch of people. (93)

It would be possible of course to doubt the premises: are the French really freer, more expressive than the British? Are the differences class differences rather than national differences? Is it rather that, being in a freer situation, the students project on to the French their own diminished inhibition and justify it to themselves? This seems to be what this student is saying:

> In France I had so much freedom and so little inhibition. Here everyone knows your background and everyone knows your family. I could have gone out to France saying my father is in prison and my mother was the Queen of England and I was a raving homosexual and they would have believed me. It was a total freedom to go out there and be. It was a really authentic experience, because I was who I wanted to be. Here, you come back and straightaway I am my father's son, my brother's brother. They can't even tell your personality really because you've got a different medium and you're talking as a foreigner in French. It was great. (59)

Others express it differently in terms of aspects of their own personality which are discovered or released:

> In Avignon I was a different Peter, more forceful, a much stronger, outgoing personality, talkative, much less timid. That Peter would talk to artistic people, journalists, whereas the English one has scientific friends. I like the other Peter more. (94)

> After about five months in Germany I lost touch with my English and I found that I was learning and reading and making general experiences but they were in German and it was difficult to express those new experiences in English. In Mexico I played the English Spanish speaker, playing on words, saying things with a funny accent . . . I had a lot of fun with the Spanish language. I got a big kick out of language jokes, playing on words. I am not very good at that in English, but when it is not your own language you can say something in an outrageous accent in the middle of a sentence and get everyone to laugh. (95)

The experience is so formative because it involves basic issues of identity. At every turn a post-adolescent or young adult is being required to identify, disidentify or withhold judgement; he or she is challenged to say 'That is me', 'That is not me' or 'I don't know'. Individual identity is discovered and constructed by a process of identification and disidentification with significant individuals and/or groups in situations where emotions are engaged. The student who discovers her essential Englishness:

> To all intents and purposes I think I'm English, my character, my upbringing. I prefer to stay in England. (94)

is constructing an identity as much as the person who cherishes a non-standard Spanish accent:

> I refuse to give up speaking with a Mexican accent. I refuse to speak Castillano. The accent is all I have left of my time in Mexico, apart from a scrap book and a photo album. (95)

or the one who says 'Spanish is me. I am more me speaking Spanish than English. I felt wrong speaking English' (51).

The student who develops a clear preference for France or Spain over Germany or for Germany over Italy (and this seems to be very much the rule – biculturalism is common, but never triculturalism) is constructing an identity, balancing out, through experience, oppositions between rule and freedom, work and pleasure.

What these students have in common and what distinguishes them from other students of other disciplines is a distance from their own culture, a capacity to see the world from another's point of view, to find it strange and yet not to reject it, even to enjoy it, to be happy:

> It is a typical British tendency to look at the foreigners and think *they* are the ones who are trying to stop things happening. We seem to have a great

ability to be able to say when *we* don't want things, but when it applies to other countries no-one seems able to get around to saying what it is going to do to them. (87)

I would like to live in a hot climate. I feel so happy abroad, really lively. (97)

For these students, cultural difference ends up being associated with pleasure and, not surprisingly, compounded with sexual difference.

Here is an account, by a female student, which brings out very clearly the way in which learning is bound up with difference, the way national difference and sexual difference become merged, the way that difference produces anxiety and excitement, in short the erotic nature of the year abroad:

We used to go down to the beach every day. Right from the start the Italian boys came out and started to chat to us, and groups formed. Myself and one other girl ended up going around with three or four Italians. We spent most of the time with them . . . we'd sit and talk for hours, these boys didn't speak English. I really love hot weather. The day before the exam I had been for a swim with this bloke, and I said 'I really must do some work' and he came back and said 'I'll help you revise' and I had my Italian grammar book and he tested me on my Italian verbs. I thought that was a good way to learn . . . The worst experience was being scared of the Italian males. I thought 'I want to go home, I can't stand these people' but I did like all the attention, because we were different, we were blonde, obviously not Italian, we did get a lot of attention, although it got a bit much. If people say 'hallo' to me normally I say 'hallo' back, but I'd do that and they would just grab me. But you learn to handle it. (56)

Another student summed up:

Everyone who comes back is in love with somebody from some country. (96)

After a learning experience of this magnitude, settling down to a final year is not easy. For some, Britain takes on a new attraction as they rediscover the delights of orderly queues, emotional restraint and understatement. However, for the majority there is period of rejection:

When I came back I hated this place. I couldn't stand the cold, the people, I couldn't stand anything. (51)

which, as the quotation from the English student at the beginning of this section shows, can provoke irritation.

Some students will complete their degree and return to the country. They may marry, they may actually decide to change identities, to become French or German. Others will work towards biculturalism. This adult process is one we can look at best through the experience of staff in Part Two. But first we must attempt to make some general statements about these students and about their choice of subject.

3

Reflections

Our view is that, whereas each student is in some respect like all other students and in some respects like no other student, it may very well turn out that . . . it would be best to consider the ways in which he is like *some* other students. (Donald Brown: 'Some Educational Patterns' in Sanford 1956, p. 59)

1 Theories of development and personality

(a) On theories

So far, I have done little more than report what Modern Languages students have told me about the experience of choosing and living their discipline. The order I have imposed on the material has been the minimum required for clarity. But the process of acquiring knowledge has two necessary stages – experience and reflection.

In order to reflect on experience one needs theory. In an area like the one into which we are venturing, which concerns on the one hand human personality and development and on the other the social organization of knowledge, theories abound. The rational myth has the researcher and problem-solver checking out all the theories and using those theories and those parts of theories which best make objective sense of the particular data. In reality, the choice of theory, like any other choice, is subjective as well as objective: a statement about a theoretical stance is perforce autobiographical, the result of one's own intellectual history.

What I shall do is to give an account of the theoretical approaches which I have found useful. My aim is not to improve on these theories, even less to create new syntheses, but to *use* them in a particular instance. This is, I imagine, what their creators intended. Theories in this area are valuable to the extent that they are practical aids to reducing confusion; they are guides in the jungle of fact. In the second part of the chapter, I shall attempt some generalizations in answer to the question: What sort of people are modern languages students?

(b) Personality[1]

I have already expressed my views about the theoretical and practical limitations of personality testing. But it would be needlessly self-denying to ignore this work since it does supply a vocabulary, which enables us to make some sense of the diversity of human beings and their choices. So, concepts like affiliative (or integrative) motivation compared with instrumental motivation, tolerance or intolerance of ambiguity, field-dependence or field-independence (scanning or focusing), extraversion or introversion, authoritarianism, empathy, 'anomie' or ethnocentricity, yielding, convergence or divergence,[2] are, irrespective of their origins, inventions which have descriptive and explanatory power.

Their drawback is that they can be used as static principles of classification: the creators may have been aware of this danger and issued warnings against it,[3] but users reify. The temptation is to pose (and therefore answer) questions in the form 'Are modern linguists convergers or divergers? Extroverts or introverts?'. Tests (which are snapshots) encourage this.

This is why theories which are dynamic rather than static seem to me more helpful. They build on traits, of course: but instead of asking whether linguists are convergers or divergers, one converts these 'ideal types' into 'ideal' developmental stages and one can then ask where this particular individual or this particular group stands on that developmental scale and make surmises about their trajectory.

This is the contribution of the social psychologists. Writers like Mead (1934), Sullivan (1955), or Goffman (1959) are concerned with the ways in which social identities are formed by a process of identification and disidentification – with individuals in early childhood but very quickly with groups. Gender-identity, class-identity, regional or national identity, generation identity are all constructed in this way as *performances*, through a process which is largely unconscious and based less on objective reality than on fantasy and myth. Writers differ according to whether they view this process as a supreme human achievement (like the authors mentioned above) or whether they view it as a process of alienation, which is the position of Laing (1961: 1971) and Sartre (1957). Laing puts it concisely: 'we learn to be whom we are told we are' (p. 95) and 'the usual state of affairs is to be in a tenable position in phantasy systems of a nexus. This is usually called having an "identity" or "personality"' (p. 40). For Sartre, this process of identity formation is a process of bad faith and denial, a process whereby a formlessness, the original and permanent nothingness of consciousness, the *pour soi*, is given the shape and hardness of the *en soi*. However, Sartre's theoretical positions are undermined by his imaginative writings, where the advantages of having a fixed identity are fictionally recognized. The complex reality of human development, it seems to me, has to be dynamic, like Lewin's view of change in general (Elton, 1981), a process of freezing, unfreezing, refreezing, unfreezing . . . or in Sartre's terms, a series of *en soi* positions which are successfully dissolved by the corrosive actions of the *pour soi*, the process taking place, as he also saw, not in a linear way, but in a spiral, and accompanied by doubt and fear. I have made sense of this for myself by viewing the creation of a social self as a process whereby a 'me' (accusative case) is created through group identification, while an 'I', with its origins somewhere in infancy, looks on. Figure 3.1 is my attempt to visualize this process of identity formation.

Figure 3.1: *Sense of self*

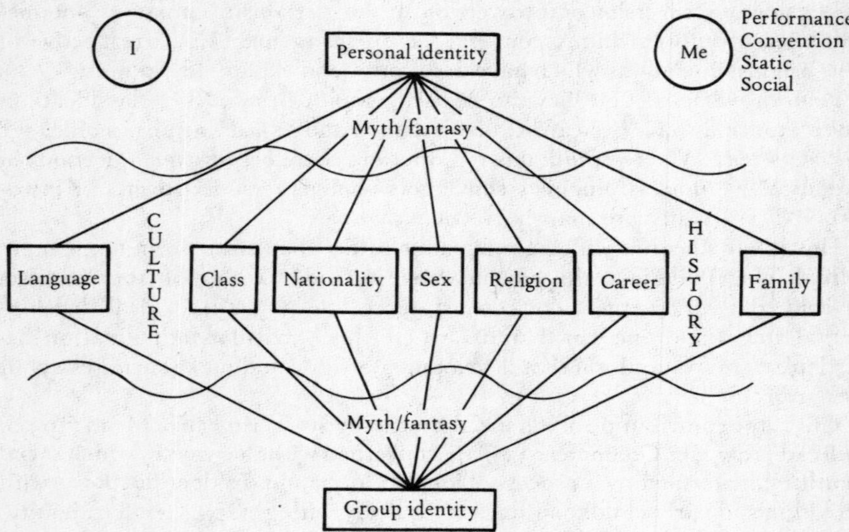

We can focus on identity through career and subject choice, which is our particular concern, thanks to the achievement of Nevitt Sanford in *The American College* (1962) and that of Arthur Chickering and his associates in *The Modern American College* (published in 1981, with a foreword by Sanford). The contributors to these collective works (there are 80 of them in all) share a particular view:

> Let us put it boldly. We propose that colleges and universities concern themselves more deliberately and explicitly with human development. We go further. We propose that the values and aims of human development be taken as unifying purposes, as organising frameworks for all institutional efforts. (Chickering, 1981, p. 9.)

Their belief or bias, which I share, is that all human beings develop, more or less quickly, more or less far, but that the facilitation of this development is the business of education and that education unnecessarily limits itself if it confines its conscious attention to cognitive development alone. They also believe that the various disciplines contribute differentially to growth and development:

> All curricula either favour or hamper personality development, regardless of whether they were designed with such development in mind . . . Much of the individual's knowledge is peripheral to the personality in the sense that it is readily forgotten, and much other knowledge remains superficial in the sense that it does not become integrated with the individual's inner needs. Our major concern is with the kind of learning in College that can

bring about a development change in the personality structure. (Sanford, 1962, p. 425).

The theoretical background of their work is mainly the various descriptions of the life-cycles; they seem only marginally concerned with early childhood which is the territory of the social psychologists and psychoanalysts. But, in the American educational context, they are concerned (especially in Chickering's book) with the entire adult life-span and believe that higher education should be involved in this. Writing in a British context, where, in spite of the Open University, higher education is still the domain of the young, I take from their work the part which concerns the period of the life-cycle from 18–22 years, from post-adolescence to young adulthood.

Here in a schematic form derived from Sanford and Chickering's books are some of the developmental models (Table 3.1).

It can readily be seen that here too there is a danger of treating these stages as if they were clear categories or rungs on a ladder. Erikson warns against this in a footnote (1950: 1963, p. 265). But the temptation to see psychic development as linear and irreversible like somatic development, is hard to resist. Unlike Sartre, who gives full weight to the tragic, the alienated and the irremediable, the American theorists can seem rather blandly normative and melioristic. As with personality traits, developmental stages need to be viewed dynamically. The image of the spiral is again appropriate since the individual goes through the same stages, but from a different perspective (this is the case with Erikson's stages as the blank cells in his scheme indicate (p. 264)); he or she can also regress or anticipate (through imagination and play) and, of course, the spiral can flatten to a circle; people get stuck or permanently frozen at one stage. We could think of other metaphors – helter-skelters or snakes and ladders.

Nevertheless, having made these reservations, I will conclude by saying that the actual goals and values described by the life-cycle theorists – autonomy, integration, tolerance of ambiguity, objectivity, relativism with commitment – seem non-controversial. These are indeed, I think, the goals that most of us would claim to be pursuing for ourselves and our students. There are difficulties about this normative approach with respect to disciplines; for example, natural science and mathematics majors are said to find 'some refuge from intellectual questioning and uncertainty' in their subject: they are 'late maturers' (Sanford, 1956, p. 40) and this seems to favour liberal arts disciplines above others. Nevertheless, a criterion for a discipline can well be the extent to which it facilitates or hampers progress towards these goals, provided one acknowledges that refuges as well as springboards may have a role to play in growth. The issue of specialization (which may meet society's needs but not necessarily those of the individual) versus general studies (which may meet the individual's needs for growth, but not necessarily society's needs) is an issue we will discuss in the third part of this book. Jung, who stated that 'the social goal is attained only at the cost of personality' (Jung, 1983, p. 72), has a lot to say about this. For the moment, we will use the theoretical notions described in this section to illuminate the specific experience of modern languages students.

Table 3.1: *The life cycle*

Chronological age	*Erikson*[1]	*Chickering*[2] *(based on McCoy, Havighurst, Gould Sheehy)*		*Perry*[3]	*Sanford*[4]	*Kohlberg/ Loeringer/*[5] *Weathersby*
17		Leaving parents Breaking out Pulling up roots		Basic dualism	Impulse life checked by primitive methods of control (Freshmen)	*Conventional*
	Stage 5 identity vs role confusion (adolescence)	Achieving emotional independence		Dualism modified		Conformist
		Preparing for marriage and family life		Multiplicity	Gains in expression of impulse & mechanisms of control	Conscientious/ conformist or self-aware
↓		Choosing and preparing for a career	Ginsberg (1963) [fantasy choice] tentative choice realistic, choice compromises	Relativism		Conscientious
	Stage 6				(Seniors)	

	Intimacy vs isolation	Developing an ethical system		Commitment	On the road to autonomy	*Post-conventional*
					'less certain of identity'	Autonomous individualistic
	[early adulthood]	Leaving parents Staying out	↓		'more unstable because there is more to be stabilized'	Integrated (Maslow, 1971)
22		Putting down roots	↓			

1) Erikson 1963[1950], p. 252–257;
2) Chickering (1981), p. 21, 31, 774;
3) Perry (1981), p. 79;
4) Sanford (1956) p. 41–42 and Katz and Sanford (1962) p. 418–440;
5) Weathersby (1981), p. 53–54.

2 Modern Languages students: life cycle and personality

(a) Life cycle

(i) 'Breaking out'

There are a minority (7.4% in 1983) of mature students (defined as over 23 years of age at admission): they may already have had jobs, been married or divorced, had children. They were not necessarily good at languages at school, but in most cases they lived abroad subsequently, 'acquired' a language, became attached to a foreign culture, and, when they decided to do a degree, used this skill and enthusiasm as their launching pad.

Their presence in modern languages departments serves to highlight the developmental stage of the majority of the students, who are indeed not 'mature'. Staff are permanently uncertain about whether to call them 'boys and girls' or 'men and women'. They themselves will speak of 'the girls and boys in the group' rather than 'the men and women in the group'. They come to University as post-adolescents, and leave as young adults. First year students are very much engaged in the task of 'breaking out', 'pulling up roots', leaving families. Indeed, one of the unacknowledged tasks that British higher education performs on behalf of society is to manage the watershed which is the separation of post-adolescent children and their families. By the end of their year abroad they are 'staying out' and the emotional separation from their family has been achieved:

> The contacts have been severed, I don't mean on a personal level, I get on well with my family, it's nice to know they will be there wherever I am, but they don't play a big part. (93)

Most transitions are imperceptible, like Spring into Summer. But anyone involved with modern languages students sees this change dramatically every October as the post-adolescents, last seen 15 months ago, return as young adults, having 'broken out'.

(ii) 'Preparation for marriage'

Before discussing this 'task' an important general point has to be made. As Chickering says (p. 17) 'these findings, with some important exceptions, come from studies of white, middle and upper class men'. Hudson's research was carried out almost exclusively on schoolboys; Erikson and Sartre mostly assume the masculine includes the feminine, and so on. But, as already noted, the fact is that three out of every four modern languages students are female (Powell, 1986, p. 27). One can simply ignore this (which is more or less what happens in higher education which plays down the fact that Arts departments are largely places where young women are educated by middle-aged men) or one can acknowledge that the life-cycle of young women may be different from that of young men and that gender determines the experience of the subject. Angrist and Alquist see uncertainty as the most important fact during the student years:

> These college women . . . are groping for handles on the future, they cannot predict . . . while the big pieces (husband, children) are missing. (in Chickering, p. 262).

and Bourdieu and Passeron in the context of their general critique of higher education have this to say about women students in France:

> Because their present is dominated by the image of a future which belies it or questions it, female students cannot unconditionally espouse the values of the intelligentsia and are less successful than men in concealing from themselves the unreality of their present . . . scholastic docility constitutes a felicitous reinterpretation of the traditional role of female dependence which, in this case, perfectly matches the expectations of a higher education system which has remained traditional (and male-orientated) in its spirit and its teaching staff. (Bourdieu and Passeron, 1979, p. 62).

In Britain, Helen Weinreich-Haste (1984) has considered the situation of women undergraduates with specific reference to their under-representation in Science courses and over-representation in the Humanities (no-one is researching the under- and over-representation of males). She asked her female respondents from all disciplines to give their views about the relative importance of career and family. One finding is particularly interesting for our purposes: *all* female students rated family life as more important than career *but the gap was greatest for modern linguists* (N = 80) (p. 125). Modern linguists gave greatest weight to the intention to have children and were most likely to resign and follow their spouse in a situation where there was a career conflict; they were found to be the most traditionally 'feminine'.[4] McDonough (1981, p. 146), reviewing the work on 'need for achievement' underlines male/female differences, specifically as regards language learning. There are two kinds of learners, those whose prime motivation is success and those for whom avoidance of failure is the more important. McDonough seems to be saying that girls are more likely in general to opt for avoidance of failure but that language learning is an exception (he cites Burstall) and he explains this by conventional social factors:

> Striving for success for a woman brings her into conflict with societal expectations; which is not the case for a man; however, learning a language does not conflict with society's norms for educated girls.

Gilligan, however, (1982) adopts a much more radical position. Criticizing the life-cycle theorists for being essentially concerned with the *male* life-cycle, she claims that *differences* have been given value. Following Chodorow, she claims that the male tendency to separation and individuation, the 'defensive firming of experienced ego boundaries' is considered a more advanced developmental stage, valued above the female tendency to empathy and a more diffuse identity:

> Consequently, relationships, and particularly issues of dependency, are experienced differently by women and men. For boys and men, separation and individuation are critically tied to gender identity since separation from the mother is essential for the development of masculinity. For girls

> and women, issues of femininity or feminine identity do not depend on the achievement of separation from the mother or on the progress of individuation. Since masculinity is defined through separation while femininity is defined through attachment, male gender identity is threatened by intimacy while female gender identity is threatened by separation. Thus males tend to have difficulty with relationships, while females tend to have problems with individuation. The quality of embeddedness in social interaction and personal relationships that characterizes women's lives in contrast to men's, however, becomes not only a descriptive difference but also a developmental liability when the milestones of childhood and adolescent development in the psychological literature are markers of increasing separation. Women's failure to separate then becomes by definition a failure to develop.

Yet again I am reminded that this book is in part about the experience of women students in a masculine institution and that Modern Languages is a way of living that tension.

The fact that I made no enquiries about students' personal lives means that I have little data of my own to offer which might supplement or update the findings I have listed. There are the informal sources – conversations and confidences – and relevant information was often offered in response to my question 'Would you consider marrying a person from another culture?'. Very few respondents balked at this question (though one male student did reply: 'I can't imagine marrying anyone, from anywhere'); a sizeable minority said it was not relevant because they were already engaged or about to be married (sometimes to 'a person of another culture'); one told me that her future husband would have to follow *her* in any career conflict which, according to Weinreich-Haste, is very unusual; staff often assured me that they saw no difference between males and females as regards career orientation (both being, in one professor's opinion, 'equally hardnosed'). And this is what puzzles me about the whole gender issue. In a pilot version of my interview schedule I included questions about gender and language learning but I omitted them from the final version because they seemed to produce nothing: (Interviewer: 'What do you think about the fact that most of the teachers here are male?'. Woman student: 'Are they? I hadn't noticed'. (56)). On reflection, I think this 'nothing' was something; it reveals a certain degendering which is a specific case of depersonalizing, denial of difference, and emphasis on the sexlessly cognitive. It may also say something about young women's needs to deny their gender identity in order to participate in higher education, and male tutors' collusion with this denial. Weinreich-Haste's findings about the 'feminine' orientation of modern linguists cannot be discounted, but the fact that this is not something women students reveal spontaneously or readily is also significant.

For male students, I may add, it does not seem to be a preoccupation at all. The gender issue is not one which can be dealt with solely in terms of students; we will reconsider it when we have looked at the whole system: student–staff–institution.

(iii) 'Choosing and preparing for a career'

'Choosing and preparing for a career' is somewhat more straightforward. As we have seen, modern linguists choose the subject partly because of its utilitarian nature – it is indeed the only practical Arts subject. The student who might have done English chooses modern languages instead, because it looks a safer bet vocationally, because it offers a demonstrable, saleable skill at the end. A student who started Law switches to modern languages because they are not vocational like Law, because they postpone that degree of specialized commitment. The process seems to be that the subject ends up being perceived more as an Arts subject. Salford students to some extent and Cardiff ECS students to a considerable extent by their final year have doubts about the vocational aspect and see themselves as having done an arts degree which requires further training and specialization. Some regret that they didn't go for a 'pure' Arts degree, in English, say, because they now feel that their modern languages degree is in fact no better (though indeed no worse) vocationally than any other Arts degree.

Here we come up against another difficult question. Are the Cardiff ECS students right when they think at the *beginning* of their degree that their study of Economics or Law will give them an advantage over Arts students in employers' eyes, or are they right at the *end* when they think that employers will give preference to specialists? Careers advisers I consulted seem to be as uncertain about recruiters' views as the students. They point out that Britain is unique in that commercial firms do not expect to recruit specialists but go for people with desirable personal qualities who they will then train on the job. At least 40% of jobs for graduates are 'any discipline'. Which means that modern linguists on graduation can and do get jobs as accountants, bankers, computer programmers, supermarket executives or immigration officers. This is in striking contrast to continental countries where a modern linguist has virtually no career opportunities other than teaching. The British system is unique in the way that employers have faith in the University's capacity to educate (this is not the case in France, for example) and in their own ability to train. The faith may be exaggerated in both cases. And it may be a conservative force in British firms: they are free to socialize their new recruits in their own ways without having to compromise with what recruits bring with them from their education. And the recruiters or 'gatekeepers' themselves, may be looking for 'University' qualities which may or may not be those required for the firms to succeed; indeed, the gatekeepers as a group may be over-attached to 'University' values and not completely espouse the values of the firm.[5] Roizen and Jepson (1985), in a book which should be required reading for undergraduate job-seekers, point out how little is known about 'the micro-processes of graduate recruitment' (p. 13). Their own book is full of fascinating confidences from recruiters but has, of course, no specific reference to modern linguists or indeed to any particular discipline. The authors admit that 'the degree to which they [the recruiters] represent the perceptions of their colleagues is an unknown' (p. 25). Nevertheless, the book confirms that 'the importance of non-academic characteristics . . . can hardly be exaggerated' (p. 164): 'What we're really looking for [in our management trainees] is a strong personality' (p. 52). 'The "ology" doesn't count. Analytic development which can be transferred to whatever field he or she is dealing with is important' (p. 53).

Faith, hope and hearsay are important in the carrying out of this career task for all students of all disciplines. However, modern linguists have two advantages: one is that they may have already had a job during their year abroad; this is important both as an opportunity for them to try a particular kind of work and as a reassurance to potential employers; another is that they have lived abroad – for many employers and for many jobs this is a vital qualification.

On the other hand, there is the possibility that 'putting down roots' may be particularly difficult for modern linguists – there may be a prolonged stage of 'gallivanting'. Unfortunately University Statistical Record (USR) statistics only give information about the employment of graduates 12 months after graduation; one would need a much longer period in order to test this hypothesis, since there is a high turnover in all disciplines in this first year. Statistics are hard to find but Atton's research (1983) on Science graduates showed that 1 in 4 changed job during the first twelve months and the proportion is likely to be higher in Arts. Taylor (1986) describes in some detail the weakness of 'first destination' data.

(iv) 'Development of an ethical system'

Not all academics would agree that the tasks we have discussed so far are the proper concern of the educational process. Higher education institutions certainly provide career advice; counselling services would consider questions of 'leaving the family' and 'preparing for marriage' very much their province. But these services are considered as support services, rather than part of the educational process. What of the next task: 'development of an ethical system' or, as Erikson (p. 255) puts it, the move 'from morality to ethics' (from inherited conventional values to internalized personal values)? Is this the business of another non-academic support service – the Chaplaincy? Few academics, in Arts at least, would say that it was, and even Science departments have been known to offer courses on the ethical implications of science. And yet, as with the gender issue, there seems to be a silence around the question. I caught echoes of passionate discussions about the role of women, for example, but such discussions took place in student flats not seminar rooms. My impression is that this is not a task that modern language students are actively engaged in. They describe themselves as not being concerned with politics or current affairs. Their newspaper reading is limited.[6] My own experience of teaching a writing course where the form is proposed but not the topic is that many of the students would actually prefer to be given a topic.[7] In literature or film seminars, once they are speaking freely, I find that their attitudes, values and tastes are mainly conventional and conformist. I also find that the work of developing this personal ethical system has more or less to be started from scratch and they have to learn how to learn in this way. This is less true of final year students, but they seem rather to have reached a kind of temporizing stage, where they no longer wholly espouse family values, where they are aware of the existence of other competing values but where their response is tolerance and acceptance rather than self questioning or commitment. When it comes to expressing opinions about literature, we have seen how difficult they find it to give their own view. It is difficult to say whether this means they have views but feel inhibited about expressing them or that the system serves as a convenient rationale for avoiding having to express views. The non-literary students are in no way occupied with working out their own political or ethical systems via their studies: they see the work not as assimilation and digestion but as spoon-feeding followed by regurgitation. Arts students are somewhat more involved, certainly concerned, for example, with the existence of different critical views of the text but they shy away from personal judgement. Even on texts like *Le rouge et le noir* or *Adolphe* they will give an 'objective' assessment of the views which might plausibly be held ('for some Julien will seem . . . but on the other hand others will . . .') or they will deal with aesthetic considerations ('Whatever we may think of Adolphe as a character, Constant's brilliant narrative technique . . .'). They will hardly ever write 'I think . . .' or 'I feel . . .'. Modern literary theory can give powerful support to this ethical neutrality of course. And when one takes into account the language learning, which is, by definition, completely divorced from any ethical concern, it seems reasonable to conclude that modern languages students are not greatly involved in this particular developmental task. In the terms of Table 3.1 they start at the conformist stage where their impulse life is certainly 'checked by primitive methods of control'; they become conscientious/conformist or self-aware. It is not at all sure that they are autonomous and individualistic in Kohlberg's sense or that very great gains have been made in the expression of impulse. As we saw in the last chapter, they have made great progress in one area which the life-cycle theorists omit because their stage-by-stage emphasis assumes that it has been dealt with once and for all during childhood; this is control of the external environment. Their experience abroad has certainly helped them to reach the multiplicity and relativism stage. However, it is as if the confidence which has accrued from this has somehow not carried over into their intellectual life.

Perry's scheme is worth looking at in greater detail (see Table 3.2). Modern languages students differentiate themselves very clearly from Position 1 – the dualist position – which they see as being that of scientists, engineers and medical students – who are also at a pre-ethical stage. Here are two Arts students: the first came from a very religious family and school, and had been amazed in her first year at University to find that there were so many non-believers: she was forced to question her beliefs:

> It is funny to talk to people [Engineers] who haven't looked at things . . . they have still got their established views they have had since they were children. (68)

> I see things in much more complex ways than any of them, which means I am much worse at making decisions. I share with a girl, also a linguist. She is very different from me in some ways, but she sees things in complex ways, and can't make decisions either . . . I can see all sides of an

Figure 3.2: *Scheme of cognitive and ethical development*

Dualism modified	Position 1	Authorities know, and if we work hard, read every word, and learn Right Answers, all will be well.
	Transition	But what about those Others I hear about? And different opinions? And Uncertainties? Some of our own Authorities disagree with each other or don't seem to know, and some give us problems instead of Answers.
	Position 2	True Authorities must be Right, the others are frauds. We remain Right. Others must be different and Wrong. Good Authorities give us problems so we can learn to find the Right Answer by our own independent thought.
	Transition	But even Good Authorities admit they don't know all the answers *yet*?
	Position 3	Then some uncertainties and different opinions are real and legitimate *temporarily*, even for Authorities. They're working on them to get to the Truth.
	Transition	But there are *so many* things they don't know the Answers to! And they won't for a long time.
	Position 4a	Where Authorities don't know the Right Answers, everyone has a right to his own opinion; no one is wrong!
	Transition (and/or)	But some of my friends ask me to support my opinions with facts and reasons.
	Transition	Then what right have They to grade us? About what?
Relativism discovered	Position 4b	In certain courses Authorities are not asking for the Right Answer; They want us to *think* about things in a certain way, *supporting* opinion with data. That's what they grade us on.
	Transition	But this 'way' seems to *work* in most courses, and even outside them.
	Position 5	Then *all* thinking must be like this, even for Them. Everything is relative but not equally valid. You have to understand how each context works. Theories are not Truth but metaphors to interpret data with. You have to think about your thinking.
	Transition	But if everything is relative, am I relative too? How can I know I'm making the Right Choice?
Commitments in Relativism developed	Position 6	I see I'm going to have to make my own decisions in an uncertain world with no one to tell me I'm Right.
	Transition	I'm lost if I don't. When I decide on my career (or marriage or values) everything will straighten out.
	Position 7	Well, I've made my first Commitment!
	Transition	Why didn't that settle everything?
	Position 8	I've made several commitments. I've got to balance them – how many, how deep? How certain, how tentative?
	Transition	Things are getting contradictory. I can't make logical sense out of life's dilemmas.

Position 9	This is how life will be. I must be wholehearted while tentative, fight for my values yet respect others, believe my deepest values right yet be ready to learn. I see that I shall be retracing this whole journey over and over – but, I hope, more wisely.

(W. G. Perry in Chickering, page 79)

> argument very easily. I am different from all of them in that. We have an argument about marriage, say. Their attitude is very black and white. Normally, I can see all the different sides, which means I am quite diplomatic. (63)

Between arts and science there is the usual stigmatizing. The scientists call the arts people workshy:

> The Engineers do give us a bit of stick; they call us dossers. I think we work as hard as they do. (67)

> There's always stigma attached to being a language student . . . 'Oh you're just girls doing languages!' People don't appreciate how much reading's involved and the fact that there are no barriers. (60)

> A lot of them seemed quite amused by me. Sitting in all day reading. 'You don't do any work' they said. (64)

And the arts people pity the scientists:

> [Engineering students] have far more lecture time. They don't enjoy their work at all. It's a very functional course. (64)

> I've got quite a few medical friends. They are force-fed everything. They don't have the capacity to think in the same way. Everything has one correct answer. In English you can interpret it in your own way. With finals coming up, part of me wishes we had right answers, because it would be much easier to revise. But I feel sorry for them, having to learn like that. You can't work creatively in medicine. It is a heart attack or it is not. (100)

But, as we saw, some of the Salford students talked about fellow language students in similar ways, saying that they behaved and were treated like scientists. As regards language work, *all* students are at the dualism stage. They have gone beyond the 'it's a subjunctive because it is after *il faut que*' position, but not very far, and this is largely because of the domination of translation. Few translation classes actually reach relativism and, as we saw, dogmatism, the authority of one person, can take over, especially if that person is a native speaker. The only way language study can move to the stage of relativism and commitment is when speech and writing are freely composed, when the writer or speaker struggles with the tension between rule and creativity, chooses the right word on his or her own authority: so long as writing and speaking are

Figure 3.3

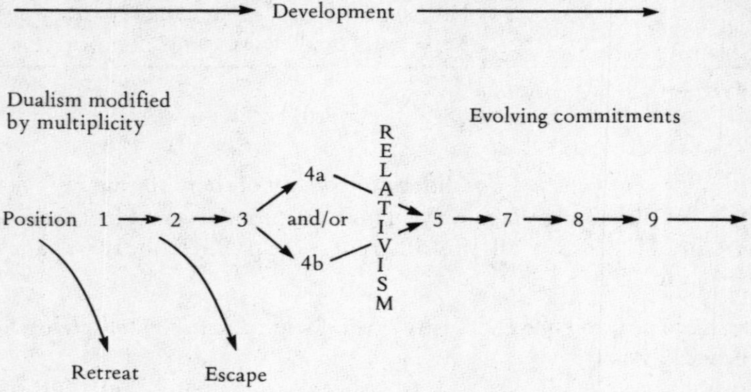

subordinated to translating and interpretation, the student is stuck around Perry's Stage 2 (which is incidentally quite a good description of a translation class). Perry draws a striking picture of this shown in Figure 3.3.

His picture of relativism as a barrier to commitment seems very illuminative and the strategies of *Temporizing* ('postponement of movement for a year or more'), *Escape* ('exploitation of multiplicity and relativism for avoidance of commitment') are very apposite (but not, I think, *Retreat* – 'avoidance of complexity and ambivalence by regression to dualism, coloured by hatred of others').

It could be that the stage of commitment is not something which students in British society normally reach. It could be that modern linguists are particularly reluctant to make this step. But it is more likely to be a wider phenomenon involving the whole process of British higher education, a thicket we will plunge into in the third part of this book.

(b) Personality

Having looked at modern languages students in terms of the life-cycle and developmental tasks let us now look at them in terms of personality. One of the triggers for this book was the opposition between convergers and divergers, and it still seems to me the most operational of the various concepts I listed at the beginning of this chapter. I can deal quickly with the others: I see British modern languages students as being largely affiliative and integrative in their motivation; though there are differences between literary and non-literary students, no-one in Britain would choose to study languages for purely instrumental reasons. British students are clearly not ethnocentric and I saw no evidence of *anomie*, strong disaffection with one's own culture, or what Gardner

(1979) calls 'subtractive bilingualism' – loss of identity through loss of one's native culture. The bilingualism of British modern languages students is clearly 'additive'. All the other items can be grouped for my purposes in the converger–diverger opposition, with the exception of extraversion/introversion. This has a venerable ancestry and a well-known personality test (Eysenck) but I find it completely confusing in practice because of the co-existence of three usages – the original Jungian one, the technical trait-based one, and that of the man in the street. Converger/diverger is situated just at the right spot on the technical–common usage cline for my purposes. I ignore Kolb's (Chickering, 1981, ch. 10) four-way division: converger, diverger, assimilator, accommodator: although it could be made to provide a useful distinction between types of converger (abstract and concrete) it doesn't help at all with divergers and the gain in subtlety is outweighed, in my opinion, by the loss of clarity.

Here then are the converger and the diverger presented schematically. I rely mainly on Hudson but the organization into boxes is mine and items marked * are additions of mine without test evidence (Table 3.2).

The striking thing about these two lists is, I think, that the converger one is a much better likeness. Box B contains a reasonable intellectual portrait of the majority of students. Box 2 is rare. A configuration A/B/C would be fairly typical of many literary students, though A/B/3 is possible, since the language activity can, it seems, be split from the intellectual functions. 1/B/C or 1/B/3 could both be portraits of Arts students (though 'wide interests' is rare) and 1/B/3 is the more likely of the two.

There are various conclusions to be drawn from this. One is connected with girls' choices of subjects. Hudson points out (1968, p. 23) that whereas convergent boys will go in for science and divergent girls will go in for arts (and presumably divergent boys will go in for arts too) *convergent girls* are equally likely to go into the *Arts* or Physical science. In other words, *modern languages may be a refuge for convergent girls who are not independent minded enough to challenge social assumptions*. Hudson adds (p. 25, note 1)

> One would predict . . . that the feminine approach to arts subjects would embody much of the precision that one would associate with the convergent male.

which is exactly what one finds in modern languages, especially with regard to the actual language work.

The other possible conclusion is that modern linguists are late developers, by which I mean that they are late crystallizers.[8] It could be that modern linguists are actually delaying being anything. The boxes B and 2, C and 3 are to be seen as being in a tension. B is not indicative of a fixed identity, as it might be for a student scientist, but of a holding operation. It is likely that modern linguists are 'all-rounders' in Hudson's terms.[9] It is as if the developing self is protected by the outer shell of a convergent identity: certain disciplines or career choices can make this outer shell permanent ('not so much a shell with a soft marrow, as bone all through', Hudson 1966, p. 101), but it seems to me that the discipline of

Table 3.2: *Convergers and divergers*

	Converger	*Diverger*
PAST	**A** Did not have wide interests as a child Was good at Maths Was poor at English* Did Economics Did Classics	**1** Had wide interests as a child Was hopeless at Maths Was good at English Did Art Did Drama
PERSONALITY (intellectual/ emotional functioning in content area)	**B** Is cautious conscientious submissive 'yielding' emotionally inhibited intolerant of ambiguity, wants right answers 'sylb' likes precise, logical argument field-independent (focusser) love of detail not imaginative or creative or fluent (few uses for a brick) instrumental motivation, concern for career tolerant of boredom prefers lectures, private study sets clear boundaries between work/pleasure Quiet, reserved	**2** Is adventurous capable of delinquent behaviour independent-minded challenging emotionally uninhibited tolerant of ambiguity, there are no right answers 'sylph' intolerant of precision, logical argument field-dependent (scanner) impatient of detail imaginative, creative, fluent (many uses for a brick) expressive motivation (not concerned about career) intolerant of boredom prefers seminars loose boundaries pleasure/work outgoing, communicative
LANGUAGE	**C** chooses accuracy over expressiveness* prefers writing to speaking (more easily controlled) attracted by structure, rule, grammar 'learns' language	**3** expressiveness over accuracy* prefers speaking to writing (less easily controlled by others) collects or 'acquires' languages, catch-phrases, accents, plays with language

* Author's additions without test evidence.

modern languages is special in the way that the absence of content precludes this. The defence has to be temporary.

If one listens carefully to the students one can hear the crepitation, the tension between self-protection and growth:

> There are very few people I open myself up to. I don't like talking about my emotions. I don't need to, basically. French people seem to talk to each other on a much deeper level. I enjoy that actually. Perhaps it is because I feel that when I speak in French it is not my true self that comes out. (63)

Here the student expresses one convergent aspect of her personality, reserve and caution with regard to the expression of emotions, denies that there is any need to overcome that caution, then expresses satisfaction at overcoming it (as a result of identification with a group whose value it is perceived to be) and ascribes this change to another 'self'. This self is not a 'true' self at the moment and only time will tell whether it ever becomes a true self. The same student revealed the same tensions and the same choice of models in her family:

> My father is very reserved. I'm quite like him. My mother is quite shy but she always gets over it and is very chatty. My sister is more outgoing than I am. (63)

So she has the (surely unconscious) choice between being like her father, which is her 'true' (i.e. presently dominant) self or like her mother, who is like she is in France, with a chatty (not true?) self or like her sister (twin sister, incidentally) who may have actually changed.

The same sort of analysis could be made of most of the students. We saw how often their contact with latin countries was an occasion for them to develop a more emotional, less inhibited self. They are anything but fixed and static, but they are pretty equally poised between desiring change and fearing it. Here is a striking case of a student who had an A at English at A-level and who considered doing Psychology (she is described quite well by Box 1):

> I was thinking of doing Psychology, but I am too much of a deep thinker anyway . . . I would get too involved. You can get too paranoid or too involved in things. I will sit down in a room and I will analyse them anyway and if I was doing that full time . . . You reach a point when you know you should not think anymore.

She dropped English, decided against Psychology and decided to do the Cardiff ECS course:

> The sociology was quite superficial really. It was just what I needed.

But she then found the Economics and Politics 'boring, tedious' ('I was forcing myself to do it – I missed the literature') and finally opted for single honours French partly because she felt there was the possibility of good personal relationship: 'I freeze up without relationship: it's horrific' (53).

This fear of depth is also the fear of change and the fear of ambiguity. What is typical about this example is the initial flight from depth, identified (rightly or wrongly) with Psychology, the move towards complete safety in the Social Sciences, the fear of 'freezing' (being stuck), represented by boredom, and the final move to a situation where there was the potential for a relationship, i.e. some kind of safety while change took place. Autonomy, expressiveness, is undoubtedly the goal, but students are aware of the risks and also of the frequent mismatch between that goal and the requirement to perform well in examinations (see the quotations on p. 30). It may be that the ambivalent attitude to reading is explicable in these terms.

These students are not very different from students of other disciplines in experiencing this tension. They are, as I said, distinguished as a group rather by their readiness to hold on to the tension without closure or commitment. As we saw, even those students who appeared close at the outset are more fluid, diffuse and uncertain after their year abroad. There is a sense in which everything for them is provisional, to be tried and sampled; they are (to introduce another venerable binary division) foxes, not hedgehogs. They do not want to know (or be) one big thing, they want to known (and be) many things – provisionally at least.[10]

> If you do go into one thing in a great depth you would be missing so many other things. I think I am far too young to be concentrating on one thing. I am much more interested in learning things about lots of things and then presumably one thing will interest me more than any other. (68)

One can see why the world is their oyster, how they can be blank screens or permeable membranes, why they are attracted to translating and interpreting the words of others (who exist, have identity, are fixed and crystallized) but are also repelled by this. They escape the Sartrean opprobrium: they do not 'exist', they are not frozen in a constructed identity which is a defence against non-identity. They are prepared, provisionally, to be non-entities, poised somewhere between I and me. Unlike the mathematicians and natural science students in Sanford's study quoted above, modern languages students are questioning – but cautiously. They have avoided the specialization which can make the refuge permanent. Above all, they have given themselves the unique possibility of using expressive foreign cultures to escape the constrictions of their own. Like the students described by Sanford (1956), they are in a state of 'exceptional educability'. Their future development may well depend to a great extent on how they deal with the career question. My enquiries have not extended much beyond graduation but, as I suggested earlier, my guess is that modern linguists are likely to have special difficulty with the process of putting down roots. Commitment may always be provisional.

What is the right time for crystallization, for commitment? When is too early? When is too late? Each individual, each generation perhaps, has to decide this on the basis of what the real world is like. There is at least a case to be made for delaying crystallization, or, to put it more colloquially, for keeping your options open in a world as subject to rapid change as ours. It has also been suggested that women have always kept their ego boundaries diffuse in order to be able to shape their commitments to conform to husband and family (Chickering,

1981, p. 22, p. 30). I think this is probably true but I am suggesting that it has wider implications and that 'diffuse ego boundaries' can be given positive connotations in terms of ego development whereas the sharp ego boundaries demanded by certain disciplines and typically required of males are anti-developmental.

I will conclude this chapter with a preliminary reflection on the question of language and identity. The schema I presented in Figure 3.1 has 'language' as one of the identity-giving processes. There would be an argument for putting this at a different hierarchical level from the others. It is not only a question of my identity as a member of the group-of-speakers-of-English (which is analogous to the other boxes). The more crucial aspect of language is that it is the medium of all the other processes since it underlies the culture and phantasy aspects represented by wavy lines in the diagram. The initial choice to put into question the process by which identity is mediated must have consequences for the linguist's identity. Again I can do no more here than raise the question. More light will be thrown on it by some of the interviews with staff.

I can also mention here two articles. The first is Peter Harder's paper (1980) on 'The reduced personality of the second language learner' which is basically a contribution to an underresearched topic, the relatedness of native and foreign speakers.[11] His point is that language learning entails acceptance of a temporary identity which is 'coarse and primitive': 'in order to be a wit in a foreign language you have to go through the stage of being a half-wit – there is no other way' (p. 269). Back in 1936, Brachfeld claimed that language study depended less on intelligence than on what he called *courage* and this still seems to me to be a good word to describe the acceptance, not only of a diminution as Harder sees it, but, much more radically, of a temporary identity loss. We will pursue this difficult question of language and loss of identity in Part Two, using as our starting point reflections made by lecturers, and invoking some little known research in which language learning was used as therapy with schizophrenic patients.

Part 2

Staff

4

Choice

Là, tout n'est qu'ordre et beauté
Luxe, calme et volupté. (Baudelaire, *L'Invitation au Voyage*)

1 A thought experiment

Let us start with a thought experiment. I bring together in a large room all the students I interviewed. Then I bring in all the staff. The two groups look at each other across the room. The student group is much more homogenous: with the exception of a few 'mature' students (most of whom are in fact not much older than 25), they are all young. In the staff group there are some young faces, a phalanx of the middle-aged and some of retirement age. If I now bring in families (rather like a degree day) the student group is joined by parents (usually, but by no means always, two), boyfriends, girlfriends, rarely husbands and wives, rarely children. The staff group has fewer parents, but they are joined by husbands, wives, ex-husbands, ex-wives, lovers, children, grandchildren. If I now ask for signs of achievement, the student group barely changes (though the A level computer print-out sheets add a *pointilliste* touch). The staff group is transformed by robes of many colours, discreet rosettes: books and off-prints are piled up in front of some (not all).

What these two extremely disparate groups have in common is their choice of subject. If we ask them now to pair up (the families having been invited to go next door to their champagne lunch) and discuss how they got into modern languages, we find a striking similarity. Staff, like students, often had some kind of language background or early linguistic experience. A professor of German tells his partner:

> One of my early experiences was hearing my grandfather having a conversation in French with two visiting French nuns. This I found deeply impressive. I was six or seven. (16)

They talk, like the students, of chance factors: a woman lecturer in Italian says she took up Italian in school to get out of hockey (7). They describe the influence of teachers: a Germanist:

> My French master stood for 2 years at A level, translating Racine line by line, and we took it down line by line. We all got grade A, and we were all put off French for life. The German master sang German songs to us and we didn't live in fear of him. (27)

They tell the students that they too were no good at Science; some were good at maths though most were not. A professor of French admits

> I wasn't good at sums. I was and am absolutely innumerate. (46)

Some were attracted to the arts, especially music, but retreated cautiously:

> I realised how much practical talent especially there was [in Music]. That may have swung me against it, I felt the weakest one in the music department, whereas where French was concerned I was one of the strongest. (3)

Like the students they were postponing a career choice:

> By studying languages I was not making a career decision, I was really postponing one. (16)

Like the students they have a half-serious rivalry with other disciplines:

> Chaps will pull my leg at lunch time. 'You actually in today and it is the vacation, we thought you arts chaps never came in in the vacation, what about your garden, isn't it suffering from your absence?' They are only here because they have got stuff cooking and they have to keep an eye on it to see that it doesn't boil over. It is not tremendous intellectual commitment . . . I can read at home. (32)

Above all they had early experiences abroad which created powerful emotional bonds with the *culture*. The decision to study the *subject* was a function of those bonds, not vice versa:

> I went to Paris for a year before going to University. I had a marvellous experience. University on the whole was not a terribly edifying experience. I didn't get the enthusiasm that I had that year in Paris. (3)

> It was a fabulous exchange. It was a Paris doctor. I spent a week in Paris then drove to the country estate where he had three enormous houses and a farm. About a hundred people there, tennis court, river running through the property, 30 or 40 people at every meal. Fantastic. (2)

By now, staff and students are in language groups, exchanging stories: tales of bureaucracy in France, seduction in Italy, political activism in Germany. Wine is flowing, there are pizzas and camemberts, wurst and sangria. The sun is hot and the sea outside looks suspiciously like the Mediterranean. A few individuals withdraw at this stage, muttering something about reviews or essays to finish, but most go out into the sun. Hedonism is a shared value.

2 Hedonism

For many of the students, the interview with me was the first occasion on which they had given any thought to questions of choice. The staff, on the other hand, had often thought deeply about the issues I was raising. This means that the interviews with the staff enable us to investigate the same phenomena at greater depth. Take the question of hedonism: students, as we saw, talk of 'fun'. Staff use the same word: 'It was fun as an undergraduate' (2). 'I just find French fun' (3). 'If you specialize life is less fun . . . specializing is bound to make you miserable' (31).

But one picks up from the staff a different word and a different theme – happiness:

> I am not a prestige person. I am a person who needs to be happy. (3)

> [in Florence] I would take a hot shower and then go out about 8.30 to have dinner. [Because of my health] I would never dare to do this in this country. I would go out in the square with this big open air cafe and music and the passagiata. The very setting of the place conspired with the balmy air and gave me confidence. I felt happy. (4)

> I fell in love with the food, the music, it was cerises à l'eau de vie, goat's cheese, being up in the Auvergne, those high mountains, I used to hear Brassens, I listened to it all day, I was given the words, I loved the tunes, I translated it, I came home with the record. They used to play Sydney Bechet in the evenings, and we used to dance to it, it was the summer. It was August, the weather was 90 degrees, we were going swimming everyday. We were having picnics, French picnics. The mother was a typical Franco-Italian, warm-hearted, maternal, just being domestic and seemingly being happily domestic in a way that my mother had never been. I would sit in the car looking at this countryside through the windows, it was so beautiful. She would let me curl up and put my head on her ample bosom. It was a daughter–mother thing all mixed up with it. That was why it was so good. She was a very motherly woman. I wasn't there long enough to detect the pain and undercurrents in that family, I just knew enough to take a delight in a very happy French family life. They probably were a united and quite happy family, they were middle class, they were catholic, they had very strong roots and bonds. (8)

In this vivid account, elements of 'fun' and 'happiness' (as well as another aspect, response to beauty) are blended: 'Fun' is the food, the *cerises à l'eau de vie*, the dancing, the swimming, the songs: the happiness is the family, the ample bosom, the acceptance, the invisibility of pain – all of which makes possible the response to the beauty of the mountains in the comforting warmth of the sun.

It is quite striking that what the adults recall is not the excitement of individual adventure and exploration, but the experience of a new family, more open, more loving. The last respondent is now aware of the idealization, but at the time it was real. In accounts like this I get the sense of a blissful discovery of a benign world. Young people, breaking away from a family in which they have been closeted, for better or worse, for 18 years, leave their parents, go into a totally different world and discover that it is not only safe, but pleasurable and beautiful, that it is not only exciting and erotic but that it also contains people who, without any ties of blood, will be loving and nurturing. As a result, the whole world becomes available for exploration:

> I was going around like a sponge, absorbing things, listening to people, talking to people who swept the streets . . . I eavesdropped constantly in restaurants. Your senses are sharpened when you're abroad. It's active eavesdropping and nosiness and feretting things out. (7)

> There is a great deal in the foreign country which is grist to one's curiosity. The setting up of one's own hypotheses about certain tendencies and national characteristics. The first time I saw a public clock in Germany showing the wrong time, this was a great insight into a certain change in the German national character. (5)

> The basic fact of curiosity, and I see mine as avid and rabid, and in many ways indecent and scandalous. I would break every closed door if I dared. (13)

3 English

The staff interviews also throw light on the choice of modern languages compared to English. Almost all of the staff respondents were 'literary'. Why didn't they do English?:

> I think I didn't feel special enough at English . . . I was really outstandingly good at French, and that distinguished me from everyone else . . . I was good at English, I loved it, I did well, but I had a sense that if I went out into the world with it and entered into competition with others, given my background which was Welsh working-class, which didn't have a rich input of culture . . . I had a canny sense that once I left my Welsh school, where I could be one of the best, and got out into the world, into university, I would be competing with cultured middle class English people, and I had a feeling that I would fall by the wayside, a small fish in a large pond. Whereas really, unless they had done some exceptional travelling in France, or unless they were bilingual, I was on an equal footing with people who would be studying French, and, given my passion, my overwhelming interest in it, I thought that wherever I went in the country really it would take some doing to find people who had the same degree of commitment and the same degree of interest. (8)

I have no data on the social origins of modern linguists compared with their colleagues in English Departments. But my guess is that even those who are British-born are more *marginal* in terms of class and even geography, that there are more Celts, more Northerners, more people from modest backgrounds. The previous respondent was Welsh. Here is a professor whose background is Irish:

> I decided I would never make it if I didn't have more to offer than all those English people, their sophistication and their cleverness. I felt very much

on the Celtic fringe, so I thought 'why don't I do two degrees?'. So I did two degrees. (32)

and a young lecturer from Newcastle:

Coming from a working-class background and faced with an array of traditional English literature courses, you have a class reflex *vis à vis* these things. I enjoyed A-level English a lot. I still think it was part of an ideology of Britian and British history I couldn't fully identify with. It was easier to enter the foreign culture than your own. (29)

Scotland has always had a special relationship with things French. A professor (Jewish):

French in Scotland is part of a fantasy national identity, the auld alliance. Frenchness or awareness of France is something that separates them from the English and at the same time is the most obvious and accessible escape from being Scots . . . success for a lot of Scots people is getting out and yet defeat is going to London. (31)

In other words, the social realities of Britain, the class divisions which are symbolically replicated by geographical divisions, North/South, home counties/celtic fringe, are operative in subject choice, and to opt for a foreign culture is to opt against an English one. A Glaswegian lecturer in Italian:

I like the French and the Italians more than I like the English, who tend to be duplicitous and hypocritical. You can quote that. (18)

Modern languages offers an extraordinarily felicitous means of by-passing class-deprivation. To gain entry into higher education in order to study 'English' requires a certain cultural background, which is a class background. The question of 'interests' epitomizes this:

I got to this bit of the form about interests . . . *You* try to have interests in Black Hall Colliery. You couldn't go to the cinema because it was the flea pit and Mum wouldn't let you, there wasn't a theatre, there wasn't a concert you could go to, how the hell do you have interests if you don't like sport? I used to feel like writing 'mind your own bloody business'. You only got University accommodation if you pretended you had interests. I've got interests now, but I didn't then because I didn't have access to interests. (38)

Here is a vivid description of how a working-class Welsh girl pursued 'interests' that were highly relevant to modern languages, but which were far removed from girl guides or the violin, the way she escaped her own restrictive culture without espousing an English middle-class one:

I think in some way I wanted to be removed from my family, my society, my culture, my language, it was like offering a new start. I probably was good at it because these things unconsciously were being fed into my approach to it. I then found that it did actually put me in contact in my

> society with foreigners who started giving me a glimpse of a different way of life . . . It was quite indiscriminate who they were really, provided they were French. And it became such a passion, such an excitement, that if a French ship docked . . . I would be quite bold and I would pick up French sailors and befriend them, just to practise my French on them and there were quite a lot of difficult moments when I realized that these sailors were not interested in this little 16 year old because she knew good French idioms, but for other reasons! (8)

The subject 'English' is used as a support during the period when the foreign teacher is incapable of providing a real experience:

> Already I loved *King Lear*, I loved the English poets, and I had a very strong emotional approach to English literature from about the age of 12. I did an act of faith really with my teachers of French literature. I believed them, because I was fond of them, I knew if they were telling me that Balzac was great I would believe them and I would reproduce all this for them, and I did it. (8)

But in the long run it is seen as not offering the same possibilities in terms of a satisfactory identity as the choice of foreign languages.

Sefton Goldberg, the hero of Jacobson's *Coming from Behind* (1985), desperate to escape from teaching English at Wrottesley Polytechnic, applies for a job at Holy Christ Hall in Cambridge, in the belief that the job is only open to Jews 'and that provided he didn't spill too much food over himself or say anything detrimental to Jesus the job would be his'. Then he discovers there are five other candidates and realizes they can't all be Jewish because 'this was England, not America. Here literature and criticism were still *goyische* pursuits, tied up with solemn attitudes to marriage and standards' (p. 201). If this book were about the subject of English it would be interesting to speculate at this point on the way in which the subject may have been protected from challenge and change for many years by this 'goyische' status and to consider the impact of feminism and structuralism in this light.

As far as Modern Languages are concerned the essential point is that they are not 'goyische' to anything like the same extent. The subject is alternative and marginal.

4 Language and identity: the singing of silent children

> I think another reason why I was so attracted to a foreign language was that there was quite a lot of anxiety or unease in my associations with my mother tongue. This was associated with my family life. My mother, with whom I learned to speak the language, was unsatisfied and unfilled and quite an angry person and a lot of those undertones were picked up by me in the use of the language. English, my mother tongue, was slightly

> contaminated by the emotional input from my family. So there were lots of phrases and lots of expressions that used to make me anxious. When I discovered another language, French, I could learn these idioms, I could learn these expressions and the use of them was in some way delightful, new and not emotionally laden. I could put my own emotional content into those phrases, those expressions, they could be fun, they could be light, whereas an awful lot of the idiomatic use of English to me was laden with my mother's experience and I needed to get away from that. It had to be something I could make my own that didn't belong to my mother. But that was all at an unconscious level. (8)

In the previous section I suggested that the choice of a foreign culture was significant for individuals in terms of their search for an identity different from that offered by their community. However, there is something which is in a sense *prior* to culture and that is language.

As I suggested when discussing Figure 3.1 language is not merely an aspect of identity (I am a member of the group of English speakers, German speakers, etc.) but the principal means by which the process of identity formation takes place. As Foucault puts it: 'Language speaks me'. To learn a new language is to create a new identity *irrespective of the foreign culture or foreign experience*. The words will not have the same depth and resonance, but they will be in some sense innocent, fresh, free of all the accretions which characterize the words of the mother tongue, *les mots de la tribu*.

Social psychologists have given these matters some consideration. R. C. Gardner (1979) insists that the study of a second language is unlike any other curriculum topic: whereas other topics reinforce the learner's own culture, language-learning 'involves imposing elements of another culture into one's own life space'.

However, although Gardner's model is interesting, the actual process whereby language creates personal identity within a culture or against a culture, the way in which a 'life space' is constructed, is not something which the social psychologists deal with in any depth, since their concern is with groups. The same can be said even for psycho-linguists who are mainly interested in questions such as brain-functioning, code-switching, and the hypothetical possession by bi-linguals of separate mental lexicons.

The most serious consideration of these questions comes from a rather surprising quarter. On various occasions, individual psychoanalysts working with object relations theory or ego theory have turned their attention to language questions. In many cases there was a personal motive in that they themselves had been forced to leave their own country. For example, in 1939, Erwin Stengel, reading a paper before the British Psychoanalytical Society 'On Learning a New Language', began: 'This problem is of especially great importance for a psychoanalyst who has to continue his work in a new country'. Stengel observes that

> Our libidinal relation to an object denoted by a word in a foreign language is somewhat different to our relation to the same object denoted by a word

in the native language . . . our relations to an object change at the moment at which it obtains a new name.

(It should be noted that, like all the object relations theorists, Stengel uses 'object', oddly perhaps, to refer to persons as well as things). There is resistance, he says, to any change in object relations, therefore there is normally resistance to new names. He explains this resistance to new language as stemming from shame at the inevitable regression (cf. Harder's 'Reduced personality'), but also from fear of the magical nature of language and its connection with primary processes. Idioms (see the quotation at the head of this section) are particularly significant. They are like petrified jokes or dreams: 'they force on us the pictorial thinking which we experience as a temptation as well as a danger'. In other words, in the foreign language the purely instrumental, code-like and predictable aspects of familiar language may be replaced by restored imagery and creative play which is characteristic of childhood. While our response to this is ambivalent (temptation and danger) it would seem that the norm is resistance (i.e. the sense of danger). Good language learners are exceptional, it seems, in that they have preserved childhood characteristics (such as being prepared to talk nonsense). Language is 'the highest accomplishment of the ego' but it seems that learners of foreign languages may be less resistant than most to changes in the ego brought about by changes in language.

Edith Baxbaum is another analyst whose native tongue was German. In a paper read in Washington in 1949, she discusses the analysis of four bilingual (German–English) patients and sketches a theory linking language and ego-development ('The role of a second language in the formation of Ego and Superego', (1949)). She starts from a statement by Sterba that language expresses mental contents a) consciously (what the ego wants to communicate), b) unconsciously, via associations, verbal choice (or style, we might say), slips of the tongue, and c) via pronunciation, which is the deepest level, the least under conscious control, 'knit into the character structure'. The theory depends on the notion that the superego, inventor of the defence mechanisms, forbids access to unconscious, repressed experience in order to protect the ego and enable the person to function in the real world. But there is a price to be paid for this adaptation and this protection: the denial produces an 'amputated ego identity', a neurosis. This neurosis can take a linguistic form, stammering or, in the case of the two children treated, the inappropriate clinging to a foreign accent (which disappeared during the analysis). To 'master the neurosis' it is necessary to release the repressed experience into consciousness and this is done through language (psychoanalysis is the talking cure). The experience of the past is revived and accepted by being verbalized, by being made into a story, and the symbolic, magical capacities of language are invoked for this. Baxbaum doesn't spell this out, but her cases illustrate situations in which the original experience was fixed somehow by language and must therefore be unfixed by language.

However, the superego combats such attempts to revive the past: 'the superego uses its power to counteract the magic of speech'. The resistance may take the form of imposing silence. This is where Baxbaum's account becomes particularly relevant. She claims that the foreign language is an *alternative to silence*:

> although the women discussed here used a second language as a language of repression, it saved them from having to resort to long periods of silence . . . children who for neurotic reasons are unable to talk are nearly always able to sing the words of songs. *A second language might be compared to the singing of silent children: both free the words of the emotinal charge which burdens and inhibits the use of the native tongue.* With the help of the new language the superego was circumvented, its efficacy was weakened to some extent. [my italics].

And this is the contradictory aspect: it seems that the foreign language can be *both* an additional defence mechanism, reinforcing the repression, (since it enables apparent escape from the past into a new world, while preserving a neurosis) *and* a means of weakening the strength of the superego (presumably, though Baxbaum doesn't make this very clear, by providing an alternative to silence while the individual 're-establishes the past within the ego identity, reconciling the past with the present'. Learning a foreign language may support the superego in its attempt to deny access to repressed experience (associated inescapably with the mother tongue) but may also provide an alternative to silence, a kind of haven. There is also the possibility (which Baxbaum doesn't develop and which is clearer in Stengel) that the foreign language may activate the magic of speech in a particularly powerful assault on the superego.[1]

Anatole Matulis, a Lithuanian analyst working in America, reported in 1977 on work with schizophrenic patients (as well as describing the importance of foreign languages in his own analysis). Matulis takes the process of identity through language back to the beginning of the child's second year:

> Language, with its labelling of inner states, enhances the separateness between the inner and outer worlds thus providing a better mastery of both.

Schizophrenics regress to the period when both ego and language are unformed. Matulis uses language-learning with patients as an aid to reforming the ego, enabling it to deal with reality by divesting it of the threatening associations:

> In learning a new language the patient would once again initiate the activity of labelling, adapting a 'new' reality which obviously is the 'old' one but with different foreign names. Consequently this new foreign *réalité* would not possess any of the past conflicts, hostility, threats and unbearable emotional injuries . . . this newly acquired foreign language would become a sort of cathartic sponge . . . it would provide the schizophrenic patient with a temporary linguistic shelter from any emotional turmoil.

The foreign language is a 'linguistic tranquilliser'. Patients who cannot express feelings, who use circumlocutions or whose language is syntactically corrupt, speak 'normally' in the language which is, as one patient put it, 'the least emotional to me'.

This is not incompatible with Baxbaum's positions. She, presumably, would say that, in the case of schizophrenics, the superego has been too comprehensively defeated, the ego made too vulnerable, the regression to an infantile, magical world of primary process, too radical. In this case the ego needs to be restored. Language needs to be given its early (superego?) function of aiding adaptation to reality via separation, and the foreign language can do this for emotionally disturbed individuals. Matulis's 'temporary linguistic shelter', is Baxbaum's 'singing of silent children'; foreign languages are an alternative both to silence and babble.

Further metaphors for this holding function are offered by Adelson (1962), discussing the notion of identification in general:

> Identifications provide the means by which needed restructuring or crystallisations of personality can take place. In some cases the student can become himself only by becoming someone else . . . the identification is used as a *prop, a crutch, a smokescreen, a shield*; once it has served its purpose it is dissolved. [my italics].

The work of A. Guiora also relies on the theory of ego development but is rooted in experimental rather than clinical psychology. Guiora attempts to give construct validity to the notion of empathy by 'transpositional research', that is, the linking of something that is difficult to measure (empathy) with something which is easier to measure (in this case, pronunciation of a foreign language). The studies are ingenious, involving Michigan students in the experimental consumption of alcohol and reaching a conclusion (which most linguists could have predicted) that drink in moderation improves your accent. What is of interest to us is the theoretical basis. Guiora, like the other authors I have referred to, believes that learning a language means being able to take on a new identity and accept 'modification of one of the basic modes of identification by the self and others, the way we sound'. As a speaker of a foreign language, 'partially and temporarily one gives up one's separateness of identity'. Guiora makes a distinction between, on the one hand, syntax, grammar, and vocabulary which are the result of 'integrated ego-functioning' and, on the other, pronunciation which (like Baxbaum) he believes to be much less under conscious control: modification at this deep level implies 'flexibility of psychic processes'. To be able, after childhood, to develop a native-like accent is psychically remarkable. So it is pronunciation in particular, rather than language ability in general, which Guiora sees as being a sign of permeability of the ego boundary, the capacity for temporary fusion of self-object boundaries. He has coined the term 'language ego' on the model of 'body ego' and makes an interesting comparison with gifted racing drivers who possess unusual permeability of body ego (i.e. who become one with the car). Linguists would be similar as regards language ego. Guiora views this permeabililty positively: for him the individual who is capable of speaking a foreign language 'without an accent' is likely to be capable of 'an immediate emotional apprehension of another, this sensing being used by the cognitive function to gain understanding of the other', a capacity which, it seems, comes from the retention in some way (not made clear) of early patterns of object relations, the mother–child fusion. The other aspect, language as a defence, aiding repression, is not something Guiora acknowledges, though presumably there is no logical contradiction: an individual may be empathic with others while still using language defensively in terms of his or her own neurosis.

5 Cross-cultural marriage

> Harriet wondered 'How did I come to marry someone so different from myself?' But she had married him; and perhaps unawares, it was the difference she had married. (Olivia Manning, *Balkan Trilogy*, p. 755, Penguin)

> La dot des vrais couples est la même que celle des couples faux le désaccord originel. Hector est le contraire de moi . . . Nous passons notre journée ou à nous vaincre l'un l'autre ou à nous sacrifier. Les époux amoureux n'ont pas le visage clair. (Giraudoux, *La Guerre de Troie n'aura pas lieu*, II, 8)

About one in three of my staff informants' first marriages were cross-cultural. Many linguists espouse the culture literally or more generally espouse difference. The Office of Population Censuses and Surveys does not keep figures of cross-cultural marriages and the Labour Force Survey which Coleman has used (1985) is useful only for racially mixed marriages. However, one in three, though not surprising, is obviously a very high proportion. My small sample includes the following first marriages: English–Ghanaian; Spanish–German; Scottish–Polish and several French–British. There were some divorces (one since the interviews were conducted) and several remarriages (cross-cultural in one case).

There is not a lot of research on cross-cultural marriage. However the Institute of Marital Studies (IMS) has reported on work with five such couples who sought help from the Institute (Cohen, 1982). The theoretical concepts used by the IMS are particularly useful for attempting to understand how linguists live their lives, since they are centrally concerned with difference and sameness and their role in the process of individuation. I am not suggesting there is complete homology between subject choice, career choice and choice of marriage partner; indeed it may be that in the psychic economy of an individual different aspects are managed by work and marriage. However, it seems that where choice is possible an individual makes choices which are significantly related, so that understanding choice in one area throws light on choice in another area. Indeed, the IMS is currently conducting research on this basis: a preliminary report has been published by Daniell, 'Love and Work: complementary aspects of personal identity' (1985).

I should also perhaps make the point that in this section, as in the previous one, I am using studies of individuals who have sought professional help, on the assumption that there is a continuum and that the same processes are at work in all of us, the distinction being that in some cases they are handled without professional assistance and in other cases they are not.

I will start by describing the model of development underlying the work of the IMS. I derive this from Cohen's article and from an earlier book by Mattinson and Sinclair, *Mate and Stalemate* (1979). Their model is compatible with models discussed in the first part of this book, but is more radical in the sense of incorporating childhood experience.

Life is a process of individuation or differentiation. This process begins around four or five months when the initial fusion ends and when the baby becomes aware of being separate from the mother. There follows the long process of growth and development through identification. This process is inherently difficult since the reality is always one of past separation and loss: gain is in the future. After the dashing of their hopes and the loss of their sense of oneness, the couples Cohen worked with felt 'different, abandoned, alone'. They were thus temporarily returned to the point humans start from and from which they journey by a succession of identifications. The process of identification by which individuation takes place can be *narcissistic* or *anaclitic* (Freud's terms). In narcissistic identification, the sense of self is enhanced by relation to what is the *same* (same-sex parent, homosexual partner). In anaclitic identification, identification is with what is different, those aspects which the individual lacks or to which he or she aspires (opposite-sex parent, heterosexual partner). The point is, however, that in both cases the reality of uniqueness and difference is inescapable. Even (to take an extreme case) in homosexual partners from the same culture, there is inevitable difference. While sameness is a group matter, difference is individual. The process of development is one of learning to be unique in a group. One difficulty comes from the fact that the more I differentiate myself the more separate and lonely I become; but the more I become a member of a group the more enveloped I am and the more I fear loss of my identity and a return to fusion (since what is appropriate for the baby is not appropriate for the adult). So the separation has to be accepted. Difference is *inside* the individual. Development consists of learning to accept this, tolerating the ambivalence – the fact, for example, that one loves and hates the same object. This is difficult so we resort to various defences. One is splitting and projecting: our inner ambivalence is denied by projecting a repudiated part (the love or the hate, the good or the bad, the free or the fettered) out onto some other person (or culture), in order to achieve a (delusional) internal sameness for ourselves. Another is a return to the original state of fusion by a romantic attachment. Cohen, in a nice phrase, speaks of 'delusional omnipotent fusion' and, while (somewhat grudgingly) accepting that being in love is something that happens to lots of people, sees it as a defence and, in particular, as the principal defence of cross-cultural couples. They all seem to have been, in conventional terms, very much in love, denying vehemently any difference between them, experiencing total, wordless empathy and spontaneity and the magical cessation of the need to relate across a gap, using language; they had what Godard in *Le Mépris* calls 'une inadvertance folle, une complicité ravie'. They had the sense that between them as *individuals* there was no difference.

They delighted in the cultural differences, language, skin colour, convinced that 'under the culture' they were the same.

Cohen's hypothesis concerning these couples is startling and throws a new light on the question of why people choose a foreign culture, language or partner. She suggests that the choice of the partner from a different culture is a means of *avoiding* difference. The couples she worked with had not satisfactorily differentiated themselves within their own culture as unique individuals within the sameness of their community: the cultural differences provide a boundary which makes the insecure identity more secure (see also Morley, 1975). They have, she says,

> an underlying need . . . to escape their own world and espouse a different one . . . the marriage out of their own culture provided them with a more definite identity while at the same time giving them a valid reason to avoid the difficulties inherent in the process of developing their individuality within their original culture.

They could

> avoid knowing about individual difference while [having] a semblance of a distinct identity.

The idyllic empathy, the 'illusory sameness' was shattered by the intrusion of outside reality (typically babies), revealing inner difference as something inescapable. At this time the disappointment was in proportion to the initial hope and promise; where before *everything* had been fused in sameness, now *everything* was different. Difference meant loss of relationship. A couple might divorce at this stage but re-marriage was again likely to be cross-cultural.[2]

Cohen concentrates on the defence of fusion, but I think the notion of projection can also be invoked. We could say that the notion of difference, of inner conflict, is projected out on to the cultures or on to the groups, leaving the individuals free to have their conflict-free and difference-free fusion and to enjoy in delight and excitement the pro-fusion of the world:

> The cross-cultural marriage protects the partners from the painful uncertainties of who they are while also holding out the promise of *potential resolution of the problem.*

Inevitably, Cohen underplays the *promise*. But many cross-cultural marriages fulfil their promise, and most of the couples with whom she was working were contemplating change rather than separation. In other words, the metaphors we used to describe the use of foreign languages might be applied to cross-cultural marriages: they can be seen as havens, protection during growth which may be particularly difficult because the integration to be achieved is particularly great. The 'promise' is considerable as is the hope. It may be that, as Cohen implies, differentiation is most easily achieved in a stable community (she refers to the Manus people 'living in a culture firmly held by three generations') and same-culture marriages (through narcissistic identification). But this position is essentially conservative. The high-risk alternative represented by cross-cultural marriage (and careers) confronts head-on the greater problems of anaclitic identification and the whole business of splitting and projection. It offers indeed the *promise* of acceptance of greater difference both in the individuals (in terms of diffuse ego boundaries, ambivalence and flexible response to the world) and between individuals and cultures. The idyllic fusion can be seen as a kind of protective compensation for this long term effort. Since these things often sound better in German, I would christen it the *Belohnungseffekt*. The effort must indeed involve 'reclaiming rejected roots', or 'accepting the past', as Baxbaum put it, but it is also concerned with freedom, change and movement and fulfils a systemic function. There may be illusion, but the illusion can, like works of art, be functional, keeping alive a certain hope of resolution, Messianic perhaps, but necessary if difference between individuals and between cultures is to be accepted and if the dialectic of same and different is to be worked out peacefully. Hope is the smiling face of dissatisfaction. These couples have 'married the problem' and the problem is difference. It may be that in some way linguists are working at difference on behalf of society, that this is their 'specialized work task', a possibility we will consider in the third part of this book when we look at the discipline.

6 What's your topic?

If we take the staff respondents back to their student days and thus create an imaginary student group, the result is like no group of students that ever was. They were the academic high achievers, the Firsts, different from their peers in various ways, more highly motivated, more interested in intellectual matters in general and in literature in particular, less interested in language for its own sake. In many cases, they were less compliant, more autonomous, to the point of rebellion even (though this does not apply to the women, who in most cases seem to have been successful at intuiting what was required of them rather than challenging anything).

In all cases they met the particular criteria for excellence which the value system of the University determines. Whatever other qualities they may or may not have had, they were academic and were rewarded by being invited to remain in academe.

The rite of passage was doctoral research. Not all students who get Firsts choose to do research and this investigation is not concerned with those who chose some other career. I am interested here in a sub-group of a sub-group: those linguists who, having done exceptionally well academically, get a research grant and start on a PhD, usually returning to the foreign country for a second bite of the cherry.

This is where the final choice of discipline is made, and also where a career as a university teacher is chosen. In a Science subject, a PhD is still a preparation for a career in industry; in an Arts subject its principal meaning is as a necessary qualification for teaching in higher education.

In theory, it would be possible at this stage to move towards obtaining legitimation in another discipline: history, sociology, psychology, linguistics. In practice, the socializing power of a first degree is such that shifts like this are rare. The first thing a modern languages graduate does when contemplating research is to 'look for an author'. In other words, postgraduate work in modern languages, even more than undergraduate work, is literary (and author-centred) as regards its subject matter, although the particular discipline whose aid will be invoked may vary.

So we are again looking at a crucial choice. Here, as always, chance plays a role:

> By chance I met Mme Romain Rolland at a party. 'My boy, I have endless papers of my husband's. Why don't you write a thesis?' (32)

But at this stage the chance elements are more apparent than real. Given a totally free choice in the whole field of literary and intellectual studies, people choose, it seems to me, subjects which are closest to their need to understand themselves. Sometimes this is obvious:

> Well, I had started looking at Simone de Beauvoir for pleasure. It seems absurd because there she was, a cultured, French middle-class girl, at a Catholic private school, with a lawyer for a father, and a rich childhood of literary input and wealth and care. A happy childhood in comparison with me, a totally different childhood, totally different background, totally different experience. But somehow or other, what she was striving towards in her own context and her own way was exactly what I was striving towards, so there was an exciting sort of exploration of who Simone de Beauvoir was, who I was. In retrospect I can see now that here is a picture of a woman showing another woman how she came to establish her false male identity. In such a way that I began to recognize where I'd gone wrong and what I had been doing. (8)

But it can also be quite obscure at the time and only emerge much later in retrospect, as in the case of a lecturer in French whose dilemma as a postgraduate was whether to attempt a career as an artist and who chose to study an author who was also a painter; or the philologist whose topic was a particular peasant dialect, who went and lived with these peasants in France and whose unconscious wish was to understand his own Shropshire origins. Then, there is also the compensating choice, the shy, withdrawn young Cambridge woman who chose Rabelais:

> I've not got a lot of imagination of my own, which is why I am impressed by other people's imagination, perhaps. (23)

I have reflected elsewhere (1981) on my own choice of subject which I now see as being uncannily apt. Only in a world where the scientific illusion reigns, where there is a belief that the terrain of literature and ideas can be mapped comprehensively and areas staked out, as in entomology or chemistry, is it possible to ignore the evident truth that the choice of a research topic or of an author is similar to the choice of a discipline or of a marriage partner. The unconscious processes – identification of both types, splitting and projection – are likely to be involved in any work that is meaningful for the researcher. The most 'objective', scholarly PhD is an act of self revelation and frequently autobiographical in the Lejeune sense (1971), an act of self-discovery through writing. But, unlike in autobiography, the self-discovery is not made explicit:

> I started off with the assumption that it didn't really matter what you were working on. Anything you were working on became interesting by the fact that you were working on it. Then I got disabused of that. It seemed to me subsequently that if you were working on something that you felt congenial, there never came a point when you had to say why it was you found it congenial. It was difficult to write on something you were not on the same wavelength as. There were implicit value judgements that one could have tracked down, but that I didn't bother to track down . . . you don't have to make explicit your own feelings. (24)

The comparison with research in a scientific discipline is dramatic. There are no nursery slopes. 20 year olds grapple with vast questions:

> The PhD subject was about one writer who started out by an appreciative historical account of the leading Jew, Spinoza and who later on turned out as one of the figureheads of Nazism. How does a man make a development like that and what has this to tell us about the historical development of Germany? (5)

This is where the original rebellious reasons for choosing modern languages begin to make sense. Modern languages enable highly intelligent people to study in a variety of fields *without accepting the official (British) definition of those fields and their institutionalization.* Modern languages scholars distance themselves not from Philosophy but from British Philosophy, not from Psychology but from British Psychology. They reject a certain narrowness and also, it seems, a certain lack of moral seriousness:

> In the sixth form we had a general studies course in which we would read philosophical aspects and discuss problems of morality. This was in the early fifties. The moral problems raised by World War Two were very much in people's minds. We had some very good discussions, I enjoyed it [Philosophy] at University. But I also saw that I could pursue that sort of thing side by side with literature. Both the German and French departments had courses on French thought, German thought. With philosophy I would have been doing the philosophy of language, that sort of thing. Later I became very interested in Schopenhauer and Jung, who were looked down upon by the Philosophy and Psychology departments. Nor would it have been possible to combine them in either one of those departments. Whereas in the language department it was just as legitimate to go into Jung as it was to go into Schopenhauer. (16)

> I was shocked by the dilettantism. I had been to some lectures in Philosophy [in Oxford] I had really been turned off by Anglo-Saxon

> philosophy because it was very boring, irrelevant . . . it didn't address real moral issues. Existentialism did address moral issues . . . I decided that I wanted to pursue these areas, but I didn't want to pursue them in the tradition of philosophical departments of British Universities. So I thought the only way around it is to go into a language department . . . you are outside the mainstream of British Philosophy. (10)

> The course [in German] was explicitly and overtly concerned with theoretical political questions. I don't think I would have been aware at that stage that English was so different. I am very much aware of it now, that if I had studied English, I would have been studying Leavisite criticism predominantly . . . Kafka, Camus, Sartre raise questions much more obviously than an awful lot of English Literature does. (17)

What was attractive about modern languages was the possibility of a cultural, intellectual life which was not British, indeed which constituted an escape from what was perceived as a non-intellectual culture. In the intellectual area, as in the areas of culture, language and choice of marriage partner, foreign languages offer the possibility of a choice which affirms difference and separateness but which requires much greater powers of integration:

> Any modern writer may have interested himself in any area of human knowledge and you have got to be able to follow him. (5)

7 The job

After several years of research and an extended experience of living in a foreign country the next thing is a job. Here we do not usually have to deal with the complexities of choice. Things may have been easier in the 1960s; people may have refrained from applying for jobs in certain places which they may have considered above them or beneath them, but on the whole people took what was going. At this stage, a postgraduate may make a last bid to change disciplines. One of my respondents, after doing mainly historical research, was interviewed for a job in a history department, but it happened to be the most conservative one in Britain and he was turned down because he had a modern languages degree and was not 'a proper historian'. However, another, a Germanist, after failing to get a job in various German departments, joined the Industrial Relations Department of LSE. He had done research on German theatre in the 1920s and therefore on labour history. He is now a senior lecturer in Sociology:

> I never regret having done a modern language degree. You concentrate on getting inside the language. That as a jumping ground for doing what I do is ideal. (27)

But such shifts are rare.

In Britain the postgraduate will expect to go directly into higher education. Few of my respondents did PGCE courses or had a vocation as a teacher; this quotation, from a man who is talking about his feelings after active service in World War Two is unusual:

> My desire to teach was a moral decision. A desire to change the world. (25)

More typical is this attitude, from a younger man:

> The academic thing becomes a necessity in order to survive within it. You can't just go on drinking wine and having nice times in France, you've got to earn money . . . if you want to carry on with these things you enjoy doing you have got to put some work into it. (2)

University teaching was, and still is to a certain extent, prestigious and desirable, but it is rarely a vocation. It would not be meaningful in my opinion to even consider this 'choice' in the way we have considered other choices in this chapter. University modern linguists make their career choice, when they make it, by default. These lovers of difference return to the same world they inhabited as post-adolescent students, sometimes to the same institutions. They will move infrequently in their career; very few will leave for a different occupation. This is where they will live their professional lives.[3]

5

Experience

It seems that Faculty are not a bad lot once you get to know them, but the culture within which they labour has to be changed. (Nevitt Sanford, 1982)

He's bowled much better than his figures indicate. (Fred Trueman, BBC Radio)

1 The personal, the professional and the outside world

We are now looking at the central span of an individual's life. It is central in two ways: first, because the years between getting a first job and retirement are the years of active adulthood, the years when one actually lives one's life, largely out of sight of its beginning and of its end; secondly, because, for most people, but especially for professionals and more especially for University teachers, a career dominates a life – in terms of time, energy invested, opportunities for personal development, exerting influence and satisfying aspirations. So, in this chapter, I am attempting to describe how certain highly gifted men and women live the central part of their lives and the role played by the particular discipline and career they have chosen.

The problem of the interaction between the personal and the professional is crucial and is particularly acute in the case of modern linguists. My dentist recently had a baby. For three months there was a locum in her surgery. Then she returned, having employed a person to look after the child. I imagine (dentist–patient communication is fraught), that there are times when the personal fact of having a baby encroaches on her work (lack of sleep, anxiety if the child is ill . . .) and she may even have doubts about pursuing her career. But the job itself remains the same, and the boundaries (time, place, task) between her private life and her professional life are unambiguous.

For University teachers, on the contrary, the boundaries are sometimes so blurred as to be non-existent. University teachers have vastly more freedom to organize their own boundaries than any other professional group. When the AUT called a strike recently, difficult questions arose: if someone had no lectures and no committee meetings that day, could they be on strike at home and would reading professional books, as distinct, say, from books about golf, be strike-breaking? In other words, whether an individual was on strike or working was a matter for self-definition. This is unthinkable for most working people and is a situation more akin to that of a free-lance author or consultant. At any moment, a university teacher can be making choices between one activity and another – this meeting (cancel class) or this class (apologies to meeting); take the child to the doctor this morning (do the marking this evening). There are very few sanctions and the job is largely what an individual makes it. It is no longer true to say as 'Bruce Truscot' said (1951, p. 99) that 'The life of a well-established, middle-aged professor in the Arts Faculty of a modern university, can, if he likes to make it so, be one of the softest jobs to be found on the earth's surface': administration sees to that, and government policy. But it can still be true of other ranks. The range is enormous: from the individual who does no research, a minimum of administration and delivers the same lectures every year, to someone whose diary looks like that of a cabinet minister and whose list of publications is like the bibliography of this book.

I am not suggesting that University teachers are alone in having to manage the personal/professional boundary: a bus driver has to take care that a quarrel with his wife over breakfast doesn't affect the standing passengers. But I am saying that the way this boundary is managed by individuals and the nature of the difficulty in each career is important for the understanding of the way people live their lives (and incidentally for understanding the significance of redundancy and retirement) and I am saying that the degree of flexibility, uncertainty and freedom to interpret, while delightful, is also productive of stress.

I have the sense that the whole subject is in some way taboo: the fantasy has to be maintained that the boundary between professional and personal is never crossed or blurred. Presumably the notion that politicians could suffer from pre-menstrual tension, surgeons from aggressive impulses, or senior policemen from mid-life depression is too disturbing to contemplate. And yet the reality is that life events impinge and they impinge more on the job of the university lecturer because the job potentially involves so much more of the person than dentistry or airline piloting, brain surgery or bus driving. Modern linguists, because they are involved in teaching, that is, in interpersonal, intergenerational communication, and because they teach language and literature, that is, potentially the whole range of human experience and symbolic representation of that human experience, are inevitably deeply and inextricably involved in the personal. A marriage, a divorce, a birth alters the teacher/student relationship, as does the death of a parent or the birth of a grandchild. The job is not the same for a 25-year-old single person whose students are not much younger, for a 30-year-old struggling to finish a thesis in the midst of babies and power-tools, a 40-year-old experiencing Eliott Jaques's 'mid-life crisis' (1965), a 50-year-old with adolescent or post-adolescent children. Life is lived through a career and through an institution; but a career and an institution are also lived through a life.

While this applies particularly to teaching and to the changing age-difference, it also applies to research. One's creativity, what one is able and willing to work on or to write about, changes constantly as one grows older (as Jaques demonstrates in the article quoted above).

There is biology and there is politics. Even in a world as traditional, as isolated and as ponderous as higher education, things happen over the 40 years of a career. Whole new institutions are created in a Robbins rush of expansion and confidence (or 'in a fit half of absent-mindedness, half of acquisitive imperialism' as Peter Scott puts it (1984, p. 1)); plate-glass-and-concrete universities join red-brick and dreaming-spires; polytechnics are born.

Then the cosy consensus, whereby universities and government agree that higher education is a Good Thing – like the Church of England and Marks and Spencer – is cruelly destroyed; suddenly higher education is under threat, rudely challenged to justify itself in economic terms, required to defend an ethos that was previously an article of faith:

> The University ethos, the pursuit of knowledge and beauty for its own sake – and beauty is even more of a luxury than knowledge – somebody has got to keep up the standards of beauty and knowledge. (23)

Declarations like this suddenly seem like colours bravely and forlornly nailed to the mast. Some of my older respondents (like the one quoted above) had their early careers in the 1940s interrupted by World War Two. Less dramatically, the 1980s have also demonstrated that in the course of a career the world changes and does not consult with individuals. Halsey and Trow's book on *The British Academics* (1971) seems positively quaint today with its questions about attitudes to expansion and a 10 page index without 'unemployment', 'early retirement', 'redundancy' or 'cuts'.

> Unemployment? . . . I didn't think of it. I came from an area with the highest unemployment in England, but we didn't give it a thought . . . we didn't expect to have 40 year old academics sitting and worrying about whether they were going to be made redundant. (38)

The above quotation is from a lecturer in Salford, the university hardest hit by the cuts. But here is a senior academic in Cambridge:

> We had a tremendous personnel crisis as a result of government policies. A department of 21 shrank to 14. (46)

And a professor in Sussex:

> There is a general problem of morale in universities, because people assumed for many years that if they were teaching in universities it was a respectable thing, it wasn't queried very much. The atmosphere of the last 8 years or so, the general sense that the Universities are being criticized, that they are not loved as they were, all of that at a time when the values of the traditional humanities are being questioned from other places, that combines to create rather low morale in the arts in general and not least in modern languages. There is a social crisis and questioning which does affect us and how we see the future of our subject. (32)

Nevertheless, whatever the tribulations in the South, the most dramatic example of how the world can change almost overnight is still Salford. The head of the department of modern languages at the beginning of my visit there:

> If you don't understand the effects of the cuts in 1981, you don't understand anything about this place. You might as well go home now. (42)

In 1981 Salford University was faced with a massive 44% cut in its income from the University Grants Committee (UGC). The modern languages department had to lose 8 out of 40 jobs. Voluntary redundancies (which left hardly anyone over the age of 50) took place. In order to operate within the new constraints, they chose to develop income-generating courses. Courses like the MA in Applied Linguistics or the MA in Interpretation (English/Arabic/English) are aimed specifically at the Arab world. The Advanced Certificate in English as a Foreign Language (CEFL) is also directed at foreign students. An intensive course takes place in July and all members of the department are expected to contribute – without remuneration. Even the departmental play makes a profit.

The department's feeling about the crisis is surprisingly mixed. There is anger, since they feel that Salford was unfairly singled out and that the stress is excessive, but there is also recognition that the external threat was somehow salutory:

> In this university we have gone from being a bit complacent to being under such stress that we can't really benefit. But some changes being forced upon you is a good thing, because, unless you are very thrusting and dynamic, you probably don't thrust actual work-type changes upon yourself. You might go and leave husbands and wives, but you don't think 'I am going to teach in a radically different way now'. (38)

> Everything happens at 100 mph in this department. The expectations that everybody has of everybody else's behaviour have perhaps been raised, a certain amount of sloppiness which perhaps might have been put down to 'we are all academics and we muck along', well we haven't been able to do much mucking along. Things have had to be very precise and a lot of us have had to learn to do things we never thought we would have to learn to do. Financial management for example. That is making it sound as if the cuts were a good idea, but that is not the way to do it. There are other ways to do it. There are other means of achieving the same ends. (36)

The main point about the Salford example is the fact of outside pressure on individuals' experience:

> Until this year I never considered going back to France, but now, with no promotion, no money, summer courses to generate money . . . I would like things to ease up. (39)

> I feel guilty about being in the job I got in 1966. But the job has changed beyond all recognition. I don't need to go somewhere else. I am somewhere else. (38)

An institution which represented a radical, practical alternative when it was set up 20 years ago and which had not basically changed during that period, suddenly found itself somehow hoist with its own petard, the guinea-pig in an experiment designed to demonstrate that universities could operate in the market place like businesses. The effect has certainly been to increase efficiency and there is a great deal of pride in achievement at Salford:

> You can't come to this department and fall asleep. You ring up this department between 9 and 5 and someone will always answer. How many departments can you say that of? I ring up Spanish departments up and down the country. Wednesday afternoons there is nobody there, Friday afternoons there is nobody there. The other departments seem so self-centred. We do look out . . . it is traditionally considered in many universities that languages are floppy, soppy, frilly, mess-abouty. Our department is none of those, thrusting, forthright, doing it, getting the money in, getting the students in, getting the prestige in. If you are competing within the university, you have got to compete on those terms. (40)

> I console myself by saying that we have a very good reputation. We've got 1100 applications for 80 places. (39)

But, as a result of the external pressure, not only are individuals who might have been expecting another 15 years of being 'in it' now digging their gardens, but those who are still 'in it' are living it in a very different way. Above all, they live with the fundamental doubt about whether what they are doing is admirable, or in some way a surrender of basic values:

> Now we give students a smaller proportion of our time, energy and enthusiasm. I don't think that getting your thoughts published is going to change the world, but what is bad and what does effect your teaching is if you don't have time to have those thoughts . . . If you don't have time to find out something new for yourself, how are you going to teach something new? (38)

One wonders how to read the quotation placed on the first page of the Salford graduate prospectus: '"May I express my faith in Salford University and in the work that it is doing . . ." Right Honourable Margaret Thatcher, PC, MP, Prime Minister'.

Salford is not alone and it would be possible to multiply examples of individuals in modern languages whose personal lives have been radically changed – usually for the worse – by the economic climate. For example, the division of languages at Brunel University which ran the degree in Modern Languages and Engineering was dispersed in 1982. Linguists simply ceased to be linguists:

> X took early retirement. He was in his 50s. Y is now Public Relations Officer. He no longer teaches Russian. Z was asked to go into Production Technology. I am now senior tutor in the Engineering department, an

administrative job; I have to organize the Tutorial system, draw up examinations schedules . . . (20)

It seemed essential to me to describe the general context of university life – the lack of boundaries and the hostile economic climate – before going on to consider more specific aspects of the experience of modern linguists in the rest of this chapter. However, the general question of the place of the discipline in the university and in society is one we will examine in the final part of the book.

2 Towards Ambi-culturalism

The language I have learn'd these forty years,
My native English, now I must forgo:
And now my tongue's use is to me no more
Than an unstringed viol or a harp;
Or like a cunning instrument cased up,
Or, being open, put into his hands
That knows no touch to tune the harmony:
Within my mouth you have engaol'd my tongue,
Doubly portcullis'd with my teeth and lips;
And dull unfeeling barren ignorance
Is made my gaoler to attend on me.
I am too old to fawn upon a nurse,
Too far in years to be a pupil now:
What is thy sentence then but speechless death,
Which robs my tongue from breathing native breath?
Shakespeare, *Richard II*, I, iii
(Mowbray on his banishment)

The career of people who have chosen to become specialists in another language and culture is inevitably bound up with the history of their relationship with that language and culture.

Some, a minority, always had a detached, scholarly attitude to the foreign culture:

> The country had no connotations. It was not good or bad. It was somewhere else. (33)

> I was never attracted to France or distanced from it. I think of it as an attractive, interesting, and in many ways beautiful person whom I would like to study. There is an element of detachment in that isn't there? I am at home in libraries where, as Montaigne puts it, 'I hold converse with the great minds of previous centuries'. I am not very good at conversing with 1985 people. I am bad at making French friends. (23)

For this respondent, the relationship does not change very much. There has been a movement away from France. 'I have found France, in the last 10 years, more and more difficult to get on with', but basically the stance remains that of detachment:

> If it came to war between France and Britain, I would attempt to judge morally and historically which was in the right and if I couldn't agree to either I would be a conscientious objector. (23)

For others, detachment – if that is the right word – takes the form of a kind of passionate oscillation. One culture is tolerable, enjoyable even, because the other exists as an alternative. Rootedness is avoided, initially at least:

> I have never been completely at home in one place, England, France. When I am in one place I am always conscious of another place which makes me see the place I'm in in a certain way. I have this critical distance which enhances enjoyment. I always feel the comparison going on . . . I'd never want to live in one place for more than 7 years. In 3 years I could be a French citizen. (29)

> My love is France. My wife is French. I have been accused by my parents of being more French than English. My children are bilingual. It is half of my life. I couldn't imagine my life without that being there. I used to see it as a conflict – even my English: people said I had a South African accent and so on. I've learnt to live with it. I used to be highly critical of Britain when I was in France and highly critical of France when I was in Britain. But you cannot maintain that hypercritical position. (36)

This notion of rootedness seems central. There is a simultaneous search for and avoidance of roots.

The most common situation seems to be that the rootedness of parents is used to facilitate the next generation's mobility: one respondent's parents were in Guernsey where he returns every summer; this enables him to feel rooted in the city where he works. But for some the situation is more complicated. The example of British-born Italians, often found on the staff of Italian departments, is particularly striking. One of my respondents did a degree in French but switched to Italian:

> If your name is Francesco Damiano Marengo and you don't speak Italian, there is something wrong. (18)

Another was born in London in 1940, in Little Italy. He also has an Italian name. He remembers, as a child, being insulted for being Italian: he and his friends had to defend themselves against charges of cowardice, for example. He described how, one summer, he visited the area up in the Apennine Mountains where his parents came from:

> When I go there I get this tremendous sense of belonging. It is quite extraordinary. It takes my breath away. I could stay there for ever. And there is *nothing* there for me. A normal person would be bored out of his mind. I speak the dialect, of course. I feel so close to these people. I went into an Osteria, all these odd guys with trilby hats, suddenly I broke into

> the dialect. Their expressions changed, they started smiling. They must have thought of me as being from the city. Then, to hear me speak in the dialect, the language I was brought up on, they warmed to me. (10)

But in Rome he experienced the conflict which came from the fact that Italians who met him assumed from his appearance that he was Italian, but he could not meet their expectations:

> There has always been a conflict, because when they see me they don't think I am English. They always look at me and they think I am Italian when they hear me since my accent is quite good . . . and yet they can tell there is something odd about this guy. But they never dream that I am British. It is not something you can escape. You can't make yourself a stock student of Italian because you are not treated like that. Your own self-definition is partly what people make you. You decide you want to be a straight English foreigner in Italy. But there is no way I can do that . . . I haven't worked these things out, they don't interest me in an introspective sense. I don't spend any time thinking about it. But if I did I am sure I would discover all sorts of interesting things about communities – a sense of belonging and languages. But the overriding fact is that there is no simple way out of this. I am not Italian, I am not British in any clear sense of either of those. I am somewhere in between. I have accepted that now. I have struggled to be Italian. Then I struggled to be English. But you are struggling to be what you are not. (10)

This case is interesting because the split is, so to speak, given not chosen and the choice of modern languages is a way of living the unavoidable. Acceptance means acceptance of a split identity.

Another experience is that of the 'exiles', those individuals who have chosen to live and have their career in the foreign country. I have done no research on British people abroad, but I did interview French and Spanish people who came to Britain as language assistants and who got jobs as lecturers in language departments. One of these described himself as a 'natural exile'. His own country, France, was not congenial for reasons which are oddly complementary to the dissatisfaction with British culture which British people express. For these, Britain is too unemotional, too cold, too unintellectual. For him, this was just what was required, since France was too emotional, too 'hot':

> I was getting a bit hysterical in France. Coming to Britain was coming to a world where I didn't feel responsible for what surrounded me and it enabled me to relax and to come to a much happier relationship with the world around myself and with people in general. (13)

The choice of a less emotional culture parallels the choice of a less emotional language which we discussed in the previous chapter.

Another 'exile', a Spaniard, came to Britain to avoid the Spanish system of competitive examinations:

> I said 'If I can avoid going through this mill, I will' (12)

He had the opportunity of returning to Spain after the death of Franco (another example of the world changing and affecting individuals) but he chose to stay in Britain for very pragmatic reasons, connected with the under-development of the Spanish University system. But, although he has lived and worked in Britain for 20 years, he still rejects the idea of being British and sees himself as a Spaniard (or a Catalan), living abroad, but publishing in Spain with roots in the 'invisible college' of scholars. Assimilation is not an option: 'You never learn enough to be a British person' (12).

Some of my British respondents referred to a period when they were tempted to become 'exiles' and chose not to: 'I never married my Frenchman'. Even after making this choice, some maintain the love affair: the foreign culture continues to offer something which the native one does not:

> If I couldn't go to France again I would feel anonymous. I think what France has given me is part of my own personality which I wouldn't get if it were not for France. I identify with France. I love acting the Frenchman, not consciously doing it, but acting the Frenchman when I am among them. Wanting to be one of them. I just found France fun. (3)

> I went to a friend's wedding. This friend I have had since I was 11, and her mother put her arm around me and said 'I am so glad you are with us for our last family lunch together before she goes away' and we both started crying on each other's shoulder . . . I suppose most of my best experiences have to do with feeling part of a French family. If I had been in England nobody would have said that to me and I would have cried on nobody's shoulder, because that sort of emotion does not surface as much in this country and it doesn't surface in me as much in this country as in France. There I can let that side come out. (1)

It may be significant that both the above respondents are unmarried. For many linguists, especially those in mid-career who have put down roots in the form of family, children, there is a move away from the foreign culture. The romantic idealization goes: either through others' experience or through one's own:

> In school that was my ambition. I wanted to live in France. Having seen people who had gone through that and hadn't found it all that easy, now I don't know. (37)

The next respondent married a French woman; the marriage ended in divorce:

> The trouble is that once you get to know France the glamour goes, the reality is not what you imagined it to be. (2)

There is even a move away from the language:

> When you are role playing and mimicing in that way . . . you are keeping yourself on a kind of superficial level of feeling. (8)

and the choice of subject:

> At the time, getting a First in French seemed like the ultimate accolade, the final stamp of recognition. There was a kind of elation associated with it as if I had reached a kind of pinnacle, but the pinnacle was snow-capped, there was ice on it and the ice started melting, and it has been melting ever since. There was no pinnacle when the sun came out. Just who I was then, how I functioned then has been so dismantled, the identity which revolved around that label, 'first class honours in French', has been totally dismantled. I can't value it now, it doesn't signify anything. It signifies my ability to please my teachers, to fabricate, to trump up, to tune into the psyches of various people, to intuit what they wanted. With just the occasional moment when I didn't know what was wanted and I had to do it in the dark. (8)

and a speciality:

> I used to think philology was useful. But all that's gone. (22)

There are almost as many ways of dealing with this sort of loss and change as there are University linguists. At one extreme is the (rare) person who changes subjects or jobs in mid-career, at the other the person (also rare) who avoids or denies the loss, who manages to maintain the same feeling and attitude to the foreign culture as he or she had as a student or even manages a career as an academic in a foreign country. In between are most people, who live their three-legged university lives, teaching, researching, administrating, changing the proportions as best they can according to the life-cycle ebb and flow of their energies and abilities and the pressures of the outside world. Sometimes what I call the 'artesian well phenomenon' occurs: individuals who chose foreign languages as a temporary shelter manage, under that broad roof, to pursue professionally the real interests which they were not sufficiently confident to choose earlier – art, history, politics, philosophy, psychology . . .

The original foreign culture may lose its importance and another take its place. Emotion can become deeper. The following quotation is in striking contrast with the accounts of experiences abroad given by students and reported in Chapter 3:

> I went for a month to Greece, in the spring. I met a woman, a modern languages teacher, much older than I am. She had certain troubles in her life and she opened her heart to me to a certain extent and I to her. Once, when we were out at Lindos, I said to her I suddenly felt like crying, the beauty of Greece, the realization that man has left all this and what types of men, plus all this beauty and I can't get hold of it, I can't possess it. It's evanescent, it's going to pass. It made me sad, ineffably sad, and she said 'I understand', and she did. Greece, emotionally and aesthetically was overwhelming. I could have gone overboard. The idea was, throw up your job, learn Greek, adore the Greeks, but of course, reality comes in, 'there's your pension, lad, and superannuation'. It spoke to my soul, I was a bit frightened. It could have turned topsy turvy if I had given in to it. Perhaps

there are areas in me that are squashed and repressed, perhaps Greece would have brought them out . . . (4)

A distinction is sometimes made between being *ambilingual* and being *bilingual*. The first refers to a state of near native ability, reached after *learning* the language, usually in school; the second is a result of being exposed to two languages in childhood. On the analogy of these terms, I suggest that the itinerary followed by most university linguists involves the recognition of the impossibility of *bi-culturalism* and is towards *ambi-culturalism*. The native culture is recognized as being primary and the foreign one is being used to illuminate it, although there is also the recognition that the outsider sees things to which the native is blind, as when one of my French respondents said about the British:

British people are tolerant because they hate confrontation. It is to avoid argument and embarrassment. (33)

The following quotations illustrate different stages of this journey towards ambi-culturalism. The order is that of increasing age:

I needed to get away from British culture in order to understand it . . . I see that it is something to hide behind. Some people need a transition between their adolescent state and the tackling of problems associated with their society . . . Modern languages enabled me to be able to handle difference and to use it in a positive way. A difference which is not wishy-washily pluralistic, but which you can use in order to judge and make your own decisions. (29)

Some people actually claim that they operate as well in one country as another. I doubt it very much. I think the best teacher of a language is one who admits he is different from the person in the target country. If you go on aping, pretending to be a little Frenchman or a little German, you become a bad teacher. In the beginning you try, you go through a phase where you think 'this is it, I've absorbed it all', but you realize ultimately you can't, you can't be the same. You've got to admit you are different, and that what you are offering is different from what a French person is offering. (2)

An Italian would put his arm around you. Then you see how it is perfectly natural to walk down the street arm in arm with a man when you have got a certain affinity. It would be wrong here, and it is right there. I become more Italian when I go to Italy, I ape the Italians. Not just because I wanted to please Italians, but because I saw and understood certain things in the Italian soul or culture which made me more ready to accept. We are all islands. When you go abroad you maintain your own values, you maintain your own hard surface. And although you are admiring and excited by the exoticism of the place you are in you really believe in those hard-learned truths which you have got in your own cultural climate and only slowly does that break up and you start absorbing real cultural

> inputs. It takes a long time. You have got to have deep relationships. It can't be done in a holiday atmosphere. Gradually you become an amalgam. (18)

> So I said 'Well I am not French, so I've got the right to speak, I've got nothing to fear, it doesn't matter what I say.' I could be impartial and stand outside the argument. I see myself as blending with French culture when I am in France and yet being slightly different. I think the pretence we have among academics that we can become pseudo Frenchmen is not really true. We are from a different culture. (6)

> If I was really honest I don't have a particularly strong devotion to French as such. It is more to a certain kind of idea, partly theological, partly philosophical, I would be as interested in reading those things in English or German . . . As a young postgraduate, my ideal was to work in France. All that is gone. I am very happy to work in England. I find myself very different from young colleagues in that. German departments have regarded themselves as Englishmen looking in on Germany and studying it. Whereas French departments try to become almost French. I find that ridiculous. To try to create a little French enclave. (32)

> I was offered a job in Germany, but I felt I was more useful as a journalist, so to speak, working here than working in Germany. Here I can interpret and mediate German culture for a readership or a group of students whose cultural assumptions I understand and share. (16)

3 Language-teaching

The experience of university linguists is founded on a contradiction. In the eyes of the world (government, colleagues, their own students) they are language teachers, but, with a few exceptions, this is not at all obvious to themselves. When they were undergraduates, language, particularly spoken language, may have had a very low priority:

> I came out of university with a first class degree, unable to speak the language. (34)

And this suited many people very well:

> The language teaching was non-existent there . . . that wasn't what it was about. I was never that interested in language and linguistics anyway. (17)

Some do not see themselves as linguists at all:

> I'm a rotten linguist . . . I am a linguist by force of circumstance. I don't particularly enjoy that part. (13)

> One thing I am not, in that precise sense, is a linguist. (6)

> I am slow at learning languages . . . especially orally . . . the reason I don't converse fluently with foreigners is that I spend 10 minutes looking for the exact word which I want to convey to them and another 10 minutes thinking of the exact implications of the word they have used in reply. (23)

> The language side of it was very peripheral to me. I was one of the best at French but I have never actually enjoyed my language teaching. It has never been any pleasure whatsoever. (10)

They may be interested in languages but it is an interest in structure and pattern:

> I am interested in the organization and the structure more than rattling off phrases parrot-fashion . . . a historical, comparative, cultural interest in the way the language works more than the wish to speak it. (23)

> I am very interested in railways, order, method, things slotted in. You can look at the pattern of trains emerging from Waterloo in the rush hour. It is like a Bach fugue. (25)

The previous quotations are from native speakers and from older respondents. Younger people put a higher value on their language ability:

> There was a good emphasis on language [in Scotland]. There was none of this Oxbridge rubbish that if you speak the language well there must be something wrong with you . . . I feel superior to the majority because I have this linguistic ability which so many so-called pre-eminent Italianists don't have. They can't bloody well speak Italian. (18)

Most people would claim to be ambi-lingual, to be highly proficient in their foreign language; but nevertheless they do not see themselves as 'natural linguists' and they do not value particularly the ability to learn languages. One compares herself to her businessman husband:

> He picks up a language every six months. He is a dabbler, he has a natural gift. We were in the Basque country, he found a butcher who spoke Basque. We came back with children's books in Basque, Basque grammars, Basque dictionaries . . . (7)

The most common position is a certain contempt for 'pure language':

> I don't like languages just for their own sake. This philologist I know would plug into the radio and learn Mandarin Chinese for three weeks. I am not like that. (22)

> I did have the ability to pick up languages really quickly and I did have a gift for mimicry. I rejected that as not really being the route for me. I decided it wasn't really worth going for. (8)

> If you are a natural linguist and you learn it rather fast the problem is what do you do with your mind? (13)

> On its own it's not enough. The study of pure language is not enough for most human beings. It doesn't satisfy their needs. They need something else, they need to be doing something with the language. (9)

Understanding a foreign language is not a matter of decoding; words have connotations and most meaning is contextual. You have to know the context and the context is the whole culture:

> If they don't know the context they miss the whole point. I have seen people translating a whole passage without making a single mistake but when I discussed the subject, they didn't understand it was humour. It was supposed to be funny. (12)

Individuals vary greatly, of course, in the way they develop, but it seems that for most people the pleasures of using the foreign language become less as they get older. It is as if, as they move towards the stage of commitments, they achieve more of an integrated identity, as if aspects of both cultures are amalgamated into one personality, which means that they are themselves whatever the actual language they are speaking; the language is of minor importance. Greenson (1950), reporting on the analysis of a bi-lingual Austrian who had had two quite different identities ('in German, I am a scared, dirty child, in English I am a nervous, refined woman'), states that 'towards the end of the analysis, there was no difference in her productions, no matter which language she spoke'.

An extreme case of rejection of the 'pure language' aspects of bilingual performance is that of the conference interpreter who gave up the job in mid-career and became an academic (at a considerably reduced salary) because he could no longer bear to go on being what he called a 'non-person', 'a channel for others'. The change coincided with his own strong personal commitment to a particular cause, nuclear disarmament. His hostility to interpreting is based on a moral judgement:

> Interpreting is a way of avoiding knowing yourself and people who don't know themselves end up in Nuremberg or launching missiles. (44)

This hostility to pure language is a basic fact of linguists' experience and this is true not only at Cambridge or Southampton, but also at Salford where most of the students' time is taken up translating and interpreting. Not surprisingly, this contrast between practice and belief causes considerable conflict:

> The student perception of this place is far more instrumentalist than the place actually is. I would quarrel with what the students want. They can be very materialistic. They simply do not understand that a degree involves intellectual, imaginative, feeling development. I would say it is language being used in whatever area a student can be persuaded to take off. What we have got to do is persuade them to take off . . . we were always looking at language for its own sake, taking language apart and everybody in all the classes was explaining the subjunctive or going on about the agreement of past-participles, but it was all language for its own sake, not language to communicate anything. If you have been in contact with ESP

> or anything in Applied Linguistics it's screaming at you that that's not enough, that's language as system, not language as communication . . . it doesn't matter what area people are taught to think in, as long as they are taught to think, as long as they can put two ideas together. Lots of language teaching doesn't do that. (36)

> The trouble with the students is that they will question the value of stylistics, the value of literature, but they never question the value of translation. By definition, translation is useful and everything else is rubbish. It is a pretty stupid view. (38)

Even more striking perhaps is the attachment to literature-teaching in language centres, where one might assume 'pure language' to flourish. The former head of the now-defunct Division of Modern Languages at Brunel:

> I did a course called the French classical heritage. I did a broad course of recommended readings, selections and extracts, going right back to the Renaissance and coming up to the 19th century novel and I included Gide and Proust in that as well. (20)

The head of the language centre at Southampton had had to give a great deal of thought to the differences between his operation and that of a language department. His position is that literature is the best content even if your goal is language ability:

> If you talk to students in a foreign language about politics you are out of their reach. They are interested but they can't argue it. They are going to reproduce the notes. But literature, they do know what they think, they don't mind being wrong. Literature is a useful vehicle. You don't need literature teachers to do it . . . I am prepared to allow anybody to teach literature so long as they are prepared to produce discussion. (26)

But the language departments look askance at this. Literature has to be taught by specialists:

> There is opposition to doing things that are academically inferior for the sake of the language content. They would like me to teach language in the absence of any reference to anything. I had to promise that any literature we read would be read exclusively for the sake of the language . . . they say 'you don't teach what you are not an expert in'. That's a huge difference. I say you teach what the students need whether or not you are an expert in it. To teach beginners you are better off with a non-expert who is himself a learner. (26)

The anomaly of language centres brings out clearly one aspect of the experience of modern linguists in higher education, the clash between their role as teachers and their role as expert researchers. In theory, language centre people are teachers, and only teachers. In a university this is an anomaly:

> This is the one place where there are people teaching who are of a different category and status, with no further career possibilities within the

> language centre. They are not required to do research. But, at least three of them are PhDs now. It is embarrassing. (32)

> We don't have to publish because it is valueless and it is ephemeral. So we are inferior in the eyes of literary people and historical linguists. If you do Old High German that is not going to change. You can publish that . . . they are the majority and they are producing fundamental truths. We are producing teaching materials and they consider us inferior. The pure teaching activity is suspect because there is no certainty in teaching. There are too many variables to make any experiments. Education is totally despised by the prigs in other faculties. (26)

People working in language centres have, of course, their own problems and their own contradictions:

> Good people in language centres want to do linguistic research, psychological research, or, privately, go on with their literary research in the hope of getting into a literature department . . . (26)

but their role in the teaching of language and literature is coherent.

What would be a coherent position for the person in a language department? One might expect it to run something like this: staff in modern languages departments, sensitive to accusations of being nothing more than teachers in language schools and having reached a mature ambi-lingualism (having never been particularly interested in languages as such) are now basically interested in literature and ideas and in developing and exchanging their own specialized knowledge, though they may also have an interest in language as a system and a structure; they are not trained as language teachers and for them language teaching is a chore, a distraction. They resent and are in conflict with the students whom they see as being obsessed with language to the exclusion of higher things. Language teaching, as one professorial respondent put it, 'is a task for a helot'. Language centres are staffed by people who see their primary concern as teaching language, who may have expertise in applied linguistics, in educational theory, communication, who develop teaching and testing materials, who can claim, it seems with justice, that, unlike other university linguists, language teaching is their prime concern. So language centres should do the language teaching and the academics should do the rest, behaving, to all intents and purposes like their colleagues in English, History, or Sociology.

In fact, this coherent position is held by nobody. Almost everyone answered my question 'Would you like to see all the language teaching done in a language centre?' with a very firm 'No'.

> I'd love that in theory but I try to resist that tendency because language is too serious to be left to professional teachers of language. (32)

An important aspect of the experience of this group of academics is that they find it difficult to have a coherent view of their role. In answer to the question 'How do you describe yourself in terms of job and discipline?' they reply, overwhelmingly, 'As a teacher'. They may go on to qualify this, but it is clear that in most cases research and scholarship take a back seat to teaching and to the relationship with students:

> I enjoy the teaching more than research. You can do different things. I adored my subject when I started a PhD but I got so bored with it. I don't see myself as a scholar, I don't take myself that seriously. (7)

> I am not much of a researcher. What I enjoy doing is teaching or getting up things to teach, the articles are a spin-off on the way. (24)

> I am a good second-rate scholar. (23)

> The best bit is my relationship with the students. (11)

> I see myself as someone whose function it is to reveal certain aspects of cultural life and at the same time to create some excitement and enthusiasm for that. That is what I see my function as being. (13)

> I see myself predominantly as a teacher. It is no longer dangerous to say this. One of our colleagues took early retirement because he thought teaching was not sufficiently highly regarded. (25)

So, the dominant part of the role is the teacher part. But, as we have seen, the demand from the students is for *language* teaching. Between staff and students there is, as regards literature, a gap. What happens then, it seems, is that the one thing which brings people together is, in spite of all the misgivings, language teaching and language learning. This, as the Americans say, is the bottom line:

> Language gives us something to talk about in a way that the other things do not. One shows a mild interest in one's colleagues' research activities but they tend to be remote. (24)

> When the chips are down, language is your discipline . . . although we spend our time getting out of language classes which we see as chores. (22)

> One should have an overall view of the students. You can't actually split them in two. It is a whole. You can enjoy the contact with the students because they feel this is why they are here. (22)

> You have to keep in touch with the actual language. Every sculptor has to know something about the quality of stone or marble. I am a professional language teacher. (4)

Lecturers who may be teaching students Dante, Molière or Kafka, say that it is in the language classes that they get to know them:

> The language work is a form of contact. They have to do the work. If they don't hand in the work there is trouble, whereas if they don't hand in an essay on Molière or whatever, well . . . (25)

The language centre staff explain language departments' wish to teach the language, in spite of their own low opinion of language teaching, as imperialism. Indeed, in times of threat, to have students to teach and something legitimate to teach them is not to be dismissed lightly. But this does not seem to me the most important part of the story. The basic fact is the desire for a clear, unambiguous role and for real contact (and contract) with the students. Given the students' reluctance with regard to literature, this contact is only possible and the role only unambiguous in the language teaching where a shared enthusiasm (former for the staff, current for the students) brings them together.

But what exactly is the language work which is done there and which brings about this meeting? It is of a very special kind: it is not communication; it is not oral language; it is not self-expression through writing; it is essentially *translation*, in particular, translation from English into the foreign language. The predominance and resilience of 'prose translation' as the central defining activity of British modern language departments from Cambridge to Salford is a most amazing phenomenon. I cannot bring myself to rehearse again all the arguments against this exercise as a method of language acquisition. No serious linguist or language learning theorist would defend it and its proponents no longer try. On the other hand, very few, staff or students, ever question it. It is an article of faith. Here, exceptionally, is an expression of doubt:

> By the final year one is hooked into this business of translating passages from one language into another. By definition the whole exercise seems to be impossible. (28)

It is clear that forces are at work which have very little to do with language learning and the above quotation gives perhaps a clue to some of these forces.

The impossibility: the exercise provides a guarantee for all concerned that nothing is ever complete, there will always be work to be done, there will always be room for improvement. Its quality of ancient ritual, its derivation from Classics, gives it a hallowed, almost religious function; its insistence on the microscopic and the ineffable means that the moment when language has to be considered 'good enough' to be used to say something that commits the writer can be indefinitely postponed. Translation, which dominates language departments, which takes up so much of the time and energy of staff and students, is a massive, collusive escape into busyness, time-structuring and reassurance. It is a flight from engagement, from uncertainty, language activity at its 'purest', i.e. its most pointless. The sad thing is that staff and students only feel able to meet at this level. The translation of literary passages serves as a shaky bridge between two quite heterogenous activities. The coexistence of these two activities, of two quite different sub-roles, is simultaneously perceived as providing satisfying variety and as creating additional stress. The following extract shows the tensions and contractions very well:

> We are actually teaching two degrees. We are teaching a language degree and a culture/literature degree. They require a different mental approach and in terms of work it is plus a third. We combine very pleasantly the feelings people teaching a vocational degree must get plus the feelings that people teaching Arts degrees get, that they are broadening people's minds. We have got the best of both worlds. I like the variety. We are gifted amateurs in terms of language teaching. We are just thrown into it.

> It is disgraceful, scandalous. In 17 years there has been very little movement in terms of training. We have this image of ourselves as gifted amateurs . . . and yet when I think about it I am incredibly professional but there is no way I can prove it to anyone. (2)

Language teaching seems to provide a sure, 'professional' role, but the fear of being 'amateur' even undercuts this security:

> I don't think we are producing people who are proficient enough in the language. We have an amateur approach to language teaching and I would like to see a much more rigorous approach. (10)

> We are always depressed, through all our efforts at teaching French, at how poor linguistically examination answers in French are after four years. Having to express themselves in French limits so many of them in what they can say. (22)

It now takes more and more energy to ignore developments elsewhere (in English as a foreign language, for example); departments themselves are often split between ritual translation activities and new communicative techniques which solve the problem of 'pure' language by making sure that everyone has something real to communicate about and a context in which to do it.

The experience of the university teacher of modern languages is, then, in part, the experience of role-confusion: the part of the role which is most salient is the part which is least valued. There is a very real sense in which language people are *not* language people. The effect of this is to produce insecurity.

4 Insecurity

The job is such that, in theory, anything can be changed, anything can be improved, anything can be done. You could write an article, you could re-write your lectures, you could devise new language-teaching methods. In practice, the energy and the time that any individual has are finite. Ritual rules, no-one complains, but guilt is everywhere. 'Guilt' is my gloss, since the words used tend to be ones like 'depressed', 'embarrassed', 'worried' . . . The range of things to be guilty about is considerable. There is the inability to interest students with one's subject, 'I always feel rather embarrassed at boring the students' (23). The fear of being seen as a 'dabbler' by colleagues:

> I am worried about people like myself, who are basically trained in French literature and language, dabbling in politics, sociology, economics. We may work very hard to try to give ourselves some sort of grounding, but it seems ridiculous when you have genuine trained people across the road. (28)

However, the greatest sense of guilt concerns research:

> My research has got fantastically behind and this is an embarrassment to me. (46)

> I haven't published as much as I should. That is why I have a sense of guilt. (11)

The university values research above all else. In other words, to be *valued* by your peers entails publishing (this will also entail being envied by your peers, as Jacobson demonstrates, with very little exaggeration, in *Coming from Behind*: for many, the quarterly reading of *French Studies* is torture; however, that is another matter and to be among the envied rather than the envying is still the basic objective). But, as we have seen, most modern languages lecturers see themselves as *teachers* and even (under pressure from students) as *language* teachers. This is fatal. Teachers, even very good teachers, cast a short shadow (and are never promoted):

> Someone who is a very active language teacher, even publishing articles on language teaching (though it is relatively difficult if you are not an English language teacher) is not going to get a doctorate. He is not going to get the research background and therefore will not get to be a senior lecturer. He will not get to be senior lecturer here [Salford] any more than he would anywhere else without having good research and it has to be respectable research, literary research. (36)

The following extract seems to me to show clearly the mixture of feelings: anger, regret, acceptance, denial, envy perhaps:

> I am totally cynical as far as academic advancement is concerned. When I see how people get on on the basis of publication, an awful lot of weighing of paper. I have read doctoral theses that I could have written in the loo and I have seen others that are marvellous. And I have seen people getting on who deserve it, for whom I have great academic respect, and others for whom I have nothing but the deepest contempt. Administration and teaching are supposed to be taken into account and they are not. There are rules and people don't play according to the rules. Titles as such have no importance to me. If they had I might have made an effort to do the right things, the things they wanted and I might have got on and I might have been a professor. But because I don't hold very much store by it I've never really bothered. The only possible motive might be for money, but it makes so little difference . . . I am not the kind of person who can balance his life, walk out of a lecture, pick up an article, write two pages, then go to a committee and come out, write another three pages. There are people like that, they get on, they become professors very young. Their progress is inexorable and they go on and on. (18)

So modern languages lecturers see themselves as teachers rather than researchers in a peer culture which rewards researchers and ignores teachers. There is a cluster of feelings – all associated with insecurity:

> As a profession we are hyper-critical. We always think we have done a bad job. I am never satisfied. It is one of my problems. It is insecurity. (2)

> I think a lot of academics, if they were to be truthful, have got a strong sense of insecurity in them by the very nature of the work, which is public work. It is like an actor who wants applause. I can think of three of four people in my department who feel insecure. I don't mean insecure in their teaching. I couldn't pinpoint the area of their insecurity, but just insecure by their very nature. I certainly am very often. I am aware of it. (3)

I do not think that many lecturers would disagree with these statements although this is not something which is often said in public since the maintaining of a confident front is one of the basic requirements of the job: outsiders would be more likely to charge dons with arrogance than with diffidence.

The question is what are the sources of this insecurity and how is it lived? Part of the answer is to be found, I think, in an unmet need to be part of a group or a team. It is probable that the need is greater among modern linguists than among other groups, since they have, as we have seen, distanced themselves from their community, and from the community's values (those of the country at large and those of the intellectual community). Their need for a sense of community at work is likely to be proportionately greater:

> I would like to move towards students and colleagues. I am more interested in that as my contribution than writing some wonderful thesis which no-one is going to read. (1)

This is sometimes achieved:

> I am part of that team . . . it's a tribal thing, it gives you a bit of security within the faculty. (3)

> In my former department you felt you were part of a team. Everybody in the department supported everybody else. There was a general sense of togetherness. (11)

But the opposite feeling seems much more common:

> Here I feel we are constantly in a state of antagonism amongst ourselves. We're rivals. That to me is deadly. That is what stops me publishing. (11)

The desire is for intellectual support and collaboration, the reality a feeling of isolation:

> A certain sense of isolation . . . here there doesn't seem to be any intellectual life. People do their own thing. Most people seem to plough their specialized furrow. Intellectual exchanges are fairly rare. (22)

There may be a certain idealization; the intellectual grass is greener elsewhere:

> It is different here from Cambridge. There I spent a lot of time talking about what I was doing to people within different disciplines. (24)

There is a sense of inferiority:

> There aren't a lot of great minds, great names, teaching French in Universities, compared with other subjects. If you said 'where can we get

a professor who will run a national enquiry?' it's the medical boys, the science chaps who seem to be of the standing to do that. They live in a different kind of world, they interact with industry. The devoted literary scholar – that is not his experience at all. You can get by on the humanities side with a fairly mediocre mind . . . There is usually some little group of academics who meet regularly to have sharp discussions about something or other. There is never anyone from French there. The ones who are really lit up by ideas and want to test themselves out against others intellectually tend not to be modern linguists. I have immensely nice colleagues, but they are not world-beaters. (32)

What emerges from the above quotation is the awareness of the lack of outside experience. University linguists have gone from university to university, from student to lecturer. Those who have had any other sort of job are in a minority, whereas Engineers (Salford for example) are required to have worked in industry before becoming academics. This sense of unreality contributes to the insecurity.

Another reason seems to be connected with the hedonist theme. Modern linguists are reluctant to do work which is not based in genuine desire:

When I have written for publication it was because I felt the urge to say something. If I felt that it would further my career or be good for me academically to have published something I might settle down to writing something without the urge. But I would have to make considerable effort for that. (11)

There is a need for relationship, personal relationship:

I am not ambitious, I don't want to move up the hierarchy. It might involve me in some sort of games-playing which I don't want. Above all I don't have a relationship with anyone that would provide the human interest and energy and the sense of relatedness which seems to be a necessary component of any passionate involvement for me. (8)

Inevitably then, they are at a disadvantage compared to hard-nosed colleagues in other disciplines (and to those in their own discipline who are not like this) who *are* prepared to divide up their days, to research and publish in order to further their career and do not require passion as a prerequisite.

There is also the question of the nature of their concept of research. Successful research in Britain is a matter of specialization, normally specialization in a particular author: one becomes *the* Rabelais expert. But for many modern linguists this is anathema. This is partly because of the existence of a totally different notion of research. Here are some answers to my questions concerning the people whom my respondents admire in the discipline and their attitudes to research. The first is a professor of classics, the others are 'continentals'. They all share what I call the continental view of knowledge and oppose it to the British:

You admire people who are like yourself . . . I like people who are broad. I like people who have made links. I like people who go outside the stereotypes and the way they have been trained. I dislike people who are buried in their subject and can't get out of it. (14)

I find British people are more limited. People have one thing, one book, one little area. I don't think there is anything I am not interested in . . . There is one person I admire. He is the sort of person who knows everything, he really knows everything. (12)

The notion of specialization in Britain is something that leaves me and other continental people utterly amazed, and also in a state of indignation . . . In the cultural field people have given up: 'He wasn't a specialist, what right did he have . . .?' Somebody does something a bit out of his field and they react by fierce hostility. The sort of notion that unless you are a specialist you haven't got the right to open your trap is staggering . . . the specialist has the last word. What lies behind that is an extraordinary lack of nerve . . . I find it very difficult to decide that I am only this or only that. I like relating things to everything. (13)

This citizen-of-the-world conception of research, a free mind ranging far and wide with a UN passport, is magnificent. There is no doubt that when one is passionately interested in a problem, subject boundaries are irrelevant (*The Double Helix* is the *locus classicus*). Most people would share my respondents' admiration for individuals who 'know everything' and agree that specialization is the result of a certain 'lack of nerve'. There is indeed something miserable and artificial about specialization. As one of my respondents put it, describing an eminent colleague:

His entire work is devoted to one author and he simply will not give up until he has said everything that can possibly be said about that author. I think that is a gross misapprehension. It is an unviable position to have and it is bound to make you miserable . . . (31)

But in the real world of average people doing an average job such universalist ambitions may be unrealistic, and the cartesian, scientific method of dividing up the world into manageable, bounded bits may be the only practical method. The vast PhD subjects (Schopenhauer, Jung . . .) which seemed so exciting and challenging have a nasty habit of daunting the researcher into silence or, paradoxically, leading him, in despair, into the securities of erudition. Even in institutional terms there are problems in implementing this:

In terms of chair appointments they are not particularly interested in what specialism a chap has, they are looking for the right kind of chap who can command a broad range of subjects. They don't always manage to find that chap and when they do he often runs into problems, his position towards his own colleagues, if he really tries to implement a comparative and connective approach. It is something that it's inherently more stressful to do. (31)

Modern languages is an overlap, a point of intersection, there are fewer securities. You can't be as narrow as a historian who works on Oliver

> Cromwell. My historian colleagues ask me a lot of questions about French historians. Frenchists are expected to know about that kind of thing in a country that they are supposed to know about. I think that is very fruitful, but very difficult . . . we have to keep up with that much more. (46)

So modern linguists are expected to be specialists, but specialists not in Oliver Cromwell but in France. In addition, there is the inescapable difficulty of ambi-culturalism: individuals are torn between their awareness of the nature of the intellectual culture of the countries they study, the high value attached to polymathic abstraction, and the British culture in which they work and make their careers:

> My approach is more pragmatic than theoretical . . . very un-French. (6)

> Mine is a very British theory, veering towards that peculiarly British phenomenon, a theory of having no theory, a pragmatic approach. German departments steer clear of German theory. (5)

The requirement to be a 'specialist' in something as vast as France, this cultural split, the presence of an impossible sterilizing ideal (know the links between everything before you write) the double nature of the job (how many translations did Steiner mark every week while writing *After Babel*?), the extraordinary conflict between the microscopic language activity and the need for a broad, linking vision in research, the mis-match between an institutional world which is individualistic and competitive and people, many of whom chose the subject because of their strong needs for closeness and collaboration and who already feel isolated from their community, the basic *given* of inferiority (a British professor can be humbled by the superior cultural and linguistic knowledge of a French child of six), all this contributes to a sense of insecurity.

Add to this the institutional norms (the same for all academics) which mean that boundaries of time, place, role and task are extremely fuzzy: individuals have magnificent, untrammelled and highly stressful freedom to exercise choice so that very little can be, so to speak, handed over to some impersonal authority; there are committees but few teams, individualism is such that it can be difficult to be sure of who your allies are from one meeting to the next or even if the same people will be members of the group. There is a general suspicion of authority and reluctance to delegate. Everyone is responsible for everything which often means that no-one is responsible for anything.

All this would be difficult enough but, in addition, the dominant teaching mode for literature is the lecture. One individual stands up on a stage and monologues (often in the foreign language) for an hour. Lecturers say they like lecturing and all their references are to the satisfaction of theatricality:

> I like lecturing, Oh dear yes, I am an actor you see. (25)

> What I prefer to do is to be talking about something I feel completely confident about, perhaps it is an element of showing off. (7)

> The thing that gives me a tremendous high is lecturing to fairly large groups. (9)

> I enjoy the theatrical aspect of it. (29)

But there are doubts,

> That is all rather doubtful, the power of being an actor. (9)

> The lecture is an artificial occasion anyhow, it is not as if you are revealing your feelings about a work of literature. You are going through an act . . . when you are speaking a foreign language you aren't being yourself, you are putting on an act. (24)

There is a sense that the satisfaction is based on a false self and on a denial of the real problems which are bound up with not feeling 'completely confident', and which involve real feelings and real relationships, especially power relationships:

> Tutorials are much more difficult. I am never sure how to handle the power aspects, but lectures . . . I quite like camping it up. In lectures students can take it or leave it, whereas tutorials are much more complicated things. (29)

Doubts like these are put on one side during the virtuoso performance in which the solitary, heroic figure strives to light the cultural fires with the white heat of his charisma and superior knowledge, knowing that this is an act, knowing that it is not real, and sharing therefore the insecurity of the actor, who at least speaks someone else's script and who performs before an audience who have paid for their seats.

One of my respondents, after saying how much he enjoyed lecturing, invited me to sit in on one of his lectures. It took place in a freezing lecture theatre, 17 second year students, 13 women, 4 men, sitting on fixed benches. He was up on a stage, behind a lectern, a pleasant voice which carried easily to the back of the hall (where all the students were), perfect French. He followed his notes very closely but this wasn't at all obvious because of the distance. The subject was comedy but there were no laughs. The students seemed to take it down verbatim, their notes, the ones that I could see, looked like essays. Some of them had English versions of the French text. At the end he made a few announcements – in English. Later that day, in the corridor, he apologized for 'such an awful lecture'. But was it worse than any other? Would it have seemed awful at all if a stranger had not been there? Was it not, rather, that the presence of a silent observer made the theatrical unreality of the situation impossible to conceal?

The difficulties of the job, the feelings of insecurity it provokes among people who seem to many outsiders (and to themselves) to have the best of all possible professional situations, derive, it seems to me, from the gap between the reality and the presentation, and from an abiding uncertainty about the task and the role. An uncertain sense of identity brought people into the subject, and the subject's contradictions tend to maintain rather than reduce the individual's uncertainties, as the individual's uncertainties maintain rather than reduce the subject's contradictions.

Part 3

The Staff–Student Relation

6

Staff–Student

'They haven't been alive long enough.' (Lecturer)

'They've seen too many students.' (Student)

1 The systemic approach

Surprisingly, staff–student relations are largely unresearched.[1] There are books on academics – Caplow and McGee (1958), Halsey and Trow (1971), Bailey (1977). There are books on students – Becker (1961, 1968), Marris (1964), Bourdieu and Passeron (1979). But, in the interest of clarity and manageability of data, these all explicitly exclude one or other group from the study. The assumption is that it is possible to understand staff and students as separate groups, as one might understand separately footballers and snake-charmers. This is, of course, an illustration of the dominant research paradigm, derived from Descartes, which advises dividing something up, the better to study it. But, while footballers and snakecharmers, having only fleeting relations, may indeed be studied apart, other separations of convenience seriously damage the research: it is simply not possible to understand writers apart from readers, predators apart from prey, surgeons apart from patients or students apart from teachers. And it is not possible to study these related groups without reference to the environment in which they exist – the world of publishing, the veldt, the hospital, the university. This holistic, systemic approach is more difficult and is likely to produce less clear-cut results but it is the only way to approach reality when groups are not isolated but mutually interacting within a system and when their experience is, to a considerable extent, *their experience of each other*. To put it simply: students are what they are because staff are what they are, but staff are what they are because students are what they are; in addition, both staff and students are what they are because the university is what it is; the kind of students we have produce the kind of teachers we have who produce the kind of students we have who produce . . . and so on; staff will continue to be what they are, students will continue to be what they are, the university will continue to be what it is until into the system is introduced, in Bateson's phrase (1973) 'a difference that makes a difference'. The difference may come from outside the system, crossing the outer boundary or it may come from inside.

However, this is to anticipate my discussion, in the final part of this book, of the whole question of change in disciplines and institutions. At this stage, I am concerned with the system as it is, specifically the way in which staff and students interact within it:

> The world is not something separate from you and me; the world, society, is the relationship that we establish or seek to establish between each other. So you and I are the problem, not the world, because the world is a projection of ourselves, and to understand the world, we must understand ourselves. (Krishnamurti, 1970)

I begin by using interview material to show the ways in which staff and students perceive each other; I then go on to describe an investigation using a research method more specifically designed to help us understand inter-group phenomena; I then offer my analysis of the recursive system described above and I conclude with data of a different type again – an account of an actual teaching relation.

2 Staff perceptions of students: student perceptions of staff

> In the past men were handsome and great (now they are children and dwarfs), but this is merely one of the many facts that demonstrate the disaster of an ageing world. The young no longer want to study anything, learning is in decline, the whole world walks on its head . . . everything is on the wrong path . . . in those days, thank God, I acquired from my master the desire to learn and a sense of the straight way, which remains even when the path is tortuous. (Eco, *The Name of the Rose*, Picador, 1984)

Staff are very ready to generalize about students and do it with relish – though rarely with as much tongue-in-cheek gusto as this director of a language centre:

> (Modern language students) are less interesting, it seems to be a soft subject. They are vaguely interested in humanity, but I would rather talk with lawyers and social scientists. I get more back from them. I think they are dull and, compared with engineers, they lack initiative. The engineers are much less worried about getting things right when they speak. A linguist worries about getting his sentence right. That is a great inhibition. . . . The English Department has by far the most intelligent students; the history department has very bad linguists but they read well. They don't have much to say. The theologians are totally useless. The Classicists contain a few geniuses and the rest are very stupid people. The archaeologists play with language and never really make it. The geographers are purposeful and hardworking and unimaginative but get good results. The social scientists are a bit arrogant but very communicative all the time. The scientists and mathematicians are a mixture. (26)

Where they have the possibility of comparing modern languages students with those from other disciplines, they tend to find their own students less interesting:

> The social science students are more interesting than ours. (29)
>
> I had a lot of pupils who weren't modern linguists. A lot read English and they were notably more involved in creative writing and probably creative tourism as well. Modern languages students go abroad quite a lot but they go specifically to learn more about that language. The people doing English went to do extraordinary things which they wrote up. (46)

They presume that the very best young people will do other things:

> (As an oral examiner, I met) this marvellous pupil at X school. She could have done anything. She was going to do African Studies, something totally different. The more adventurous ones will tend to take a step into the unknown rather than want to come and do more prose and translations. (22)

Older respondents compare today's students unfavourably with previous ones:

> The standard is going steadily down . . . I've felt it coming ever since Robbins. The schools are now staffed by people who are themselves products of the Robbins principle. More means worse. (23)
>
> Our best students in French are probably as good as ever they were but they are a much smaller proportion of the whole than they were 20 years ago and we certainly take many more poor-quality students than we used to do. (34)

What are the precise complaints? First, that students (from Salford to Cambridge) lack purpose and commitment:

> We have got students here who shouldn't be here. They don't know why they are here. They tend to do their work without putting anything into it . . . only 50% are intellectually equipped and properly motivated . . . they are almost at finishing school. (22)
>
> They don't know what they are studying for. It's in a vacuum. (39)

Secondly, that they lack cultural and intellectual curiosity and enthusiasm:

> They are hot for certainties. They read less and less. They have the extraordinary notion that you can study language by itself. (25)
>
> Most of them don't catch the cultural spark. They can be a bit humdrum. A colleague of mine was talking about the difference between English and modern languages students . . . his grumble was that modern languages students go in for a lot of plain exposition and much less critical argument and abstract thought . . . people do tend to explain things rather than

argue them . . . sometimes I think they lack curiosity. There is a passivity about the way they want to learn things and that has increased. (46)

They don't argue and discuss. They tend to want to do things which are examinable. It is terribly difficult to get a lot of them to go and see films, things that are not to do with the course. (35)

Enthusiasm and curiosity are more important than high intelligence. There is not an awful lot of it . . . they don't read much, they don't even seem to think there is anything odd or wrong about not finding out about things that are not being lectured on. (7)

The passivity is what is most exasperating:

I had asked a group to read a text . . . It emerged that not one had read it. I simply kicked them out. They came waiting for Sir to do it but Sir wasn't doing it for once. (25)

If they look blank I hate it, sitting like pumpkins. (1)

They sit like puddings and give no answer, I've got to give the answer for them . . . one, at most two, in my groups is as interested as I am. Half are bored and the rest are in between. (33)

Staff attempt to understand and interpret this. A major reason, they find, is the economic climate which is making students more pragmatic and job oriented:

There has been a great change over the last three years. 18 year olds are very worried about getting jobs. One of the questions from all the interviewees is 'Do your students get jobs and what jobs?'. 18 year olds are terribly worried. (38)

Staff see this as a fundamental generational difference between them and the students. They see the students as being very different from the way they were when they were students, comparing basically the 1960s with the 1980s:

In the 60s I wasn't worrying about a career. Some of the students here seem to be obsessed with the job market. Then an Arts degree was an Arts degree. It didn't matter what it was in. (34)

We all have these 60s assumptions that it is a bad thing to be too materialistic, that being left wing is the only political stance. They are not like that at all. They must think we are hilariously funny. They think we are museum pieces, we are so different. All this 'is it useful?' is just a whole generation terrified by the idea of unemployment. 18 year olds have lived with that ever since they can remember . . . it doesn't help to say 'Look mate, you have no idea what will be useful when you are 25'. That is not really very kind. (38)

Betweeen me and the students there is a gap that is widening all the time. It seems to me that the students I am teaching at the moment are far more conservative, with a small and a big C than I am now and certainly more conservative than I was as an undergratuate. They seem to have very set ideas. Everything that we teach has to be relevant to their achievement of their goal and their goal is very well defined – the getting of a job. I've surprised myself two or three times last term by flying off the handle in class and saying 'Look this is what I am here for'. They question me about the relevance of some discussion to the examinations at the end of the day. I find this very unsettling. I don't know if it is age creeping up on me or if we are seeing a different kind of student. I don't like losing my temper. I was angry at the narrowness, the refusal to discuss. When I complain to them about lack of preparation they say 'we don't have any time'. They say 'When the course is over we will do the reading' and I say 'Well the reading is the course'. I think we must be failing somewhere. (41)

They are saying 'Our pension rights will be affected if we don't start on the ladder now'. (46)

Another line of explanation is cultural. The passivity, the narrowness are British phenomenona and a function of secondary education:

It is a British phenomenon. Young people are blinkered. My husband teaches history and politics in a comprehensive school. He came home with a wonderful quotation of the week: 'Oh sir, do we have to do Hitler? Hitler's boring Sir'. Their education has been narrow and they don't see why we are making them do those things. They don't see the relevance of it. This is the cream of the generation. (38)

A French lecteur:

They don't like to be in the front row. I think this is very British. You've got to be in the mass, unseen, protected . . . they are less involved in political issues. We used to have opinions on everything and shout about it. They keep quiet. (33)

The African students are a lot less puddingy. They are determined to do well. They have a much greater interest in politics and in the world as a whole. They find our students really boring. (37)

There is however also a recognition that the pragmatic qualities which are a cause of irritation are also valuable:

I am pleased that they are hard-nosed. It is good for the country that there should be a fair number of talented, hard-nosed people about. (46)

They probably have a more responsible attitude than my generation did. (41)

and an awareness of the other side of the 'brilliant English student' coin:

I have come across a lot of very self-conscious waffle while marking the English papers and I have asked 'Where are the actual facts?' In modern languages you do have to find out a lot more about things than if you are reading English.

Basic competence, skill and knowledge are valued:

My ideal student would be well-grounded in basics, capable of translating into French or English a passage of a suitable level with only half a dozen mistakes to the page, hard-working, perfectly happy to spend 30 hours a week with his nose in a book, pencil in his hand . . . some background in Classics, History and RK. (23)

There is some awareness, based on personal experience, of the contradictory, tentative nature of the subject choice:

Modern languages students are trying things out. They are doing it because they are rebelling. There are more rebels, albeit mealy-mouthed rebels, in modern languages possibly than in any other subject. I was one. I rebelled against classics. (18)

My subject choice was a mixture of desire to escape and being cautious, being adventurous plus remaining in a cotton-wool situation. (29)

On the whole, however, it is safe to say that staff find students erring on the side of caution and mealy-mouthedness, limited in their aspirations, reluctant to try things out, too passive and dependent. They find the gap between themselves and the students very great.

The most frequent complaint my student respondents made about staff concerned their dogmatism: 'Language people are dogmatic, set in their ways'; 'They have a fixed opinion, they have made their decisions about what they think'. The practical effect of the dogmatism is to discount students' contributions: 'They don't want to be stimulated by the student . . . they prefer to see the same old arguments churned out'. 'There are people who are totally dismissive of other people's ideas, who make you feel inferior because of your ideas'. 'There is far too much emphasis on the lecture and what the lecturer knows is good and right and the poor little students don't know anything'. Students strongly object to being silenced. 'He talked for three weeks and we couldn't say anything so I haven't been since'. They also object to what they call 'sham openness', asking for ideas in order to shoot them down. They value 'someone who is young in mind, who is prepared to accept new ideas, who isn't set in certain view-points'.

Students expected University to be different from school and were disappointed when it was not:

At School you get accepted views rammed down your throat the whole time – what to think of *L'Etranger* and what can be meant by this or that. You are expected to churn this out. (68)

In short, as we saw in Chapter 2, students perceive staff as requiring them to conform to their views and they contrast them in this respect with staff from subjects like English and Philosophy. They are suspicious of statements to the contrary. And yet there is a great deal of ambivalence around this spoon-feeding/thinking-for-yourself issue:

> It makes it a lot more difficult for students if the lecturer won't tell you what he thinks because it means you have got to think for yourself . . . a lot of people find giving their own views very intimidating. (94)

Together with the demand that lecturers should listen to student contributions, there is also the requirement that they should be inspiring, committed, stimulating:

> What works is a freshness of approach, not someone reading bits of knowledge they have known for 20 years and expecting me to follow on the production line and come out at the end of the conveyor belt processed and packaged. That is killing. You've got to be able to combine teaching with stimulating, even stimulating yourself, because some of them just stagnate, they get bored . . . Perhaps some have been here too long. They have become totally blasé, they have seen too many students. (68)

> I was very disappointed when I came to university because I had had a super teacher for the A level class . . . the teaching here wasn't as inspiring as I had thought it would be. (54)

3 The inter-group seminar

It seems clear, from the interview material alone, that there is considerable dissatisfaction and disappointment on both sides but little awareness of the ways in which each group may be contributing to the situation. I used an unorthodox method – the inter-group seminar – as a means of developing understanding of the *relatedness* of the groups. I brought together, in a residential setting, seven students and seven staff. Most were respondents previously interviewed by me. There was no question of statistically 'representative' groups, though participants came from six different institutions and there were roughly equal numbers of men and women. My invitations to quiet, shy respondents to join us were, not surprisingly, politely refused, so the student group was certainly unrepresentative of students in general, being more confident and forthcoming than the average group. I invited two consultants, one male and one female, to assist us. They both came from outside higher education but were experienced in working with people from a range of professions, including the academic, on questions of role and group relations.

The three of us had a preliminary meeting and agreed on a method of working which would, we optimistically hoped, enable everyone to begin considering staff self-perceptions, student self-perceptions, staff perceptions of students, student perceptions of staff, student perceptions of staff perceptions of students and staff perceptions of student perceptions of staff.[2]

We started with a plenary session in which, in staff–student pairs, each

Table 6.1: *Staff–student perceptions*

	Student perceptions		*Staff perceptions*	
	1. *Negative* student feeling about staff	2. *Positive* student feeling about staff	3. *Negative* staff feeling about students	4. *Positive* staff feeling about students
Academic attitudes	failure to instil enthusiasm, uninspiring	enthusiasm	no enthusiasm	enthusiasm
			lack of purpose and commitment	have purpose and commitment 'more important than high intelligence'
	closed minds, dogmatic		no intellectual curiosity, closed minds, intellectual laziness, disinclination to reflect	intellectual curiosity
			passivity (puddings), dependency, submissiveness, complacency	

Interpersonal attitudes	mercurial, moody, favouritism, weak, no authority			
	spoon-feeding, despising, humiliating, superior, snobbery, 'not treating us as adults', patronizers, condescenders, sham openness, discounting, 'putting down'	'know where you are', safe person, no moods, fascination, confident, competent, specific direction, willing to listen, adapt, doesn't put you down, responsive to students' ideas, patient, polite		
Outside world	Rejecting student functions, keeping a distance, 'don't want to know us'	interested in you as a person outside college, approachable, friendly	pragmatic, instrumental, concerned only about jobs, materialistic	responsible, hard-nosed
		been in outside world, away from narrow academic concerns		
Compared with others	less intellectually demanding, more like school-teachers		less intellectually gifted, narrower, more cautious	down to earth, practical
Physical	'N/A'	'N/A'	'N/A'	'N/A'

person briefly interviewed the partner and then introduced him or her to the whole group. Then everyone wrote descriptions, giving positive and negative perceptions of the other group; the precise brief was to write two descriptions – one of a student/staff member who 'inspires positive feelings', another of a student/staff member who 'inspires negative feelings'. The aim was to get at the personal constructs that individuals had. The next stage involved the staff role-group and the student role-group meeting in separate rooms, each with a consultant, and building group perceptions of the other group, using the previous individual writing and a grid suggested by the consultants. After this, two members from each group were to go to the other group and convey to them the picture which had emerged. The 'messengers' then withdrew and the group discussed their input. Finally (after a long period when staff and students had worked separately) the two groups came together in a plenary meeting to compare perceptions.

The data that emerged are of two kinds: there are first the statements, written and spoken, which were made and which amplify the data from the interviews; then there is the actual behaviour of individuals and groups in the particular temporary institution in which we found ourselves. The seminar was extremely modest in scope and cannot be said in 24 hours even to have dealt systematically with all the various 'perceptions' listed above. Methodologically, however, it broke new ground. It provided me with data which was more specifically group-based and above all generated hypotheses which would not have come from the interviews. On the other hand, people were, I think, more frank in the interviews than they were in the seminar; the situation there approximated more to the real world where there are constraints on what can be said without hurting oneself or others. Specifically, my impression was that in the seminar the more powerful staff group was inhibited from expressing negative feelings about students while the students felt relatively free to express negative feelings about staff.

Table 6.1 is an attempt to present schematically the findings. It enables the reader to see where values are shared, where one group or both groups are silent about an aspect which can be presumed to be relevant and in general it shows the range of values. Not surprisingly, the seminar confirmed the findings of the interviews: staff said they disliked 'closed minds', 'disinclination to reflect', 'rejection of the intellectual world', and preferred the positive counterparts, 'enthusiasm', 'chance your arm', 'intellectual curiosity', 'individuality of response', 'active participation', even 'disruptiveness'. They tended to play down basic knowledge of language or facts. They claim to dislike spoon-feeding, which they only do because they are forced into it by student passivity.

Students repeated their dislike of dogmatism, their appreciation of enthusiasm. They were able to express more clearly than in the interviews their attitudes towards staff authority. The topic which served to focus this concern was the mode of address: some students wanted to be on first-name terms with lecturers, others preferred the formality of surnames. We were surprised at what an issue this seemed to be and decided that it enacted the problem students have with staff. They wished to see them as *authoritative*; they disliked 'weak' lecturers, i.e. those who lacked authority, but at the same time they wanted to see lecturers as fellow-adults, fellow members of a community and of a discipline. Calling a lecturer 'Dr Smith' activated and satisfied the former feeling; calling a lecturer 'Chris' the second. They want to feel 'safe' with a lecturer who is 'patient and polite', 'professional', 'sympathetic to academic and personal problems', who is not 'mercurial', 'moody' or 'unpredictable'. But they also want to 'stand on their own two feet', not be spoon-fed with dogmatic views, but be allowed freedom to take risks, to challenge and try things out. They disliked condescension and patronizing attitudes. None of this is very surprising in a group of young adults whose attitudes to their own parents are in transition (from authority figures to friends and confidantes) and who are trying to achieve autonomy without excluding mature dependency. Students want from lecturers what they want from parents – reliability and dependability combined with a readiness to let go, to trust them, to let them make their own mistakes, to acknowledge their own fallibility. They want a recognition that each generation has something to give the other, an acknowledgement of reciprocal needs:

> One hope I have for this weekend [wrote a participant at the beginning of the seminar] is that the students present will realize that but for them there would be no teachers.

Although, as we have seen, there is no reluctance – particularly on the staff side – to generalize about the other group, when it comes to understanding these aspects of the relationship, everyone seems very much in the dark, aware of 'a gap that is widening all the time', but with little notion of its cause or its nature and even less awareness of how it might be reduced or bridged.

The social and cultural explanations which are offered seem inadequate because they do not take into account the reality of the interaction within a shared system. There was occasional recognition that the behaviour that staff disliked in students was a function not only (or perhaps not at all) of external forces but of staff behaviour:

> We drive the ideas out of them. We tend to put students down a lot when we teach language. The stuff they hand in has more errors than anything else, after all. (22)

One of the students at the seminar told the staff very forcibly that they got the student behaviour they deserved. If they got compliance it was because, unwittingly or not, they asked for compliance. And indeed there is a certain disingenuousness in complaining that students are only interested in succeeding in examinations while staff clearly devote a great deal of energy to matters of assessment, especially language assessment. However, staff behaviour is also a function of student pressure:

> We are being much too judgemental a lot of the time on essays. But if you ended up not giving any mark at all but just throwing up questions at the end, they wouldn't like it. (24)

In other words, the students' passivity and dependence ('like puddings') which they (at times), are ashamed of and would like to escape from, is maintained by the staff's authoritative judgement ('dogmatic') and information-giving which they (the staff) are (at times) ashamed of and would like to escape from since it implies the infantile processes of spoon-feeding and regurgitation.

The paradox is most acute in the area of marking and examining. It is not surprising that it is so painful for all concerned:

> All marking is a pain. The marking of essays really hurts . . . it is torture . . . (13)

This is where the contradiction between the high regard for autonomous, enthusiastic work, insight and original ideas and the reality of timid comformity and pragmatic concern for the cash value represented by exam success, is most acute for all concerned. Comformity, timidity, dependency, dogmatism is what no-one professes to want and what everyone colludes in producing.

How does this happen?

4 Enthusiasm: the Concert Relation and the Gift Relation

> I admire enthusiasm, tremendous enthusiasm. James, for example, never stops talking. He is absolutely fantastic. (6)

It seems to me that we can arrive at a better understanding of the staff–student relation and its paradoxes if we consider more closely the value which, as Figure 6.1 shows, is shared by both groups – enthusiasm. 'Be enthusiastic' is the demand each group makes of the other. But each group experiences disappointment and what often seems like bewilderment. There is also, beneath the surface, a great deal of anger and frustration which occasionally produces a critical incident – an outburst which would not be significant in another culture, but which in British academe, leaves the participants full of guilt and remorse.

There are two senses in which people may be said to share an enthusiasm – I propose calling them the Concert Relation and the Gift Relation.

In the Concert Relation, individuals who already have an enthusiasm – for Bach or Brittan – meet in a hall and *are enthusiastic together*: they may listen; they may participate unofficially by singing along; they may participate officially if they are in the choir at the *War Requiem*. In the Gift Relation, someone who is enthusiastic – about Bach or Brittan – *offers* (as the French say for gifts) the object of that enthusiasm to another person. The gift may take the literal form of a record or be perhaps in the form of a suggestion or an invitation. I suspect that a great deal of our personal culture comes from 'gifts' like this.

As we saw above, in their student days staff had considerable enthusiasm for their chosen foreign culture and it was this enthusiasm which brought them into the teaching profession. Students too have, on the whole, enthusiasm for the culture, as we saw. It would seem then that the conditions exist for a Concert Relation and it is certain that this underlying assumption is a very strong factor in modern languages departments – 'we all share an enthusiasm for French/German/Italian culture'. The corridors will be decorated by tourist posters, maps, paintings . . .

One difficulty is, as we saw, that staff, as they reintegrate with British culture, may have gone beyond that early enthusiasm or lost it altogether. However, the main problem is that it always has to be translated into enthusiasms for specific manifestations of the culture: staff and students cannot gather together in a concert relation to share enthusiasm for 'France'; it has to be for some aspect of France and the particular aspect is determined by the academic culture (Baudelaire is a respectable recipient of enthusiasm but Beaujolais is not). So the Concert Relation, whereby individuals who already have an enthusiasm freely gather together to celebrate it, only operates at the level of assumption and myth.

At the level of practical reality the Gift Relation operates. Now, as I rediscover every year at Christmas, this is a difficult relation to get right. One theory is that you give the recipient what *you yourself* love or desire; this has obvious limitations (my Aunt Mabel has no use for the size 11 mountain boots I currently covet and amber beads don't suit me). But the alternative – giving what the *recipient* loves or desires – implies knowledge which you often do not have and, strictly speaking, are not supposed to request. The situation is made more or less tolerable at Christmas by gift tokens and the fact that everyone is in the same boat.

The Gift Relation between staff and students excludes gift tokens and reciprocity – the staff give, the students receive. So all the onus is on the staff to get it right. Occasionally, we try to guess what the students want; very rarely we ask; but the usual method is to give what we ourselves love or used to love or think we ought to love. The mountain boots phenomenon applies here strongly since these loves are usually those of our student days and they are the loves of men. It is not surprising then that our gifts (since they can't be surreptitiously exchanged) so often languish on the top of a cupboard or end up in a jumble sale or, worst of all, get given away to others (usually Sixth-formers).

It is true that after Christmas I may have to pass some sort of an examination in the sense that when I visit Aunt Ethel I will remember to wear the pink and green angora sweater with the sheep motif she knitted me. But my visits are infrequent. Students visit Aunt Ethel all the time and are in an impossible position. The lecturer tells them how wonderful this author is, how much this book means to him, how moved he is by the ending, how beautifully constructed it all is and (a nod to the Concert Relation) how French or German. He then tells them to exercise their own independent critical judgement when writing their examination essays which he will mark. How can I tell Aunt Ethel that I dislike her sweater? I will fake enthusiasm. 'Angora is my favourite colour'. But at least Aunt Ethel won't accuse me of lacking autonomy and originality and I am not expected to develop professional expertise in knitwear.

The effect of the gift relation as practised is to encourage fake enthusiasm and to inhibit personal development:

> I've got to do an essay on Sarraute whom I dislike and I'm desperately trying to find ways of justifying that dislike. I don't feel all that domination in my relationships. I can't relate to it. But it's an assessed essay. So as I'm not capable of justifying my dislike, I'm going to have to say, 'Yes, it's OK'. (64)

One woman staff respondent sensed this and expressed doubts:

> I sometimes get the feeling that the texts we look at, Gide, Sartre, they look on them as something that is so far beyond the pale in terms of what it might actually mean to them in their own real lives that it seems a bit odd . . . I don't know how far the students ever do change their ideas. If they just listen to the talk that goes on and then remain within their confirmed opinions. (30)

Such feelings, or at least such expressions of feelings, are unusual. On the whole, it seems that staff and students collude to maintain an enthusiastic frontstage fiction while ignoring the backstage reality and the frightening possibility that very little *happens*, that between academic life and 'real' life there is little connection.

Being enthusiastic or inspiring seems such a self-evidently good thing that it takes a certain effort to question it. But questioning is essential.

The first doubt concerns the learning model. People talk of 'infectious' or 'overwhelming' enthusiasm, of being 'bowled over'. In other words, the model implies passivity: one yields swooningly to a superior force; one is moved by a gift. There may be occasions when this is an appropriate behaviour, but it certainly can hardly be said to promote autonomy and intellectual independence. Students are simultaneously attracted to this model and hostile to it as they are simultaneously attracted to autonomy and fearful of it. Lecturers are seduced by the role of the rich donor, the actor, the performer; the system (lectures) encourages them. But it ill-behoves them to go on to complain of student passivity and apathy when their chosen form of interaction is charismatic and depends, by definition, on dazzling an immature, passive audience. Jeanson, describing Orestes in Sartre's *Les Mouches*, talks of '*la classique morale des grands exemples*': 'this ethic', he says 'has been shown up for what it is: it has either paralyzed people by pointing out the distance they have to cover to be like the model or distracted them by proposing that they imitate a hero whose situation and problems are quite unrelated to their own' (1960, p. 25).

We certainly offer ourselves as models in this sense: at the level of metacommunication every lecture is an invitation to students to go forth and speak in monologues to passive throngs. It is hard to overestimate the extent of the dependency created by this lecture mode: students often strive mightily to be like tape-recorders, to get down every word; they are afraid of exercising judgement about what is important and what is peripheral.

Unfortunately – or fortunately – most of us cannot actually manage the charisma. This too remains at the level of myth and assumption, often producing disappointment and a sense of failure, but rarely achieved. It might be possible for me at the beginning of my career to be enthusiastic and inspirational most of the time. I might even manage occasional flashes every year. I certainly cannot keep it up until I retire. And if I try sincerely I may well collapse with the strain. If I simply polish my act I will escape the strain but I am likely to entertain rather than inspire. If I persist with enthusiasm I am likely to become what students dislike most – dogmatic. Dogmatism is enthusiasm growing old. Dogmatism colludes with passivity to deny autonomy.

The point I have made in this section is that the passivity which staff deplore and the dogmatism which students deplore cannot be understood by reference to the personalities and psychologies of the separate individuals and groups concerned. One has to look at the shared value system (enthusiasm) and the way it is enacted through the forms of communication which the system offers (forms which are themselves the product of a value system). And one has to consider the relatedness of the two groups as role-groups within that system.

5 Person and role

One does not ask a person in role – policeman, pilot, surgeon – to be enthusiastic. A characteristic of the demand for enthusiasm is that it is a demand made by and of a *person*. It is also frequently enthusiasm *for* a person, albeit a person of special status – the author of these poems, these plays. One hypothesis which emerged from the seminar is that staff and students are uneasy and uncertain about their role, that they long therefore for the personal.

One revealing episode took place during a session when the staff group were supposed to be collating all their individual pictures (positive and negative) of students in order that two of their number should go and brief the students who were doing the same thing for the staff in an identical room across the corridor. We were having considerable difficulty working in this group, arguing vehemently about the categories which had been offered as an aid (academic, interpersonal, physical appearance . . .), accusing the consultants of 'imposing crippling distortions' by this grid and feeling very dissatisfied with any consensus: it seemed too banal and ordinary (research has to produce original and striking results which distinguish one individual researcher from another).

Half-way through the session a lecturer made a proposal that the task should be abandoned: 'We have this marvellous opportunity to talk with students and we have been stuck in separate rooms all this time'. He proposed that the staff group should simply move in on the students and engage with them on a personal, informal, one-to-one level. There was some initial support for this but in the end the suggestion was not taken up: it was pointed out that it was being assumed the students would welcome such an intervention, but in fact they might not, and it was added that it would be embarrassing if the students succeeded in their part of the task (choose representatives and give the staff their synthesis) while the staff failed. Whereupon the two representatives were quickly chosen and the task was completed. (The students completed their task with less difficulty, though the consultant working with them reported that he had had to be very cautious about making any procedural suggestions, because he felt they would have inevitably taken them up, at the cost of their own autonomy.)

My interpretation of this episode was that staff in particular found the independent, symmetrical work situation in role-groups difficult and the member who proposed changing it to an informal, personal exchange was expressing the group's frustration at an unfamiliar situation where staff and students were relating on a group-to-group and role-to-role basis (another staff group member had previously proposed taking a lamp from the students' room on the grounds that it gave a better light than ours!). The wish to have a *personal* relationship with the students was in fact a wish to escape from a situation where an agreed task was being pursued jointly and collaboratively by persons in role and to enter into one where the interaction was personal, face-to-face and unstructured in terms of time, place and task. If we had 'invaded' the students it is possible that they would have protested; but it is unlikely. They too have a desire to deny role and to meet lecturers as persons. What would have happened is, I think, a version of the 'sherry culture'. Staff and students would have met as 'persons' and engaged in polite talk, probably dominated by the staff member. There is a kind of pseudo-mutuality[3] about such functions which is the counterpart of the gift relation in the lecture room.

What seems difficult for us all to accept is that *persons* may meet more fully in *role*, that doing away with boundaries of task and role creates only an illusion of mutuality and communality – or, to put it another way, imposes social roles (sherry giver/sherry receiver, gift-giver/gift-receiver, young/old) which may be more familiar but which are also much more restrictive and evoke much more reticence.

Individuals need to regulate the degree of intimacy between them in order to protect their private selves. In a sherry party, such regulation will have to be very strong. In a seminar, the role and the task can regulate the distance and people can thus move into personal areas without fear of being misconstrued. I can read a student a love poem in a seminar because she and I know we are studying Petrarch but if I bring out a love poem in a sherry party she will be uncertain about what is being communicated.

The social roles are inevitably difficult to manage collaboratively, given the relatedness of the participants – typically, a middle-aged male and a young female. The sexual elements of this relation are almost never acknowledged. It was quite striking that in the seminar the item 'physical appearance' in the proposed grid was ignored or completed by 'not applicable'. One member of the staff group did offer 'nice legs' but it was treated as a joke in very bad taste. Another complained jokingly of students coming to summer seminars in distractingly flimsy garments. Neither of these comments was communicated to the students. Even in the interviews, the only reference to the gender aspect was this comment from a woman lecturer:

> I'm not interested in 18 year old girls. It is alright if you are a 45 year old man, it's the facts of life. My colleagues like them. They are pretty young things [students not colleagues] . . . but dozens and dozens of nice young ladies bore me stiff. (40)

This recognition of gender seems *prima facie* closer to reality than the fiction that staff–student exchanges take place between subjects who have age but not gender. And yet, over and over again, during my interviews I had to remind myself that the 'students' who were being talked about by lecturers were in fact young women.[4] The whole gender question is an emotional and intellectual no-go area.[5]

The only model I can call on to help me understand these social aspects is the family model in which the student–lecturer role-relation is analogous to the daughter–father role-relation. What is required is that the father recognizes the daughter's femininity while the daughter recognizes the father's masculinity. What actually constitutes 'recognition' is not obvious, but the standard model implies that parents and children recognize recognition well enough. (I have insisted on the 'majority' relation (father–daughter) but there are of course, in higher education, other configurations – father–son, mother–daughter, mother–son). No-one has ever claimed that these family relations are easily managed and there are special difficulties in the higher education setting, especially now that the explicit *in loco parentis* boundary has been eroded and the proportion of students with divorced or separated parents has increased. One feature of the family configuration is that sons and daughters define their relation with the opposite-sex parent in the context of the parents being a couple. Likewise the parents' relation to the children is based on their primary relation to each other. But where in the context of higher education is the parental couple? From the students' point of view it is certainly the department; they perceive lecturers in a department as being a close parental (colleague) group, meeting occasionally in private behind closed doors to transact business. This means that students have satisfactory (sibling) relations with each other. But, as we saw, the lecturer feels more like a single parent. The job is essentially solitary. There are committees but no teams, consequently very little support, recognition or challenge from colleagues. There is also the fact, as we saw, that modern languages lecturers are likely to have uprooted themselves from their own community. It is not surprising then, that lecturers, in the absence of a sentient group of their own, look for relationship from the only people who actually work with them – the students. The students are often called upon to perform a function which is properly that of colleagues (as some children are 'parentalized' and required to substitute for the husband or the wife). Students are not aware of this or unconsciously reject the demand. I suspect also that there is some envy by staff of the students' apparently close community (this may even, paradoxically, be perceived as a parent group). This is something which lecturers can find painful:

> I give what I think is a good class. But at the end of it, when I pick up my books, they just start a conversation amongst themselves as if I wasn't

there. There is not a 'Thank you', not even at the end of a course, just nothing. They go off together to the coffee bar and I go back to my room. (8)

One of the most important aspects of work is *credit*. People will work extremely hard if they get credit, and without it they will usually perform badly and be miserable. The credit can be quite token (a gas fitter worked hard to sell me a maintenance contract, when I asked what was in it for him he told me that he got a pound for each contract, but that there was a competition between teams of fitters). University teachers, unlike gas fitters, operate in an absence of any means of obtaining automatic visible credit and of any substitute in the form of recognition by colleagues. Teaching (which specifically concerns us here) is totally unrecognized. But even published research is insufficiently acknowledged. One professor, author of several books, told me that he felt more and more 'spectral' as an author. The consequence is that staff seek credit from students in ways which are inappropriate.

In short, both staff and students have needs which they feel could be met by persons from the other group, but which in fact are rarely met. My view is that the needs would be met more satisfactorily through a clearer delineation of role.

6 Mastery and the inter-personal

The final plenary discussion of the seminar split two ways. There were those who were complaining of deficiencies of interpersonal relationships and who, by implication, were claiming that the subject was mainly *about* interpersonal relations. Then there were those who said that the task was not to improve interpersonal relations but to further scholarship: students were there to learn 'mastery of other people's difficult ideas'. They could not be limited by their own experience; they learned vicariously. The role of the staff was to instruct students via their own superior mastery and knowledge. The inter-personal position was the more popular, particularly among the students. The 'mastery' position was perceived as being rather stuffy and old-fashioned. (In general, it was striking that at this seminar the subject itself was rarely a topic. 'When I was a Chemistry student', said one of the consultants, 'I was more interested in how good my teachers were as chemists').

However, both positions are clearly legitimate and not, in theory at least, incompatible. But, in practice, the double requirement is difficult. 'Mastery' implies a clear, unambiguous subject with agreed, well-defined objectives. Whether the mastery is of other people's difficult ideas or of other people's difficult language, the situation is clear and questions of the Gift Relationship do not really arise. You do not have to agree with or even like D. H. Lawrence to translate him into Italian. You do not have to agree with Jung or Freud in order to give an accurate summary of their ideas about God. Not surprisingly, 'mastery' has great appeal to staff and students alike. It offers a kind of clarity and security. When staff say they 'know the students in a prose class' they are acknowledging the personal satisfaction of participation in a clearly defined, relatively impersonal task.

But it is not enough: first, because the task is, in the language area, frequently trivial and repetitive, so that the knowledge of each other that the participants-in-role derive is also trivial. Second, because the *subject matter* is, in fact, frequently not language or ideas but interpersonal relations. And this is the developmental concern of the students. It is possible to 'master' EEC law or Descartes perhaps, but the attempt to 'master' Dante or Goethe in the same way is inevitably reductive. One may have mastery of ideas or of language; one does not have mastery of interpersonal relations or of symbolic representations of interpersonal relations. This is a territory which can be explored but not conquered.

And yet the attitudes that accompany the mastery idea – for example, devotion to a clear, shared, impersonal task with clear objectives – are badly needed in the other area. In the absence of such attitudes the teaching of literature in particular becomes either 'personal' chat (salon, pub, or TV, according to the participants) or a version of the Gift Relation, requiring enthusiasm.

The general level of satisfaction would go up, I feel, if it were better understood that furthering interpersonal relationship *between staff and students* is not the work task. The work task entails furthering students' understanding and awareness of interpersonal relations and enhancing interpersonal skills but the lecturer's role requires detachment from the ongoing process rather than participation in it. Enthusiasm has to be for the task itself and not for any particular object (text etc.) which is being used to further the task. When the lecturer's care is for the boundaries and for the learning process itself, the students escape the double bind created by enthusiasm and are free to respond autonomously. They may reject the object of study, while being committed to the objective. Students escape the gift relation double-bind when a lecturer uses authority to prescribe a learning method which requires autonomous behaviour of them and proscribes one which does not:

> Students like doing proses. You have to refuse to give them proses. You do what you believe in and say 'tough' if they protest. You must contest the dominant way. (17)

This (unusual) statement may seem authoritarian. But it is in fact a proper exercise of authority. A proper exercise of authority in learning situations is to create a space where individuals may be free and empowered to take the opportunity to learn. The mastery is then not only of language and of difficult ideas but also of interpersonal relations: these interpersonal relations involve (on the part of the lecturer at least) awareness of staff-student relations, but this is, so to speak, an enabling objective (as learning to load a rifle enables the objective of firing it to be reached). It is not the objective of the exercise. The solution to the problem of students perceiving staff as cold and aloof and staff perceiving students as passive and unrewarding is not more coffee mornings or sherry parties but more participation in clearly defined, meaningful, shared tasks with secure boundaries. And the responsibility for initiating these tasks, creating these boundaries, as distinct from passively accepting the rituals of translation, or of the lecture and the gift relation, is the staff's. It is we who have the authority to do this. Only in this 'impersonal' (i.e. non-social) situation where the lecturer is clearly in role, can personal matters be safely shared and personal initiative be taken by students. It was striking at the seminar that the students who preferred formality (Dr Smith) were more active and autonomous than those who preferred informality (Chris). Role liberates. Role can even free people to question the role.

There is a place for enthusiasm and the gift relation where the lecturer – as a person – offers something about which he or she is enthusiastic. But the condition of this is that the lecturer renounce his or her role, i.e. authority. The student should be free to reject the gift – which means in practice no examinations. Reciprocity is also a condition – I give Bach but I get Steve Reich. In my terms, 'Concert enthusiasm' is valuable but passion for the task of learning and understanding, passion for the subject has to be separated from passion for a specific object of learning and has somehow to be combined with detachment (which must also be distinguished from indifference). The onus is on lecturers to become more aware of what is going on between them and students, to exercise authority more creatively and more appropriately and in particular to realize the extent to which we project on to students our own weaknesses (passivity, timidity, failure to chance your arm, closed minds) and our own longings (freshness, enthusiasm, originality, commitment, idealism). Students are doing their own projecting – specifically, they project all their creativity and potency out on to the staff, leaving themselves feeble and bereft. But they are unlikely to remedy this without assistance from the staff. The cultural dependency is much too strong and goes back much too far.

7 Staff and students at work: an example

In discussing the staff–student relation we are basically discussing the teaching relation and what form it should take in higher education, more specifically, in the humanities, more specifically still, in modern languages. It will be clear from this chapter that I have strong views about the extent to which present forms foster excessive dependency and this in young people whose main developmental goal is autonomy. Staff complain about a passivity which they and the system in which they operate conspire to create and maintain. I have offered my understanding of this situation and of the complex, systemic relations which end up producing results which are disappointing for all concerned.

This is not a recipe book – 'How to run better seminars – From dependency to autonomy in ten easy steps'. However, a course I have taught while writing this book has produced some unusual and relevant data about how students respond to a situation where the tutor is attempting to place the onus of learning, in the sense of personal growth and change, much more on them and where role-relations are being redefined. It also provides evidence of the difficulty the tutor has in striking a balance: too much guidance is spoon-feeding; too little is thwarting and makes students despair and lose trust.

A lecture audience is a sea of silent faces. What is going on in their heads? Graffiti on desks give occasional clues – 'Jake slept here' – but the fossil evidence is sparse. A seminar situation seems less opaque but the complexity of what is going on is greater, so, although more is said than in a lecture, the proportion of unspoken to spoken ends up by being greater. The beneath-the-surface reality of staff–student relations in a seminar is virtually *terra incognita*.

The course I am referring to is concerned with the cinema of Alain Resnais whose main theme is just this – what goes on 'beneath the surface', the life of the mind. A key image is in *Hiroshima mon amour* when the heroine sees the hand of her Japanese lover twitch in his sleep, whereupon a peremptory image is involuntarily triggered by association. The image is horrifying, but she turns to her lover, now awake, and says 'Tu veux du café?' The image remains private to her; there is no way he can know of it unless she tells him.

The class (of final year students) is quite large (12) and meets every week for one and a half hours, having watched a film the day before. There are no lectures. I occasionally divide the group up into sub-groups of various sizes but most of the work is done in the whole group. As a matter of course, every week, I ask a student to take the 'minutes' of the meeting – basically to free everyone else from compulsive note-taking and to emphasize the collaborative nature of the enquiry. The 'minutes' constitute our collective recall. Each session begins with a reading of these minutes.

This is an option course. The Concert Relation is present: it is assumed we are all enthusiastic about the cinema (though this assumption needs checking out; some students are simply unenthusiastic about other things). The Gift Relation too: I offer Resnais as an option because his films have significance for me; though I underplay this aspect. The films challenge the students' preconceptions of what the cinema is, specifically of what narrative is (these preconceptions are deeper in many ways than the corresponding literary preconceptions: people of this age have been more strongly socialized by film than by literature). They also challenge their attachment to the surface, their fear and denial of depth.

Early on, as soon as the group perceived that it was safe to do so, they expressed very negative feelings about the films. The minutes reported this but also enacted the rejection at a deeper level, remaining resolutely at the 'tu veux du café?' level: 'John said, then Mary said, then Theresa said . . .'. I suggested at one class that the problems Resnais was concerned with – narration, representation of mental activity, its difficulty and individuals' resistance to it – were being demonstrated in the writing of the minutes. The following week the minutes were largely devoted to how boring the minutes of the previous session were, as boring as the Resnais films. The following week, the minutes actually reported not what was said during the meeting, but what was going on in the minute-taker's head – largely a debate about the weekend shopping. The minute-taker was away and the minutes were read by another student. They were full of derision and my feelings were of anger at the way things dear to me were being mocked. I kept these personal feelings to myself and directed attention to the minutes as a text analogous to the films we were studying.

The next class but one produced the document on which this section is based and which I am going to reproduce with my comments. In it the student attempts to describe what is going on, not in her own head, but in the group. The following week, the group listened to these minutes in some amazement (these too were read *in absentia* which added to the sense that they were analogous to art objects, the 'artist' absenting herself, leaving the object to speak). The group recognized the representation of the previous session as accurate, but at a deeper level than that of a recording. I do not know a document which gets closer to the actual process of staff–student interaction in a teaching situation: my own description of the seminar would not have been anything like as revealing. It seems important not to edit the text in any way. These then are the complete minutes. I have added my commentary but readers will inevitably provide their own and, as observers, may well see more. This is in no way a model seminar but a relatively rare opportunity to see, through a student's eyes, the tensions of dependency and autonomy and the pleasures and pains associated with revising these staff–student relations in such a way as to combine 'mastery' and the interpersonal while avoiding both dogmatism and passivity.

Great! There is a joke – an ad. for cars with the caption 'The reality is better than the dream'[1] Gaiety turns to panic as a slip of paper[2] about the dreaded exam is produced, reminding us of the ultimate objects of this sometimes almost flippant course. There is a stony silence while reading this slip of paper – it certainly brings us back to reality. The silence becomes uncomfortable – seems to last an eternity. Why do silences always seem so uncomfortable in this group? [3]

1. A reference to a recurring theme in Resnais's work.
2. A statement spelling out in greater detail than at the beginning of the course the objectives and the requirements of the examination.
3. Partly because the tutor does not automatically fill them.

At last someone breaks the silence with a technical question about the exam, the implication being – 'Do I really have to know all these films inside out? Can't I choose the films I really like and ignore the rest?'

Again there is silence – my mind goes blank with so much silence. Looking around, I see that everybody has their eyes fixed on the sheet. I wonder, does Colin know where to go next? How much does he plan these meetings?

As usual, the initial response to this week's film – *La Guerre est finie* – is 'I couldn't understand it'. However, there is a tentative suggestion that this film is not quite so bad as others – is this because we are gradually getting used to the apparent strangeness of these films? If so, do we only fall asleep because we have established the habit of falling asleep during these films? There seems to be no agreement so far as to what is actually happening in this film. Apart from Colin, we all seem to experience such difficulty in expressing ourselves when it comes to Resnais' films.

In *La Guerre est finie*, there is an impression of chaos – so much seems to be happening that we can't actually grasp what's going on.

'Give a response to this film' – at first it seems an almost impossible task after the first viewing. It seems such an open question. We are trying to analyse why we have such difficulty understanding these films. God, I'm confused – so's everyone else – this is evident in the long, silent gaps, and the fact that everyone is fidgety.

There is a suggestion that this film is difficult because the experience is so remote from our own – I feel there is something in this – certainly I couldn't identify with anyone or anything.

There is an impression of being thrown into the middle of this film, with no explanation – I see a parallel here somewhere with being thrown into a meeting where we are commanded to give some kind of concrete response. [4]

Perhaps it is safer to fall asleep than to try to fathom out this disturbing thing which is 'the films of Alain Resnais'. Ignorance is bliss. It makes you think too much about your own condition, far more comfortable to make a joke about yet another boring Alain Resnais film. Reminds me of conversations about the

4. It would be possible to give an introduction to this film which would certainly make the first experience of viewing it much less confusing. My decision not to do this is consistent with a belief that the ability to tolerate confusion is valuable and can be learned only if the opportunities that arise are not preempted. But too much confusion produces despair.

universe and space and God when you end up with a headache and a lot of unanswered questions. [5]

Eureka! someone actually enjoyed this film – and let's not forget the 'juicy bits' – typical of a French film – trust Mark to bring that up.

Oh no, now we're being asked to tell the story of the film – something I certainly couldn't do. Why is it always difficult to remember the names of characters in these films? Even the plot is difficult to understand – a mass of false passports, false identities, arrests, the Spanish Civil War is thrown in there somewhere. Is he married? – which reminds me – who is the child tucked up in bed – another dream?

There is a cry for help from the poor individual picked upon to tell the story. I have to say that I don't agree that Diego is fantasizing about making love to Nadine. There is general agreement that this character doesn't seem to know what he wants to do.

We all seem to have extreme difficulty in retelling the story of a film we have just spent 2 hours watching. The trouble in relating events would appear to be unique to Resnais' films and is tied up with the feelings of boredom they evoke. You tend to drift off into your own little world as the film jumps from one thing to another. There is no flow, no clear narrative – they are fragmented in terms of action, plot and characters. You can never become involved in a Resnais film, it is difficult to identify with the characters' situations and consequently the whole becomes difficult to understand. I feel that I can identify with the woman in *L'Année dernière à Marienbad*, but this was not my initial reaction. I had to think about the film quite deeply before I realized that what was going on on the screen, was somehow related to my own life.

My mind is wandering – back to the meeting. Standard narrative forms do not convey the experience of a middle-aged man who

5. The crucial question – whether to change (to learn) or not, whether to accept the discomfort of having to re-align your conceptions of what is narrative, what is cinema, what is normal, what is your 'own condition', whether to live with 'unanswered questions' or take questions and answers off the peg, ready made (see Table 3.1 above, particular Perry's Phase 6).

suddenly finds he is no longer committed to a cause which has held him all his life. Resnais is trying to describe the nature of human experience, but he goes about this in too realistic a way; there is a feeling that inside information of the character's thought processes is necessary in order to hold our attention.

The recounting of an emotion or an experience distorts because it tries to give shape to something which is intangible – I feel this is what is happening as I try to grasp and write down the feelings of the group. Colin is talking a lot – there is the impression that everybody is lost and feeling rather uncomfortable – is there a sense of guilt about not understanding these films?

Is there a bored, hostile reaction to these films, because they disturb us? They make us look at our own superficial lives, make us realize the amount of time we waste making small-talk, so that we never get to know the essential part of people which exists beneath the surface? We ourselves come across as boring and mundane, just like the characters in the film. [6]

We must also look to the way in which we have got used to viewing; attachments to our methods of seeing go deep and therefore any change makes us feel uncomfortable, even insecure. [7]

6,7. Again, this sort of awareness is not something that can be achieved other than by going through the process of confusion and uncertainty referred to in the previous paragraph.

Colin starts to talk about some radical teaching group and I find that everyone is suddenly more attentive. Is this because it is something from real life, something from within our own environment? Colin is talking about changing narrative forms – this is becoming almost like a lecture.

Colin is now talking about individual films – he is giving almost a summary of each film, so everyone listens attentively – at last! Some concrete guidance as to what these films are about. [8]

8. I am surprised that I did this – something about a balance between giving and withholding 'concrete guidance'. The group was particularly anxious about examinations at this time.

I feel confused. It is extremely difficult to follow the thoughts of others while trying to sort them out sufficiently to be able to put them down on paper – does this say something about Resnais? [9]

9. The student is working on a problem presented by Resnais, experientially, through her own experience of taking and writing these minutes.

It is also extremely difficult to grasp the mood of the group. As people are not saying much, I am trying to gather something from their facial expressions but all I see is a sea of blank faces. People are attentive because a bewildering scene in the film is being explained – we see different shots of girls because Diego is wondering what Nadine looks like, having only heard her voice.

People are beginning to relate this to personal experience: eg, what you imagine when about to meet someone you haven't seen for a long time.

It is suggested that the life of the mind is taboo is most films on TV and at the cinema; they deal only with the 'tu veux du café?' level. I feel that this attitude is changing in films, reflecting the modern preoccupations with psychology and mental illness.

Again there is a sudden surge in attentiveness as Colin relates his day – we are all so nosy about the lives of our teachers – we want proof that they are in fact real people I suppose. [10]

10. So much for the person-in-role concept! The idea was to use my day as an example of the banality and insufficiency of the bare facts. The curiosity about me the person makes the bare facts interesting.

I think we ought to define 'reality' – for me, reality is what we do everyday; that which goes on in our minds at the same time is so shapeless, everchanging, that it is something other than reality. Inner experience is frightening – *Nuit et Brouillard* is mentioned – I shudder. [11]

11,12. Again, working experientially on the Resnais problem – the imagination is both creative and destructive; dream and fantasies are better *and* worse than

The very different personalities of those present begin to emerge as people try relate to the film through their own personal experiences.

In rejecting these films, I don't think there is an active denial of the life of the mind. Perhaps, like Diego, we have no time for it. There is also an element of danger in becoming too involved in the life of the mind; you tend to forget the physical needs of the body – result, complete breakdown. [12]

reality, inner experience is frightening, equated with mental illness, breakdown. This is what I mean by working on the inter-personal in role, different from 'nosiness'.

We are in a half way state – we are bored by routine, surface life, yet frightened of going into our minds – is it possible to strike a happy balance? [13]

13. This paragraph is very striking as a picture of someone or of a group, struggling with the issue of whether or not to learn, the fear of learning. The 'balance' is the teacher's responsibility.

It is so difficult to get the feelings of the group – somebody talk, for God's sake! It seems that Colin talks [14] and I try to analyse my own responses to what he is saying – these minutes are what I feel, not what anybody else is thinking – how do you get round this temptation of extreme subjectivity? My thoughts are confused, racing. It is more difficult to observe than I thought. I wonder if Colin is disappointed by our bored responses – what does he really think about us? that's something we all feel, just as he probably wonders what we all really think about these films.

14. Only an observer could say whether my talking is an appropriate balanced response to this group's anxiety and 'half way state' or to my own insecurity.

Colin is very insecure, so afraid of 'indoctrinating' us – not totally sure about his teaching methods. [15]

15. The student thinks it is insecurity – probably right but it does not seem as if my insecurity makes the student feel insecure. It is simply noted. Again

inter-personal, but shared awareness in the context of the task.

There is a suggestion that the characters in '*La Guerre est finie*' are warm, moving, perhaps more human than characters in the other films.

The discussion turns to the two love scenes, the first of which I found laughable, what with bits of body everywhere, like some crazy Picasso portrait.

Colin identifies with Diego and finds the end of the film moving – I seem to be discovering more about how Colin feels than about the feelings of the group – is this my fault? [16]

16. I was, I think, trying to give a lead.

I bet Colin's going to be hoarse at the end of one and a half hours – I think he is quite enjoying himself though – I wonder what this seminar would be like if some of our more vociferous colleagues were here? [17]

17. Very different. I am forced *by this group* to talk more. When 'the vociferous colleagues' are present, I talk less.

So, Colin has a secret desire to write – he suffers from 'the same old routine' syndrome as us. In answer to your question, Colin, yes I do feel I have a past to come to terms with – but that's all I'm saying. If the other members feel the same way, they're not letting on. There is definitely an element of inhibited behaviour, almost shyness in this group, as if they are afraid of revealing too much about themselves. Back to the film. [18]

18. The film is partly about what one reveals and what one conceals from oneself and others, and ultimately about the necessity of appropriate self disclosure. An issue as delicate as this can either be ignored or inter-personally demonstrated. Here I demonstrate (though the disclosure is not very risky) but no-one follows the lead: the description of the group is accurate – they are shy, quite inhibited. It is too

large a group and too diverse. The essential point, however, is that there is no requirement to be personal. The task is not interpersonal and it is not an encounter group. The task is understanding the problem of revelation and representation and also the way the past is present in the present and impedes the future if it is not disclosed. This understanding can be achieved by inner reflection without actual disclosure as the minute-taker has seen. The question is not 'How can feelings be expressed?', but 'how can feelings be made available for work?'.

There is admiration for the mistress in *La Guerre est finie* – she is romantic, she puts up with this macho character, she is willing to give up all her friends for him.

We're back to the business of falling asleep. When things are difficult, when we have problems, or feel unhappy we want to curl up and go to sleep – sleep is associated with warmth and security. [19]

Personal aside here:

I now like Resnais films – it is better to be uncertain, it makes you more open to new ideas and experiences.

19. The authentic response to these films – falling asleep in this case – is the way to genuine understanding of them and of the issues they raise. The tutor's job is to give the students the freedom to fall asleep or more generally (since, as was pointed out, fortunately, everyone

The music is mentioned – but nobody says what was suggested at the Tuesday viewing of the film – the music was conducive to sleep because it sounded like angels singing in heaven.

The beginning of the film suddenly becomes clear to all as Colin explains that it is a flash forward – Diego is imagining what he will be doing in a few hours hence. This is what we all do in real life – imagine little scenes that we hope will take place. This little technique also shows us something about Diego's character – he is a planner.

This all seems such a jumbled hotch-potch of predominantly my ideas – I do hope it doesn't bore everybody to death – profit from the reading of these minutes to plan your shopping trips to Sainsbury's and to catch up on your sleep – do we do anything but eat and sleep in this group?

was not asleep all the time) to express their resistance, the negative, to refuse the gift.

This can be done indirectly: 'I gave them *Parler croquant* by Claude Duneton. All the students loved this onslaught on the 17th century, this seemed to liberate them' (22) or it can be done, as in this Resnais course, by straightforward acceptance of counter-dependency and by refusing to yield to the temptation to persuade or argue, since persuasion or argument will merely produce compliance.

Going through the negative in this way with students is not easy, especially when you are privately enthusiastic about the objects of their negativity. As the minutes show, the temptation is always there to make things comfortable for everyone by transmitting authoritative information or enthusiasm – which is to opt for a lower level of learning.

This particular course is unique in the way that pedagogic issues closely mirror the subject matter. The document is a contribution to my principle purpose in this chapter which is to throw light on the lived experience of students and of staff in their working relationship. The minutes show the students as they are. Tutors either work with them as they are (in the way described or in some other way) or else they invent, in collusion with the students, some fantasized students (better or worse than the real ones) and work with those. This solution is easier for all concerned but leaves both staff and students with an obscure sense of missed opportunity.

7

Staff–Student/Male–Female

I have already referred on several occasions to the gender issue, to the fact that modern languages is a 'feminine' subject, in the basic sense that, at all levels, the majority of those choosing to study it are female. In Higher Education there are, as we saw, three women students for every male. And yet, when we consider staff, the proportion is exactly the opposite: there are three men for every woman.[1] It is true that in the university as a whole the proportion of women is even smaller (one in six),[2] nevertheless, the contrast between a predominantly female student group and a predominantly male staff group is very striking. One of the female students at the final plenary of the staff–student seminar issued this challenge to the male lecturers: 'There's us, and then suddenly there's you. Where did you all come from?'.

The experience of language people is in part the experience of this gender imbalance. This is why I am devoting a chapter to an attempt to understand the significance of gender for staff and students in modern languages.

1 Female staff

> As long as a woman is for birth and children she is different from man as body is from soul. But when she wishes to serve Christ more than the world, then she will cease to be a woman and be called a man. (St. Jerome)

On reviewing the interviews I conducted with women staff respondents I am struck by how fragmented is the record. Several of the interviews are incomplete because my respondent could only give me a limited period of time, a lunch hour for example. One interview was broken off because the children had to be collected from school. I found that women took up much more frequently than male staff (or students) my offer to use the pause button on the tape recorder: perhaps they were less confident, less trusting of me than male colleagues were; perhaps they were prepared to say more personal things. I also note that in the period since I conducted the interviews several of the women have left the job or have begun to think of leaving it. I am sure that a study of women who have left university employment prematurely would throw a great deal of light on higher education. The experience of women academics is clearly different from that of men.

This is most self-evidently true for women with small children. I was amazed at the feats of time-management that such women achieve. One respondent, Dr Knight, had three young children:

> We planned all the pregnancies so that the birth would coincide with the end of the teaching year, so that I could do the finalists' course . . . one of my highest commitments is to the students. With the last baby I went on doing some classes until the last minute: I went into hospital from here. She was 5 days early. Each time I ended up marking exam scripts in hospital. (30)

But these feats of planning are not recognized by the institution:

> I never felt that it was registered, let alone appreciated, by anybody.

Dr Knight had this to say about how her role as mother is perceived (or, rather, not perceived) by students and colleagues:

> Students that I know very well. If I am out pushing a pram they don't even see me. I think they are not expecting to see me with a pram. It happens even with colleagues. They don't make the connection.

This is the most obvious explanation of the disparity in numbers: males are in a majority mainly because males can marry and have babies without seriously disrupting their careers. A previous generation of women accepted the fact that an academic career and marriage were irreconcilable and some opted for the career. Today women are less ready to make that choice, and yet, in some ways, things have changed less than one might think. The job situation is such that many women have to choose between living with their partner and being unemployed or, like one of my respondents, having a post in a place hundreds of miles from their partner whom they see only at weekends.

As regards children, the dilemma is even more acute. Dr Knight is remarkable in her ability to combine a career and babies. For most academic women the sensible choice is not to have children. And yet Dr Knight said, 'I was not aware of being a woman until I had children'.

Acker and Piper ask 'Is Higher Education fair to women?' (1984) and, not surprisingly, conclude that it is not. In terms of recruitment and promotion, the figures clearly show that women are under-represented and it is difficult to deny that Higher Education should, on grounds of fairness, employ more women, even if this means adapting to women's life-cycle and maternal role. In Higher Education in general and in modern languages in particular, men have the power to determine structure, content, process and values. Women staff are in a minority and do not have that power. Women students, although in a majority (in Modern Languages), have, of course, even less power than women staff.

The implied argument of the Acker and Piper book seems to be that this situation should be changed because it is 'unfair'. Some members (of an undifferentiated group) are discriminated against on grounds (sex) which are not material – as if being under 5 foot tall or speaking French was a disqualification for undertaking a PhD in mathematics.

But this notion of the undifferentiated group is suspect. It implies that for the purposes of the job there are no significant differences between men and women or between men's experience and women's experience, that men and women can do the job *as presently defined* equally well. Since the job is at present defined by men, it implies that, provided artificial and unfair restraints are removed, women can operate perfectly well within this male-created world, exercising power within it as individuals and not as women.

I believe there is truth in this. Many women are able to function extremely well in a system which was created by men, on the basis of male life-experience; they work effectively within the modes and structures of men and are happy to do so.

But in fact women's experience, real and potential, is different from that of men, and women, even those referred to in the previous paragraph, are perceived differently by others. 'Masculinity' and 'femininity' are certainly constructed, but that does not mean they do not exist or that they do not determine our experience of ourselves, of others, of institutions. The group is not undifferentiated: it is comprised of men and women and it is not only that women are underrepresented but that the feminine experience is underrepresented. There is certainly a strong argument on grounds of abstract fairness but the answer to the question 'Why does the imbalance matter?' is that a better balance of the sexes seems more likely than anything else to bring about a better balance between cognitive and affective elements in the system. Far from reinforcing traditional male/female stereotypes (cognitive men/affective women) such a change might actually liberate both men and women from pressures either to conform to stereotypes or to reject them in a counter-dependent way.

The situation at present is that certain indispensable functions of the system are devolved in a sex-stereotypical way on women. The need to care for troubled students, for example:

> Somehow the men's doors are always closed; they've got important things to do. It's always my door and my shoulder . . . I say this to men: You are going to have to do your share of nurturing. You can't carry on leaving female colleagues and secretaries to do it all.[3]

And, in general, the low value placed on relationship affects women more than men. The male ideal seems to be a kind of heroic individualism, the capacity to work alone, to survive and prosper without support. Autonomy is the end and the capacity to be lonely is the means:

> In my final year I had a very enjoyable time being highly selective and irritating one or two of the older tutors quite a lot – I wouldn't attend certain lectures at all. I much preferred to be working on my own or doing something special. I worked on my own a tremendous amount. I was totally autonomous by the time I started research . . . I more or less taught myself. On the thesis part of it I had no advice at all but it didn't matter. (9)

The British PhD is the incarnation of this – an exercise in solitary masculine heroism, and provides another reason for the imbalance. Women are less able to work in this way.

> There was no-one (at first in university) you could really get deeply in contact with as I had been for six years with my teacher . . . (but) in the final year it was possible to get that real contact with two or three people which meant that someone mattered to you and was interested in you and that you were working in a relationship again. (8)

> I enjoy working in collaboration; it usually occurs because when I find somebody in my own field with whom I don't want to compete I suggest collaboration instead. (53)

I was struck by how often my women respondents had a research interest in questions of *register* in language, register which is the subtlest linguistic indicator of a relationship.

In conclusion then, we can say that the position as regards women staff in modern languages is that of any minority group. The abstract arguments for parity of numbers imply that the minority group shares or is prepared to share the values of the majority group, that the difference which excludes the minority is not a salient difference. This seems inherently implausible when the difference is gender, when the task of the system involves relationship and the study of symbolic descriptions of relationship and when one significant group of people in the system – students – have an exactly opposite lack of parity.

2 Female students

> On the whole there is no sexual difference. (Male professor)

> My ideal student would be perfectly happy to spend 30 hours a week with his (sic) nose in a book. (Female senior lecturer)

> The men aren't aware of the differences in the life experience of the women. The women are aware but the male students are not. (Female lecturer)

As I suggested earlier, the tendency is to deny the salience of gender difference. This may seem a worthy attitude: to insist on a common humanity and to ignore differences of sex or age or colour is indeed preferable to basing value-judgements on such differences. But the common humanity into which the differences are merged always ends up being virtually indistinguishable from the powerful majority group.

The reality of the experience of most students in modern languages is that they are women in a system devised and run by men. In order to prosper in that system they have to respond to men, to men's demands, to men's choices of (male) texts or (male) subjects of study, to men's ways of thinking and working. To the extent that this is seen as developmental all is well: the process of socialization into male ways is then the very process of education and civilization, analogous to that whereby children are required to respond to adult ways in order to prosper (and grow). To the extent, however, that it is seen as requiring that fundamental aspects of individuals should be denied, the process is anti-developmental and results in a fabricated identity.

Here is a striking description of a woman lecturer's experience as a student. I believe many women students will identify with it:

> I hadn't really found myself as a woman who could present her experience as a woman in words which she felt would be acceptable to the male authority figures who were judging me . . . I was having to find myself a sort of male identity . . . and that male identity was a fabrication . . . my first class degree was a product of my fabricated male identity. My real experience of literature and my real beginnings of finding myself were in the occasional tête à tête with books in French which did in some way reflect my experience as a woman and I could respond to that. But nowhere in their actual formulation or the set up of my exams or my study was there a place for that . . . I was trying to develop a sharp male intellect along the lines required by society. I didn't have an outlet for the other side of me, for some kind of creative activity. What I did then was to try to get it by having a baby. (8)

It is very striking that, at the staff–student seminar, women staff and women students identified very much with each other. The women students said that contact with the women staff was for them the most important part of the seminar. One of the things that struck me very forcibly was the extent of the deprivation experienced by women students because of the lack of role-models.

Compare for example two teaching experiences – Dr Knight:

> There was an occasion when I was visibly pregnant and we were doing Sartre's *L'Age de Raison* with its description of pregnancy – that was an odd experience for us all. (30)

and a male respondent:

> It was a group of women. I asked them about the maternal instinct. How they thought femininity might be constructed . . . I was, as a man sitting behind a desk, taking a feminist view about the maternal instinct, telling them what feminism was. There was total consensus that the maternal instinct existed. The whole thing worked extremely badly . . . (29)

It is obvious that Dr Knight is better placed to explore these issues with women students than the male seminar-leader. Women students are forced into using men as models and this makes it difficult to find authority to develop their feminine identity. I am convinced that their passivity and dependency are the result of this. An appropriate development of the feminine side might produce autonomous, collaborative, empathic behaviour which is not passive and where dependency is mutual. The current definition of autonomy is a masculine definition.

The women staff at the seminar identified very strongly with the women students, particularly with their silence and their apparent passivity:

> When I was a student I wouldn't open my mouth. I sat and hoped that no-one would ask me any questions. I used to be terrified when it was my turn to perform. I hated it. (7)

> I was quiet because I didn't have anything to say that was any better than what the lecturer was saying, so I didn't say anything. I used to sit there, so they told me later, and write down what I wanted to write down and apparently look at them sceptically all the time and not contribute anything. (38)

Unlike the male lecturers, who seem not to have had doubts or uncertainties as students or to have drawn a veil over them, the women remember how they were and how long it took to acquire some solidity. This memory causes particular problems when they teach groups of silent women with whom they identify:

> They are all people who don't believe in making loud, superficial noises . . . having been a quiet student and having got a lot out of it and not having wanted to talk in class makes it difficult for me because you are supposed to go in there and get them all talking, get them all reacting . . . the people who talk are the people who talk and some of them talk a load of rubbish, but if you are a teacher you are supposed to get them talking . . . Whether starting to talk, or starting to shut up is a sign of maturity I don't know. (38)

The answer to the question in presumably a version of Ecclesiastes – 'There is a time to talk and a time to be silent' and maturity is knowing the time, and having the choice. But the value system of the university, the very definition of 'teaching', always favours talking over listening.[4]

There is a paradox of silence. It is not necessarily the same thing as passivity. As a student put it:

> When I am silent I am not sulking, I am communicating, but men don't know how to listen.

The trouble is that silence is hard to interpret and it is not surprising that it is rarely seen as communication but always as passivity and lack of confidence. A woman lecturer is driven to wish the women students were more like men:

> I'm irritated at their unwillingness to make a move, sitting there waiting to be fed . . . the men are less dependent, I see them as very much in isolation. It irritates me when they stand out quite often as the best students. I want to kick the female students into action and say 'go and fight back, you're as good as him really, with a bit more determination and commitment'. (1)

But another sees the difference more neutrally:

> The male students have more self-confidence. The women are more aware of the subjective nature of what they are saying so they are more tentative about it whereas the men tend to build their individual experience into something more general. It is easy to notice the tentativeness in women . . . I envy in male colleagues the certainty they seem to have about all sorts of things which I feel very doubtful about. (30)

Frequently, it is this tentativeness which is being communicated. The fact is that there is a lot to be tentative about. Masculine confidence 'about all sorts of things' is the result not so much of superior night-vision as of greater readiness to leap in the dark. Women are more aware of uncertainty, ambiguity, and confusion, more in touch with their own subjectivity and with the arbitrariness of abstract intellectual constructions.

Women at the gender workshop brought up the whole question of masculine articulacy, the way that language itself could seem to be masculine, one remove from subjective experience, the way that they frequently felt excluded from this language. As Umberto Eco puts it in *The Name of the Rose*:

> There are words that give power, others that make us all the more derelict . . . there are those to whom the Lord has not granted the boon of self expression in the universal tongue of knowledge and power. (p. 330)

Women might learn to speak this language, they said, but it was compliance rather than self-expression. At one stage the workshop enacted the painful silent seminar with older men coercively interrogating in order to illicit some response from silent young women. Again, it is not that female students do not need to learn the 'language of knowledge and power' but that this language has to be part of a real, not a fabricated identity and this implies the recognition of other, different languages, including the language of silence and the language of subjective experience.

3 Balance

When Powell (1986) expresses the wish that there should be equal numbers of boys and girls doing modern languages, when attempts are made to make science more attractive to girls, when, in this chapter, I claim that departments of modern languages need more women staff, something is being expressed which is more than a wish for arithmetical equality: it is a wish not only for fairness but for wholeness. The gender issue serves to highlight a general lack of balance, therefore a lack of wholeness. Any enterprise requires cognitive powers: clear, distinct boundaries of task, place, time; conceptual, abstract thought; decisive action – in a word 'mastery'. But an enterprise also requires affective powers: recognition of the confused and the tentative, the unique and the personal. Where one set of qualities (mystery?) is denigrated and suppressed the whole enterprise is unbalanced and the other set also functions less effectively.

What is required for the enterprise of modern languages to function effectively and for people to have a satisfying experience within it is that differences *between* individuals and *between* groups (male/female, staff/student) should be acknowledged and that this acknowledgement should be seen as a stage on the way to acknowledging difference *within* each person and, ultimately, to achieving wholeness and balance.

Part 4

The Discipline

Once an object is conceptualized as the member of a given class, it is extremely difficult to see it as belonging also to another class. This class membership of an object is called its 'reality'; thus anyone who sees it as the member of another class must be mad or bad. (Watzlawick, *Change*.)

To understand the experience of language people it is not enough to consider indivduals and their psychology, nor even groups and their psychology. In Part Three we saw how two groups, staff and students, could only be understood in their relatedness. But the staff–student system which we considered there was only one constellation in the galaxy. Staff and students of modern languages are members of a particular discipline which is related in complex and multiple ways to other disciplines. Staff are members of a profession – that of University teacher – which is related to other professions and semi-professions. Students see themselves in varying degrees as future members of those professions and semi-professions. Staff and students are members of a particular institution – the University of Redbrick or Plateglass – which is one of 45 British Universities. Universities are a section of the 500 institutions which make up 'Higher Education' in Great Britain. Higher Education is part of the British educational system which, together with the media, the arts, the entertainment industry, the advertising industry and the meteorological office, maintain and transmit a national culture. Knowledge-institutions and culture-institutions are sections of the entire society – industry, commerce, medicine, agriculture, politics, religion . . .

To see clearly that any object of research – individual or group – is comprehensible only systematically,[1] that is, in terms of a set of shifting relations, is to understand why so much research isolates and fragments. The totality is daunting, and one is forced to focus on foreground. As we saw in Chapter Five, non-British academics see this as a characteristic trait of British intellectual life. We shall see that it is also one of the characteristics of the modern University and that in this respect the discipline of modern languages is anomalous or anachronistic in that its thrust seems unavoidably integrative.

Like the Resnais seminar we considered earlier, this book is what Bateson calls a metalogue – an exemplification of its own content.[2] At the risk of concussion, this modern linguist is trying to see the woods *and* a particular tree. I shall start by describing the woods – discipline, subject, university, profession. I hope that the reader will bear in mind the material of the previous chapters and thus begin the work of relating the part to the whole which will be the subject of the concluding chapter.

8

Systems

We with our quick dividing eyes
measure, distinguish and are gone.
The forest burns, the tree-frog dies,
yet one is all and all are one.
(Judith Wright, *Rain Forest* (*Phantom Dwelling*, 1985))

1 Disciplines

The literature offers a bewildering variety of terms: there are disciplines, sub-disciplines and multi-disciplines; subjects and subject-disciplines; bodies, fields, areas and universes of knowledge; bodies, fields, areas and universes of study; disciplinary cultures and sub-cultures; faculties and faculty cultures; specialisms, professions and semi-professions . . . all separated and classified by boundaries, frontiers or frames; all grouped into curricula with syllabuses (and syllabi). It is less a wood, more, as Eisner and Valance (1974) say, 'a conceptual jungle'.

The root questions are philosophical or, more specifically, epistemological; but they are sociological too, or more specifically, they concern the sociology of knowledge. And the preceding sentence is, of course, another metalogue: even the discipline of knowledge about knowledge is subject to problems of definition.

Let us start with some questions: What is knowledge? What do I need to know or want to know? What do I need or want someone else to know or not to know? Are some things more worth knowing than others? Who decides? and what exactly is a 'thing worth knowing'? Are these 'things' like bricks, or like jig-saw pieces, or like the petals of a flower? Do some 'things' have a family likeness? Are new 'things' created? If so how? and if I now know a new 'thing' how can I enable others to know it? And why does it so frequently happen that they do not want to know?

Here now is a random list of 'things to be known'. The reader may care to bring some order to the confusion (which is only a minute sample of the confusion of the world) by introducing some boundaries and categories. I suggest the following: which are things to be known in families? which in schools? which in Higher Education? which in departments of modern languages?

> Word processing, computer-programming, linguistics, song-writing, literary criticism, bluffing, thinking, Shakespeare, Germany, Geography, Arithmetic, German Literature, Acupuncture, Botany, Osteopathy,

> French irregular verbs, Historical Phonology, marketing, collaboration, Germany, Philosophy of Science, 'The Daffodils', Cybernetics, Biology, Quantum Theory, brushing your teeth properly, knowing right from wrong, killing rabbits, making mayonnaise, running a University, Zoology, Aunt Maggie's Birthday, playing the guitar, recognizing your mother's face, solving quadratic equations, loading a container ship, translating, making random lists, knowing when to stop . . .

I am not suggesting that the world ever has to be organized from chaos in this way: indeed many of the items on the list are educational labels resulting from a prior organizing process. But I believe the experience of the list makes one aware of the urge to order, the heterogeneity of the material to be ordered and, more fundamentally, the heterogeneity of the ordering processes.

The most striking example of the urge to order is to be found in the work of the curriculum theorists in the United States in the 1970s. Writers like Bloom, Bruner, Schwab, Gagné, Lowe,[1] all in their different ways, emphasized order through cognitive process. 'Disciplines' were basically coherent logical structures of thought. The cognitive process made sure that the knowledge to be acquired matched perfectly the cognitive structure which organized it. 'Studying a field of knowledge means investigating its hierarchical structure' (Lowe, 1971, p. 141). The subject matter (rocks for geologists) is important as are the typical methods of investigation and the criteria for truth, but what really counts is coherence and clear boundaries. By extension, for these writers, coherence becomes a criterion of excellence; the greater the coherence of the concepts and principles or 'foundational ideas', the more prestigious the discipline.

This concept of a discipline reflects and reinforces a scientific view; it values above all the ability to manipulate abstractions. It is essentially Platonic in its wish to have a structure of abstract concepts to whose perfection the real world aspires. These writers take the given – the various arrangements of subjects as taught and learned in institutions – and attempt to justify them at a higher level of abstraction. The subject is seen as the admittedly imperfect realization of necessary structures.

The remarkable work done in Britain around the same time starts from a radically different premiss. The authors in Michael Young's influential collection *Knowledge and Control* (1971) refute the 'objective view of knowledge', the belief that 'zones of knowledge are objects which can be considered to have meaning other than in the minds of the individuals in which they are constituted, irrespective of their realisation' (p. 75). Knowledge is not given, but socially constructed, as are all the boundaries which classify it. Basically, 'disciplines' only have abstract existence. What exists in reality are *subjects*, that is to say institutionalized, operational territories inhabited by communities of people who defend their boundaries and compete with other communities.[2]

These communities, according to Young, are part of the system through which power and control are exerted:

> Those in positions of power will attempt to defend what is to be taken as knowledge, how accessible to different groups any knowledge is, and what are the accepted relations between different knowledge areas and between those who have access to them and make them available. (p. 114)

Indeed, some of the vigour of this collection may come from the fact that it constitutes a combative affirmation on the part of one epistemic community – sociologists – of their own power to determine what is knowledge. This is implicit in all the articles, explicit in that of Blum.

For our purposes, the concepts elaborated by Basil Bernstein in his contribution (1972, pp. 47–69) are the most valuable. He points out that the British education system operates with what he calls the 'collection code'. There are very strong boundaries between contents (subjects), producing high levels of specialization and subject loyalty together with hostility towards 'mixed categories and blurred identities' – because these 'represent a potential openness, an ambiguity which makes the consequences of previous socialization problematic' (p. 55). Not only are subjects in Britain strongly differentiated (strong classification) but they are also strongly 'framed', that is to say the boundary between what is and what is not considered knowledge is very rigid (the reader may care to refer back to my random list – it should not be difficult to distinguish school knowledge from community knowledge there). 'Strong framing entails reduced options; weak framing entails a range of options' (p. 50). The fact that the high status University qualification was until recently a Single Honours degree with a common syllabus is an example of strong framing in Britain.

Bernstein hints at the religious aspect of the classification code (Bourdieu elaborates the parallel further). Subjects are to be kept 'pure' and the weakening of frames of classification represents a 'pollution, endangering the sacred' (p. 56).

British education then is characterized by extremely strong classification and framing of knowledge, having the effect of creating the powerful subject identities and loyalties which Lacey (1977) discovered in his student teachers. The opposite of this collection code is the integrated code where some 'relational idea', some 'supra-content concept' (p. 60) determines what shall be known. Young's book is, in one sense, a plea for the integrated code, though Bernstein in particular underlines all the difficulties. Collection codes give everyone the illusion of a given coherence: integrated codes make it plain that we start from incoherence and ambiguity:

> The ultimate mystery of the subject is not coherence, but incoherence; not order, but disorder; not the known, but the unknown. As this mystery, under collection codes, is revealed very late in educational life – and then only to the select few who have shown the signs of successful socialization – then only the few *experience* in their bones the notion that knowledge is permeable, that its orderings are provisional, that the dialectic of knowledge is closure and openness. For the many, socialization into knowledge is socialisation into order, the existing order. (p. 57)

To sum it up, 'the collection code makes knowledge safe through the process of socialisation into the frames'. There is inherently less security and control in integrated codes.

The conclusion that seems to flow from this is that the need for security, dependency, control is very strong in Britain and the tolerance of ambiguity very low. This is confirmed in Bailey's splendid book on academic life, *Morality and Expediency* (1977), where academic fear of risk-taking and the dislike of the anomalous (exemplified by the homosexual rooster) are described *con brio*: 'people or objects or events which will not fit into a known category are likely to be regarded with fear, with contempt or with loathing' (p. 184).

It is of course a human not a national characteristic to desire predictability. We trust people to the extent that their group adherence is clear and unchanging, that the label matches the contents. It is, however, a matter of degree. The trouble is that the label on the box of student and academic says 'explorer' and we are confused to find inside the box a pair of carpet slippers.

Knowledge and Control represents a high water mark rather than a foundation stone. It can perhaps be best seen as a particularly restrained and academic contribution to the de-schooling debate, different in style from the Penguin education specials of which Illich's *De-schooling society* was the most radical (1971), but sharing their oppositional values. It is a measure of how long change takes (but also an indication that this kind of work does have an effect in the real world) that 15 years later the General Certificate of Secondary Education has now become a reality and the power of tertiary education over secondary which Bernstein deplored (p. 69) has been dramatically reduced as has the framing and to a certain extent the classification of knowledge. The effect of this on the universities remains to be seen, but the impact is likely to be considerable.

2 The University

The work we considered in the previous section was mainly concerned with the school curriculum. No theoretical work of comparable scope and quality was done for Higher Education and there seems to have been no applications of the concepts to Higher Education. Tony Becher, in *Towards a definition of disciplinary cultures* (1981), found 'little in the way of useful precedence or precept for the study', and Barnett, as recently as 1985, points to the lack of any worked-out educational theory of Higher Education: 'Higher Education is a set of theoretical practices without a theory of those practices' (p. 243).

However, there are certain features of the University which have been described. The most significant of these is the dual nature of the allegiance. Every University teacher is a member of a discipline and of a department and the degree of overlap can be quite small. On the one hand, there is the membership of the 'invisible college', a network of scholars all over the world who share the same specialism, who may meet at conferences but who may well not, since physical presence is not a requirement (Crane, 1969). On the other hand there is the actual institution, department or University. Burton Clark expresses it forcefully (1983a):

> What is most stunning about the operational level of this society is how much the main personnel are oriented to, and controlled by, an affiliation to others like themselves who are located elsewhere . . . We are confronted by a huge master matrix in which the academic person comes under dual authority, simultaneously belonging to a discipline and an enterprise. (p. 21)

Clark goes on to say that the 'primary home' is the discipline. It seems to me rather that there is a tension, within individuals and within groups: there are, as Clark himself pointed out in an earlier paper (1962) the 'localites' and the 'cosmopolites', the 'company man' and the 'itinerant expert', those whose allegiance is primarily to their department and its running – hence to teaching, to students and 'service' – and those whose allegiance is indeed to the discipline – hence to research, to publishing, to far-flung colleagues. The reality is the split and what has not been sufficiently pointed out is that it is very easy to be at home nowhere. The man who has two studies always does his best work in the other one.

The academic belongs both to the discipline and to the enterprise. But the discipline is subject to extreme fissiparity:

> Academics are rewarded primarily for going off in different directions . . . busily fragmenting as if prestige and their own version of the good life depended on it, which it does . . . members of these groups steadily cell-split to get away from each other – sociologists from anthropologists, biochemists from biologists . . . (Clark, 1983a, p. 20).[3]

The result is that in the *enterprise* the degree of subject integration and collaboration is extremely low: 'Academic departments consist in part of autocrats who individually run certain operations' (p. 22).

Tony Becher noted,

> One of the most surprising outcomes of the interviews was the very limited extent to which the academics concerned were engaged in collaborative as opposed to individual research . . . one major factor militating against team work was held to be the thin spread of specialism. (1981, p. 118)

What has not been pointed out is the simple practical point that because the invisible college of the speciality is worldwide, the individuals with whom one could in theory collaborate are largely unavailable, whilst the people with whom one could in practice collaborate (because they are on the same corridor) are considered ineligible because they belong to a different invisible college. In other words, the system is almost designed one way or another to preclude *all* collaborative intellectual work. It allows individuals to idealize the invisible college while the real college becomes, as Clark Kerr says 'a group of individuals united by a common grievance over parking' (1972, p. 20).

However, in addition to the cell-split, there is the sense of oneness of a discipline. Disciplines can in fact be distinguished by the extent to which this oneness is experienced; Becher sees History and Physics as having 'a somewhat mystical notion of oneness' while biologists and sociologists are fragmented.

Furthermore, the power of the 'enterprise' aspect may be greater in America where Burton Clark does his research than in Britain. In Britain the sense of 'collegium' is a force in all institutions. Becher and Kogan oppose it to 'hierarchy'; Bailey calls it 'community' and opposes it to 'organisation'. The governance of universities is made difficult by this duality. It is interesting to see a writer like A. K. Rice (1970), whose experience is with organizations, attempting to understand the university as if it were solely an organization, one with singularly poor leadership, poor delegation and excessive participation. Heads of Department, for example, are 'organizationally inhibited by the lack of definition of sanction for their management; culturally, they are inhibited by the pervading climate of participation in every decision-making process' (p. 91). Although Rice does not express it in this way, he seems to be saying that the problem of the University comes from attempting to maintain, in a very large organization, the structures which were only appropriate for very small ones.

Peter Scott (1984) traces the history of the University in these terms. The 'liberal' university has been transformed into the 'modern' university, but its values have not been destroyed so much as submerged. The liberal university, represented by the Oxbridge College, was marginal even in terms of producing élites. It did not see its function as producing new knowledge but in teaching students and exercising custodianship. The rise of the influential modern university parallels the rise of disciplines, 'fracturing and re-fracturing', and the rise of the ideology of science which meant that 'intuition-based disciplines' and the humanities had to undergo 'scientification' and become knowledge-based rather than culture-based in order to survive (p. 141). The fragmentation called up the need for integration, but each discipline in turn, Philosophy, History, English, Sociology, by yielding to the pressure to fragment, rendered itself incapable of providing integration. In other words, the demise of the liberal university parallels the collapse of any notion of a unified culture. The modern university is balkanized because knowledge and culture are balkanized. The experience of academics today is the experience of intellectual fragmentation and the sense that something vital has been lost in the process of developing a professionalized model of knowledge.

Until 1944, the University was marginal. Then came mandatory student grants, the Robbins Report and halycon days. For many years British Higher Education operated as a closed system, with public funds and virtually no public scrutiny. A. K. Rice said in 1970, 'present University organization is based for the most part on closed-system characteristics, in which transactions with the environment are kept to a minimum' and went on, 'but the day is passed when a University can dictate its requirements to its society and, having acquired them, could retire into its ivory tower. Under today's conditions, Universities have no alternative but to come to terms with the societies in which they exist' (p. 4). Society may be prepared to make a modest contribution to the upkeep of institutions whose task is to symbolize permanence and tradition in the midst of chaos and change (monasteries, monarchies, museums). But, after Robbins, Higher Education was too big, too expensive and attracted too much scarce talent to be treated in this way. It became an open-system. Already in 1969, Shirley Williams was demanding greater accountability and, as Kogan says (1983, p. 29), even if Labour had won in 1979, Higher Education would not have been given an easy ride. It was Tony Crosland, after all, who was responsible for University accounts being opened in theory to the inspection of the Officers of the Comptroller and Auditor-General. Universities, for better or for worse, now share with all other forms of life the need to adapt to the environment. While Rice's model – materials (students) taken in across the boundary and modified materials (graduates) exported out across the boundary – is an over-simplification, nevertheless it is true that any institution only survives if it transacts with the environment and performs some transformation (Dry beans in + Dry beans out = no Heinz). Universities are currently being required to pay great attention to what society requires both in the sense of what is attractive to students (one set of clients) and what is attractive to industry (a client both for the university's research product and for its student product).

Change takes place when the environment changes, but the effect of outside pressure is almost never to introduce novelty as such into a system but always to modify the balance of the system: marginal or minor sub-systems may be activated to deal with the new situation; major or dominant sub-systems may have their power reduced.[4]

So the current crisis in Universities will have the effect of changing the power relations not only between Universities and the rest of Higher Education (the Polytechnics, for example), but also between subjects and between competing ideologies within the subjects. This is to assume of course that the system can adapt as an organization. As Bailey says, 'an organization, since it is run on reason, can adapt itself readily and efficiently to a changing environment. But in a community on the other hand, the typical reaction to change is to build the walls higher' (p. 52). Here too, change in the environment changes the power relations between forces for organization and between forces for community, and changes them in favour of organization. The paradox is that organization is required to protect the values of community.

It is not easy to predict how the University will respond to the changing environment. Scott's analysis shows the University changing from élitist liberal humanism concerned with organic knowledge and pedagogy to 'academicism' concerned with the fissiparous knowledge of experts. This move was seen initially as being instrumentalist or even vocational. The question now is whether this is still the case. It is not of course a question of simply satisfying the needs society knows it has, since there is no consensus about what society's needs are in a post-industrial world (and it may be one of the basic functions of a university to articulate or model conflicting views). But it still seems clear that the current domination of the research mission and of research of a particular kind is no longer perceived as being indubitably instrumental or 'in the nation's interest'. As nature resists being 'forced into the conceptual boxes supplied by professional education' (Kuhn 1970, p. 24) so the problems faced by engineers, lawyers or therapists require integrated rather than fragmented approaches. As Carter says (1985, p. 144) 'in engineering most projects depend on teamwork for their success, but the emphasis in University courses is on individual unaided effort'. Scott shows how even in the natural sciences the instrumentality is uncertain. As for the humanities:

> it is not clear how growing academicism has increased their instrumentality to lay society . . . Indeed, it can be argued that the trend toward abstraction in the humanities has undermined the ability of these disciplines to serve as part of a general culture of civilisation and so in a significant sense impoverished lay society. In their case academicism seems to have been an enemy of instrumentality. (p. 84)

The needs of society may require a shift 'away from the authority of the expert towards collaborative human skills' (p. 249). And Scott concludes,

> the pursuit of knowledge narrowly conceived has overridden the cultivation of rationality within society. Perhaps for this reason Britain has only the most vestigial intelligentsia because the main role of an intelligentsia is to communicate academic learning in a sensible way to society at large, a role that is barely recognised in Britain . . . In Britain we have the clear paradox, a Higher Education of considerable academic brilliance, and a society sunk deeper in philistinism, suspicious of new ideas and scornful of rationality. (p. 262)

Rice had earlier made a case for the generalist:

> The demand for specialist qualifications to bring brighter career prospects and higher status frequently conflicts, not only with the student's own desire for a broader education, but also with society's need for those who can bring some order into the chaos caused by the increasing fragmentation of knowledge. (p. 49)

These issues are of vital importance. If the Universities' conception of the primary task is wrong the consequences could be disastrous:

> The decline of the railroads in this country [USA] has been explained as their failure to realise that they were not in the railroad business but in the transportation business. By the same token, if colleges and universities are in the business of information transmission, then we risk imminent obsolescence; technology and other providers can do it more efficiently than we can. But if we are in the human development business then we have a chance – and a reason – to survive and prosper. (Claxton and Murrell, 1984, p. 2)

The problem is that the very characteristics we have described – the divided allegiance, the cognitive emphasis, the fissiparity, the strong classification and frame, the hybrid nature of the governance, all make it extremely difficult for the University to clarify its primary task.

3 Profession and career

An individual has various reference groups. There is the discipline and the invisible college, there is the department and the *collegium* but there is also the profession. One effect of outside pressure has been to make academics much more aware of this aspect of their lives – as evidenced by overflow AUT meetings – (though the AUT is a trade union and not a professional association).

I take from the extensive literature on professions and professionalization the basic idea that professions are collective organizations competing for prestige and rewards with other professional and occupational groups on the basis of services they can provide or services society can be persuaded to believe they can provide. A group is professional according to the degree of autonomy it has specifically over its own membership (deciding who may be admitted and on what criteria) and its own rules and operating methods. The basic requirements are that there should be a body of abstract codified knowledge, a set of skills, a service which society requires for which it deems that body of knowledge relevant and an agreement that one group and only one group should be licensed or mandated to perform that service with a view to solving concrete problems of living. The professional group itself should be involved in the creation and transmission of the knowledge. Another feature of professions is that members are entitled to become privy to 'classified knowledge', intimate, non-public information about clients.[5]

The profession is then an organization for managing transactions with society. Like all such groups its strength is measured in part by its perceived cohesion, although its reality is that of a set of subgroups which differ in competence, power, and prestige. One of the functions of a profession is to protect the weak and the inept, though this self-seeking function is, of course, in conflict with its 'societal mandate' under which it receives privileges but imposes self-controls (Goode, 1969, p. 293).

Goode places university teaching with law, medicine and the ministry as one of the 'four great person-professions'. I suspect there is some subjective self-seeking in this assessment and Goode's argument seems almost to rule out the creation of new professions (they only become semi-professions). Nevertheless, the case for University teaching being a profession on the criterion of autonomy is certainly strong. No professionals exercise such freedom to control their own work. The question concerns rather the mandate. Goode points out that competition between professions is strongest where they overlap and the contrast with school-teaching is striking; school-teaching is at best, Goode says, a semi-profession like librarianship, nursing or advertising, especially because it rates low on autonomy (but it also rates low on 'body of knowledge' since pedagogy is perceived as being a trivial content). However, the status of University-teaching as a profession seems to be much less clear than in the other three cases. Goode evades the problem in an astonishing way: 'precisely because the temptation to analyse the academic at length is so strong, I shall stifle it' (p. 305). This is an example of the way that professions are reluctant to reduce the mystery on which some of their power depends. It is also an example of the monopolistic aspect of professions; only professional sociologists may write the sociology of professional sociology and they prefer not to, in order to preserve the mystery of the profession of professional sociology.

My reference to 'professional sociologists' highlights the problem of analysing the profession of University teaching. The 'invisible college' of the discipline can in many cases be perceived as the true profession. This varies from discipline to discipline, but, in engineering for example, a university teacher will also be a professional engineer (a member of the same professional organization as non-university engineers). How he or she rates the two allegiances will vary from individual to individual, but they will always exist.

The difficulty of describing the profession extends to the very nomenclature. Throughout this book I have had difficulty in finding the right word to describe the men and women I am writing about – 'academics', 'lecturers', 'tutors', 'staff', 'faculty', 'dons'. The term I have tended to use, 'University teacher' (which is also the one chosen by the trade union), is seriously misleading in that it singles out one aspect of the multiple professional role to the exclusion of the others. It may be that this aspect is the one that society sees as being the particular service which is being provided. But if this is the case there is certainly ambiguity since the University teacher's professional status comes, as we have seen, specifically from the distance established between teacher and academic. Given traditional values it has certainly been in University teachers' professional interest to play down the 'teacher' part of the role. The powerful resistance to 'professional training' in teaching skills is resistance to being socialized into the profession of teaching which is perceived as entailing a weakening of the socialization into a higher status disciplinary-based profession (sociologist, engineer, linguist). The knowledge base of pedagogy is considered not only inferior to the knowledge base of the subjects but capable of contaminating them.

The status of the profession of University teacher comes not from the teaching part of the role but from the legitimating function of the institution and from other professions which have delegated their knowledge-creation and their knowledge-dissemination functions to the University. Thus, as a profession, 'University teaching' is extremely anomalous in that

1 It has no specific body of knowledge of its own but instead claims all bodies of knowledge.
2 It lacks the cohesion which characterizes professions.
3 It aspires to legitimate all professions in so far as attaining professional status requires for an occupation (*inter alia*) university training (e.g. cookery – home economics).

The profession aspires to being a kind of meta-profession (clerics, lawyers, doctors are trained in the University). If it can continue to convince society (and other professions) that this is indeed what it is, all will be well, all manner of things will be well. But if it fails, its fall will be commensurate with the hubris.

There are signs that society is making more down-to-earth, secular demands of the profession and that the magical functions of legitimating and warranting are no longer seen as offering value for money. A recent writer, Cohen (1985) can speak of the 'disabling University'; he argues against the emphasis on theoretical aspects of professional training to the exclusion of skills, claiming that this unfits people for professional practice. He attributes this to the strength of disciplines and the consequent neglect of the interpersonal, integrative approaches. Carter, an engineer, in another recent article, considers the same opposition between the theoretical and the practical. He creates a taxonomy of objectives which includes a definition of 'knowledge' which is not solely cognitive. Paradoxically, an education for the professions which deals with the whole range of professional requirements and which is therefore more vocational and instrumental ends up by being closer to the liberal idea of a University being about the development of a whole person. Carter claims that his analysis applies to all subjects:

> The range of skills which form the hidden curriculum [of any course when it is examined in the light of this taxonomy] is very narrow and of limited relevance outside the academic world. (p. 148)

This seems to me to be a crucial point. At the moment, *pace* Goode, the profession of University teacher hardly exists. The University is the place where individuals with different disciplinary/professional allegiances meet in order to socialize young people into those disciplines. But the process of socialization, the transmission of values through pedagogy, is almost completely opaque to all concerned. The messages which are transmitted are coded and the operators do not know the code. Society is demanding that University teachers should be more professional and, as Barnett put it at the end of his article on the legitimation crisis in Higher Education (1985), 'this entails the idea of Higher Education as having as its principle task metacriticism', that is, higher-order reflection on practice, especially the practice of creating and exchanging knowledge. Transmitting knowledge is not enough.

Because Universities are large and powerful and employ large numbers of highly intelligent, even brilliant men and women, it is tempting to believe that they are immune. But morale is a tricky thing, and a profession that lives on and by ideas is more vulnerable than one whose transactions are more rooted in concrete reality. I said earlier that outside pressure almost never introduces novelty into a system. The exception is when the system dies.

9

Modern Languages

He only says 'Good fences make good neighbours.'
Spring is the mischief in me, and I wonder
If I could put a notion in his head:
'*Why* do they make good neighbours?' Isn't it
Where there are cows? But here there are no cows.
(*Mending Wall*, Robert Frost)

1 Discipline

By most of the dominant criteria, Modern Languages is not a discipline at all. The sociologist who had switched from German described to me his experience of teaching, in collaboration with Modern Linguists, a course on Fascism:

> The first year it was taught as German Fascism, Spanish Fascism, French Fascism. It was a classic example of a modern language approach to it. Theory is collapsed into history and the national culture. We agreed they should look at theory . . . otherwise it becomes just a mass of individual historical epochs or examples.

Sociology, in contrast, has

> a set of organizing concepts or ideas which give it its scientific backbone or framework off which you bounce ideas. In Sociology we have core concepts – class, power, beliefs, values, theories of social cohesion and conflict . . . if you have that as a discipline-base you can organize your study in options, but they are reference points . . . The problem with Modern Languages is that the organizing idea is just the language, which is not enough to give it intellectual coherence. You end up with a higgledy-piggledy thing. (27)

Within a system which, as we saw, values disciplines according to their theoretical coherence and hierarchical structure, Modern Languages is conspicuously lacking in either, wedded, even more than History, to the unique, the different:

> The historians were looking for what was true of 95% of the population and I was interested in what was true of the other 5%. Linguisticians are interested in the way 99% of the people talk, and I'm interested in the 1% which uses language differently. (23)

The educational system as a whole in Britain operates according to the collection code. Disciplines are countries with rigid immigration laws and clear rules for citizenship. But in Modern Languages Immigration hardly exists:

> You can put anything on a French course as long as it has some link with France, is intellectually respectable and makes the students work. (22)

There used to be rules – the content was philology and literary history – but they have fallen into disuse:

> The Strasbourg Oaths. That is the natural place to begin the study of French. If one loses the Middle Ages, why stop at the Renaissance? . . . If you are going to cut out Montaigne and Rabelais, then nothing is sacred. I don't think I believe anymore that anything is sacred. We have got rid of Flaubert. The only thing that is sacred is the language. That is the only thing that makes it a French course. (22)

> Nothing is sacrosanct. Except the language. That competence must exist. If you read the stuff in English, that's the end. (29)

It is the end also, as we saw in Chapter 5, if language is taught separately:

> It would destroy the discipline. We would be using French in relation to literature in the same way a French historian uses French in relation to history. We would all go off and do our different things – literature, history . . . – and the French specialist would be within those departments. (6)

The plausibility of this last suggestion shows, I think, how fragile, in conventional terms, the structure of the discipline is.

Ultimately, the only principle of coherence is then the language. While this provides a very clear distinction, it is also intellectually trivial since its capacity to make meaningful distinctions between contents is almost nil. Furthermore, it provides coherence only for individual languages and not for 'Modern Languages' which, on the contrary, it separates from each other as effectively as it separates each from other disciplines. As we saw, British education is also characterized by strong frames: the fence separating community knowledge and 'school' knowledge is exceptionally high. Traditionally, disciplines are valued according to their distance from what is known or taught in families or communities. Now, in one sense, Modern Languages is indeed distant – not much French gets learned in Coronation Street. But a great deal gets learned, Rue de la Reine. The act of learning a language, specifically learning to *speak* a language, is almost the prototype of family or community knowledge. Indeed, most academics and all students would agree that the foreign language is best learned, not in school or university, but in the community. Academics may complain about the 'café' French of their back-from-abroad students; they may grumble that these students are less good at prose translation when they return: in their hearts, they know that *the language, which is the principle of coherence of the discipline, is something which is best learned outside the frame of the discipline* and many spend a great deal of time and energy enabling students to do just that.

I think this basic fact explains a great deal about language teaching methods in schools and especially in Universities. Language learning in educational institutions has always been characterized by its distance from the way languages are learned in families and communities, and this is not, as is often maintained, because this is the most efficient way to learn a second language but in order to maintain a frame. Howatt (1984, p. 147) shows how reformers have always worked outside the educational system; he mentions Prendergast and West in India; one might add, Curran or Gattegno. Whenever there has been a pragmatic need to learn a language,[1] the methods have been the opposite of 'school' methods. Howatt shows how there has always been a publishers' divide between 'school' books and practical books (Assimil, Berlitz), how universities have, from earliest times, been indifferent to the practical needs of language learners. He goes so far as to regret that foreign languages were ever brought on to the school curriculum (p. 138). Wilga Rivers has even wondered whether languages should not be de-schooled.

I am not concerned here with the rights and wrongs of de-schooling Modern Languages but with the position of this discipline within the system of disciplines and with making the point that its status as 'school' knowledge is shaky, its specific content (the equivalent of the geologists' rocks) indeterminate and its principle of coherence trivial. It is not surprising that 'other disciplines look at us with a bit of a curled lip'(6) and that there is a feeling of insecurity, even inferiority which is reflected in the teaching. More secure disciplines, especially disciplines which combine a strong principle of coherence with a strong frame (typically non-school subjects) can be much more relaxed about the pedagogical aspects of the framing:

> In the social sciences, the attitude to teaching is more relaxed. Seminars and tutorials are much more a shared experience. There is less of the element of dronologue. Because the subject has not been taught before, there are no patterns of behaviour established. (28)

The system as a whole is, of course, extraordinarily conservative and authoritarian in its teaching methods, but Modern Languages, with their traditional language exercises and literature lectures, seem particularly so, especially in relation to the communicative nature of the task. Staff are also, as we saw, perceived by students as dogmatic and uncomfortable with ambiguity, while students are perceived by staff as passive and dependant. I suggest that this is, in part at least, a reaction to the insecurities I have described and which extend even to the appropriate label: not everyone is happy to be called a 'Modern Linguist'.

> The terminology is a bit lacking. It reflects our uncertainty about who we are. (2)

The experience of language people, staff and students, is powerfully determined by the quirkish nature of the discipline within the system of disciplines.

2 The University

> The University is organized on the basis of clear subject boundaries. It is to do with the way the University structures its finances, with student quotas . . . people are frightened of breaking down the barrier because they think it might have some detrimental effect upon their staffing, the amount of money they get. It tends to make people resistant to change. (28)

> It is easier to establish a firm base in a University when you can be clear to other people what it is you're doing. The rigid boundary approach is much clearer, much easier to negotiate with other groups . . . The comparative and connecting approach is inherently more stressful to do because you run into problems of relationships with other people and other specialisms more frequently, there is more negotiation to do. The concentrated, closely defined orientation towards a subject that sets itself simple, explicable objectives and declares that it has no interest in doing anything else works very well in terms of carving itself a place in an institution, setting up clear relationships with other people. Even if one thinks that the objective is positively wrong it is a very powerful position. (31)

Rice makes, in more general terms, the point that boundaries reduce uncertainty and anxiety:

> The more certainly boundaries can be located, the more easily can formal communication systems be established. (1970, p. 13)

Hence, one can presume that in institutional terms a fundamental aspect of a subject's strength will be the unity and clarity it is perceived to have, whatever the disciplinary cell-splitting at a research level.

Modern Languages is a subject with very little unity or clarity. It does not present the sense of methodological one-ness which Becher discovered in History and Physics. The loyalty of the separate languages is stronger than loyalty to 'Modern Languages', even in institutions where languages are grouped into departments or schools. And minority languages feel resentful and vulnerable (CILT, 1975, especially Joan Maw, pp. 28–33); all languages resent the arbitary dominance of French;[2] even in Spanish, there is, as we saw, opposition between Peninsularists and South Americanists. The subject inevitably reflects some of the tribal politics of the world.

But, in addition, the tribes of each language are themselves divided, which means that other communities find dealing with them difficult.

In order to illustrate this I propose now to make an anthropological excursus to the land of Emmel and to explore the tribalism of Modern Languages compared with other disciplines which seem to have achieved nationhood. Let us name the tribes.

First there are the PHILITS. They are really two tribes but the older

PHILOGS, fathers of all the tribes, were assimilated long ago.[3] They still practice here and there but their main function is honorific: they give ancestral weight to the *PHILIT* tribe. The *PHILITS*, then, are a venerable tribe, respected accordingly by other communities over the hill. For many years their dominance over all the tribes of Emmel was complete and many say this was good for Emmel's standing: other communities also revered the Gods that *PHILITS* worshipped and were happy to have them worshipped by priests who could read and praise the sacred texts and make them meaningful to the Young. Unfortunately, reverence for the Gods declined, especially among the Young who multiplied and found learning to read the sacred texts burdensome and a distraction from their main concerns which were frying other fish. *PHILITS* are an elderly tribe; fertility is low in general; dearth is in the land and this means that many *PHILITS* have been called to the Great Garden over there. And yet, though diminished, they still strive to control all the principal rituals of the Emmel community.

Other tribes are restive and are challenging that control. For example the EFCOMS, who have always been the helots of the society, are now banding together and making war-talk. They claim that Effective Communication is Emmel's real mission and they point to other tribes such as TESOLS, EFOLS, and ESPS who flourish and multiply all over the Earth, even in the Oilands. They proclaim that the sacred texts are not the only texts and that communicating with other tribes through speech, body-language and computerized smoke-signals is also good medicine. They claim that the community actually depends on them for supplies of young women. Privately (sometimes publicly) they accuse the *PHILITS* of leading Emmel to disaster and corrupting the Young: 'Literature turns some of them into nasty little snobs. They think they have the true values. Crap!' (36). The *PHILITS* point out haughtily that all other tribes despise the *EFCOMS* and claim that if it weren't for them (the *PHILITS*), *EFCOMS* would all be working in the chalk mines.

Both *EFCOMS* and *PHILITS* are ancient tribes and their edgy, Beckettian symbiosis has a long history. The POLISOX on the other hand, are a new, young, vigorous tribe. They have no hostility towards the *EFCOMS*, though they too can be condescending. On the other hand, they see the *PHILITS* as being impossibly old-fashioned. The future lies in alliance with the SOCSCI people who are high-status tribes with granaries full of concepts and theories, some of which, they say, can even be used to understand the nature of tribes. (The *PHILITS* are sceptical about this and scathingly accuse the *POLISOX* and the *SOCSCI* of forgetting that tribes are people. They also accuse them of interpreting any trivial old bit of carved stone they come across.) The *EFCOMS* make alliance with the *POLISOX* against the *PHILITS*.

Then there are the APPLESTICKS, a nomadic tribe; they have close links with the *EFCOMS* whose huts they often share. They descend from a very prestigious but rather remote tribe, the LINKSTICKS who live by analysing trees. The *APPLESTICKS* believe they can distil the wisdom of the *LINKSTICKS* and apply it to the work of the *EFCOMS*.

PHILITS, *EFCOMS*, *POLISOX*, *LINKSTICKS* and *APPLESTICKS*, all live uneasily together, occasionally quarrelling, occasionally making alliances. The *GERMANO-PHILITS* and the *FRANCO-PHILITS* sometimes join forces as do the *HISPANEFCOMS* and *ITALEFCOMS* but usually all the tribes go their own way. Emmel is a pluralist society whose emblem is a tall tower.

The surprising thing however is that this multiplicity, while confusing to the university, has actually enabled the discipline to adapt with great rapidity to the changing environment. In the late 1950s,[4] during expansion, traditional language and literature departments were seen as failing to meet a need that society had for competent linguists. The new Universities responded to this and created language centres with language laboratories and language laboratory directors. Then the Polytechnics were formed and did the same thing but more so: instead of separating off the language and the intellectual activity, they went solely for the language. They made their courses attractive to schools – at first by getting all their weaker pupils to go there and then turning them into competent linguists. But by 1976 good students were choosing to go to Bath or Bradford or Salford or even to a Polytechnic to do language training rather than to do literature and prose translation at some civic university. The currency of the society is A-level grades, and wealth is measured annually by the number of applicants multiplied by the number of grade points they achieve, multiplied by the average grade points of the students who finally enrol. In these terms, language and literature departments were facing an economic crisis. The 1976 London conference on 'The Crisis in Modern Languages in Secondary and Higher Education', convened by the Society for French Studies, was in fact about the crisis of the *PHILITS*. The *EFCOMS* (Salford, Ealing, the Polytechnics) were doing quite well. They were encouraged by the creation of new A-levels like the London syllabus B which excluded literature but they still feared that the *PHILITS*' crisis would become an Emmel crisis if the *PHILITS* did not adapt.

PHILIT-dominated departments did respond by improving their language teaching where they could. This actually meant allowing *EFCOMS* to devise new courses (the Scottish Universities project is typical of this move). They gave up the monolithic degree structure, the notion that 'it's not a degree in French if you haven't studied X or Y'. The typical degree now involves two languages and offers a whole range of options, with or without a 'core'. Options were the natural solution to conflict – a collegiate avoidance of the choice and judgement which would be exercised in a hierarchy. But the solution is effective since either an option will attract few or no students, in which case it vanishes painlessly (without conflict), or else it will continue to attract students, in which case it does meet part of a very varied demand.

The most striking example of the option strategy is the creation of new inter-disciplinary degrees. Chris Bettinson (1986) traces the history of European Studies, 'a new and vigorous young discipline', which has grown 'in the cracks' between existing disciplines and which combines *EFCOM* (and *APPLESTICK*) expertise with *POLISOX* knowledge.

This process is still going on today. The discipline is changing and adapting, but whether it is changing fast enough or in the right direction is still a matter for debate.

What seems to be happening in general is that the fragmentation, the multiplicity, the absence of coherence is being re-framed positively. On the one hand, there is the discomfort of not having a clear identity. On the other hand, there are positive advantages in pluralism, in being a 'multiple discipline'. Good management can produce complementary, inter-disciplinary departments. A head of department:

> There are people in my department with very different interests which can lead to disagreement at times on general issues but they complement one another very nicely. John and Peter are poles apart but everything slots in and forms a whole . . . The modernization of language studies has still got a little bit to run for the balance to be redressed properly but once that has taken place – and we are not far off – things can go on hand-in-hand. These differences can be a positive factor in a department as far as students are concerned . . . These difficulties when properly harmonized can be good . . . pluralism is not bought at the price of coherence, it simply becomes a different type of coherence. (18)

The idea of pluralism applies even as between institutions:

> My good friends in Bradford have a point when they say that you can't assume that an interest in and an ability to handle a foreign language automatically goes with literary interests or gifts. And why should you not associate the study of a language with a much more social or historical or political investigation of a country? I think that is right. I am all for diversity. There ought to be Salford and there ought to be Sussex and those cater for different kinds of client. One should not try to turn Salford into a kind of Sussex and one should not turn Sussex into a kind of Salford. There is room for both. (32)

It even applies at the level of professional organization. As *PHILITS* become less powerful, other tribes develop separate organizations. The Society for French Studies, a very *PHILIT* organization, sees the problem:

> French Studies feels itself slightly threatened since it sets out to be all-embracing. It wasn't the Society for French Literature, it was the society for French Studies but now there are other bodies, the Society for the Study of Modern France, the Association for French Language Studies . . . If French Studies was the all-embracing thing it is claimed to be, either there would be no need for such things or they would be sub-groups of French Studies. What is happening is that French Studies is trying to move in the direction of such things in order to be all-embracing again. (President of the Society for French Studies)

The list of separate language organizations is very long: at a recent (29–3–85) meeting of the National Council for Modern Languages in Higher and Further Education the following were represented:

Association for French Language Studies; Association of Hispanists; Association of University Professors of French; British Association for Applied Linguistics; British Association for Chinese Studies; British Association for Japanese Studies; British Association for Language Teaching; British Universities Association of Slavists; Conference of University Teachers of German in Great Britain and Ireland; Institute of Linguists; International Association of Teachers of English as a Foreign Language; Linguistics Association of Great Britain; Modern Language Association; National Association of Teachers in Higher and Further Education; Standing Conference of Heads of Modern Languages in Polytechnics and Other Colleges; Society for French Studies; Society for Italian Studies; Centre for Information on Language Teaching and Research; Joint Council for Language Associations; National Congress on Languages in Education. There is also the University Association for Contemporary European Studies and many others.

Here too the National Council of Modern Languages (NCML) and the Joint Council of Language Associations (JCLA) are attempting coordination in the same way as French Studies, but the task is daunting.

The reality of the discipline – its multiplicity and lack of coherence – is beyond dispute. What varies is the way that individuals subjectively frame that reality, which means how they see themselves now and in the future in relation to other disciplines and subjects and to the outside world. They can see themselves as others see them or they can see their pluralism as an adaptive strength and as appropriate to the world as it is. One essential factor in a group's decision about how it sees itself is its sense of its own past. The past of Modern Languages is Classics which haunts the subject like the ghost of Hamlet:

> If we don't adapt properly I see a scenario where we could end up in exactly the same position as Classics, and not that far off either. (28)

Modern Linguists know that their subject emerged victorious from the struggle which destroyed Classics and they have an Oedipal fear of history's vengeful powers, they fear that MLA presidents may soon, like Classics presidents, be pronouncing melancholy orations about 'Strength in what remains' (Rees, Presidential address delivered to the Classics Association, 1979).

There are various general accounts of the fall of Classics and the rise of Modern Languages,[5] though disappointingly few histories of specific institutions outside Oxbridge.[6] Charles Firth's account of the development of the School of Modern Languages at Oxford (Firth, 1929) is a source no less valuable for being polemical and acerbic:

> 'A period full of new hope is now at hand', prophesied the Commissioners. Here, however, it began with an attempt to prevent the building of lecture rooms for Modern Languages in order to enlarge the accommodation provided for antiquities. As I hold that to teach the living languages and literatures of Europe is a more important part of the University's duty

than to accumulate relics of the extinct civilisations of the East, I thought it desirable to explain the history of this attempt to the public in general. (p. vi)

Firth describes the debate around the proposal in 1887 to create a School of Modern European Languages. The main opponent was the Professor of Latin, Thomas Case, who clearly believed the acronym of the school to be appropriate. Firth summarizes Case's pamphlet:

> The Classics were a far superior education, and they would be endangered by the new School. 'The manner in which this danger acts is not so much by direct attack as by the multiplication of rivals to the Classics . . . students will be withdrawn from the final Classical Examination by the ease of an examination in one Modern language'. The result would be that 'all Classical Studies, Philological, Philosophical, and Historical, will suffer a common martyrdom because there will be a constant pressure to appoint teachers of Modern languages in the colleges, instead of classical teachers' . . . 'The consequent outcry for modern teachers in the Colleges will partly diminish the classical staff, and partly their stipends, and that, too, in the face of declining revenues and the difficulty of offering clever men a career'. (p. 71)

The main supporter of the proposal was Henry Nettleship, who claimed, on the contrary, that the Classics would not suffer:

> The fact is that the study of Classics never has suffered, never will suffer, from the juxtaposition of other equally serious studies. It gains from the new light it receives. (p. 73)

It may seem to us now that Nettleship's optimism was misplaced and that Case was right. But another way of looking at it is in terms of the *Selfish Gene* (Dawkins, 1978): Modern Languages is an *evolutionary development* of Classics: the genes are the value system not the particular subject in which they happen to embody themselves in order to adapt and survive.

I believe that this is a key to understanding the discipline of Modern Languages. It shares with Classics (or takes from Classics) almost all its essential characteristics: first, it is a multidiscipline – Classicists are Papyrologists, Historians, Philosophers, Archaeologists, Philologists, Literary Scholars . . . Second, it combines macroscopic breadth with exacting microscopic technical requirements (reading texts) – Like Classics it is a 'hard' subject (Keys and Ormerod, 1976). Above all, its values are integrative: compare a president of the Classical Association:

> I like people who are broad, I like people who make links, I like people who go outside the stereotypes and the way they have been trained. (14)

and a President of the Society for French Studies:

> I see the discipline as being a multiple discipline. We all keep in contact with the various parts . . . An example of the way an academic community

> ought to work is the Oxbridge College. There was an interplay of knowledge . . . just because you are a specialist in one area doesn't mean you don't talk about other areas . . . one is specialised and multiple. You are pillaging other people's expertise. A departmentalised system tends to cause difficulties. If you are perpetually standing on your dignity, claiming to be this or that . . . in a multidisciplinary society you don't have any of that. Everybody is thrilled when people move outside their discipline and do something different. I think it is always a pity if people till only one field . . . At Oxford someone with that amount of knowledge in depth would not get a job . . . people would say 'Yes, very good, but far too narrow'.

This reveals another similarity. Like Classics itself, this view of the generalist/specialist is essentially Oxbridge and Collegiate. It belongs to the liberal University, with its emphasis on small communities, on teaching and on the interplay of knowledge, not to the modern university. The difficulties of Modern Languages stem in part from the way that their need for integration is thwarted, outside Oxbridge, by the environment.

The final similarity with Classics is vocationality or instrumentality. Classics, in its heyday, was a training for professional and especially administrative life. It was the 'mandarin' discipline. It would be wrong to ignore the arguments of writers like Bourdieu that certain subjects are used primarily as selection devices so that the actual training the subject gives is subordinate to its use as a means of singling out the most intelligent or amenable students, or, alternatively, filtering out those who are not intelligent or amenable. Nevertheless, Classics did require competitiveness, adaptability, a capacity for empathy and also an ability to endure boredom and deal with minutiae. Modern Languages demands and fosters very similar qualities.

The question then is whether the new avatar is now facing extinction in its turn, whether Modern Languages can be seen as Classics' Last Stand or whether the characteristics I have described, the 'genes', have the capacity to adapt, survive and prosper. It is to the future of the discipline that we now turn.

3 Profession and career

> An historical sense is essential, which means that we must know how to be new as contrasted with repetition – psittacosis – on the one hand, and with escape from tradition – aphasia – on the other. (MacNeice, quoted by Turquet, 1975, pp. 98–9)

A profession, I have said, organizes transactions with the environment. In this final section we will consider Modern Languages in its relation with society.

The basic conflict is between, on the one hand, the desire to deny the necessity of any transaction with the environment (i.e. to deny the need for change) and, on the other, the belief that the system must respond to outside pressures even if this means accepting loss. A vivid picture of these forces at work in Modern Languages can be obtained thanks to a polemical article published in *French Studies Bulletin* (FSB) (1984, p. 11). The authors, Ceri Crossley and Dennis Wood, are *PHILITS* from the University of Birmingham French Department and their article provoked a range (and a rage) of replies from *EFCOMS* and others. Their outburst was triggered by proposals for a revised Northern Universities Joint Matriculation Board (NUJMB) A-level French syllabus and by articles in the previous *FSB* (10) by R. H. Bird of the DES and Professor Sam Taylor. The article (described as an 'academic hatchet job' and 'OTT' in subsequent replies) has the advantage of revealing the feelings of some *PHILITS* better than more measured statements or the usual silence. The authors, in tones reminiscent of Thomas Case, see the A-level syllabus as a threat to University Departments who, as 'guardians of human values' will have to resist 'the manifest philistinism' of the proposals. The danger is that Universities will be required to modify their courses in response to the needs of the new breed of A-level students:

> Let us be quite clear, the JMB syllabus creates needs which only institutions such as Polytechnics are likely to satisfy. University departments which may be tempted to ape such institutions will be conniving at their self-destruction.

The JMB syllabus is condemned for doing away with prose translation and 'making only grudging gestures to literature and horizons of value'. Matthew Arnold is invoked and parallels are drawn with English ('there is no movement to drop Shakespeare or Lawrence from English syllabuses'). The syllabus represents an 'instrumental' view of language. The range is 'impoverished and narrow', the content consists of 'banalities' and the methods involve the 'grotesque amateur theatricals' of role-playing, an activity which is 'intellectually insulting'. This may be what society wants, but, say the authors, quoting David Holbrook, 'We must educate not for society but against it'. Literature is valuable 'because it equips students to question the assumptions of society'.

The *EFCOMS*' replies, in subsequent issues, stress that they are in touch with what *is*, whereas Crossley/Wood are loftily concerned with what ought to be or once was. Ideally, perhaps, sixth formers would be reading *Phèdre* and using their intellect to question the assumptions of society, before going on to do more of the same in University language departments. In reality, in schools, 'large slices of time are spent in translating the texts in order to reach even the minimum level' (*FSB*, 13, p. 13):

> When the necessary steps in language learning are taken too fast, or even sacrificed, in order to make way for a premature encounter with literature (and this is what still happens in many, many sixth forms), everyone is the loser: the student, discouraged by the seemingly endless chore (spread over 4–6 months) of translating a book line-by-line; the teacher, driving students to express opinions they haven't got about books they cannot understand; the University, deprived of potentially able students who have mistakenly vowed never to open a French book again.

Crossley and Wood write as if the University was still a closed system and if a particular tribe with its value system could be exempt from the laws of the environment. 'There was a time', they conclude plaintively, 'when A-level candidates were encouraged to aspire'. The *EFCOMS* are saying that the aspirations of young people are no longer those of the *PHILITS* and that pious hopes do not fill the larder.

The conflict which these *FSB* articles make visible concerns the nature of change, and the most important thing we can say about change is that it inevitably implies loss. This is something that Peter Marris shows in a range of situations in his moving book *Loss and Change* (1974). I do not believe that Crossley and Wood are seriously claiming that Modern Languages can avoid all change, but the strength of feeling they display must be an indication of the loss they experience. I am reminded of the informal meeting I held after my interviews in Southampton. The two oldest members of the department of French, about to take early retirement, exchanged Biblical and Classical references and quotations in a way that none of the younger people in the room could match. Another respondent, also at Southampton, had this to say:

> Individuals conduct careers on those [specialized] lines until they hit a brick wall and then of course it all falls to pieces. That can happen, as in a sense it has happened in some places with Medieval Studies. A chap who knows everything about the *Chanson d'Alexis* might, thirty years ago, have been a department's greatest asset as a man of scholarship and eminence. Now he comes to be regarded as the department's greatest liability. (31)

Things must go; space must be made for the new; but it is essential to acknowledge the sense of loss. Marris explains how the apparent reactionaries and the apparent reformists unconsciously collaborate to manage change and, in terms of the epigraph to this section, to avoid the extremes of psittacosis and aphasia:

> Whether the crisis of disorientation effects only an individual, or a group, or society as a whole, it has a fundamentally similar dynamic. It provokes a conflict between contradictory impulses – to return to the past, and to forget it altogether. Each, in itself, would be ultimately self-destructive, either by denying the reality of present circumstances, or by denying the experience on which the sense of self rests. (p. 151)

> Conflict is a powerful organizing principle of behaviour, defining friends and enemies, good and bad, in terms of immediate, transitory purposes. At the same time, it relieves the internal tensions of loss by displacing ambivalence onto an opponent whose resistance restrains impulses which could not otherwise be so single-mindedly expressed without being self-destructive. The opposition, that is, represents aspects of the need to conserve the past or realize a different future, which the other side can then afford not to acknowledge, though it shares them, since each constrains the other's recklessness. So, like mourning, the conflict dramatizes a transition, and makes the transition itself a meaningful sequence of

actions, without needing to prescribe the forms of accommodation to which it leads. (p. 159)

What exactly is the 'reality of present circumstances'? The first thing is that value judgements about the discipline are mediated through the schools and, as we saw in Chapter 1, through decisions made by head teachers, third formers, sixth formers. Our knowledge of how these choices are made is meagre but it is clear that Universities have nothing like total control over them. What does emerge from the research we have (and from my interviews) is that sixth formers are remarkably uninterested in literature or even in reading. A recent survey concludes:

> Few show any inclination to want to read and discuss foreign literature in later life. In fact, reading a foreign language is itself not highly valued . . . Perhaps to the despair of some University teachers, students seem to want foreign language courses to equip them with practical foreign language skills. Overwhelmingly they see the development of oral skills as a top priority. (Swallow, 1986)

We saw earlier that Modern languages are not attractive to boys but that they are attractive to many girls who are not divergent, literary personalities and who might well have opted for sciences if it were not for pressures to be 'feminine'.

We also know that relevance to a future career is an important aspect of subject choice and that, of the Arts subjects, Modern Languages is chosen because it is felt to be career-related and rooted in a real (and attractive) world.

In other words, the very pluralism of Modern Languages enables it to appeal to a wide range of real students and to adapt *as a system* to fluctuations in student preferences, though this is not necessarily a comfort to those individuals and institutions within the system whose particular offerings are spurned and who are required to deal with loss on behalf of the system. According to Swallow's survey, red-brick and plate-glass universities may well be squeezed out as students polarize between the prestigious older Universities (who have always offered pluralist degrees) and the technological ones (including the Polys). Given the reality of student feeling as described in the first part of this book and confirmed by findings such as Swallow's, it seems very unlikely that the single or even the joint honours language/literature degree beloved of *PHILITS* has much of a future in the majority of Universities. Students will (as Swallow's report shows) continue to prefer Universities to Polytechnics, but they are increasingly hard-nosed about the course and will only choose the one that meets their needs as they pragmatically (and philistinely) perceive them. In terms of survival, the *EFCOMS* have a strong case and the readiness of *PHILITS* to adapt or allow adaptation, *in other words to accept loss*, may be crucial for the discipline. This is the significance of the Crossley/Wood *FSB* debate.

There are other transactions besides those with students (though students are usually indirectly involved). Employers, for example, choose graduates from all disciplines: their preferences ultimately affect student choice and government thinking.

There is unfortunately very little hard information about employers' views of graduates from different disciplines, and, as we saw in Chapter 3 (p. 59), the role of the 'gatekeepers' themselves is mysterious. However, we do know that this year (1986) 40% of all jobs open to graduates are 'any discipline' (*Graduate Post*, 15, 7, 1986). Modern Languages graduates, far from going *en masse* into teaching (which was the case when *PHILITS* ruled supreme) now compete with other graduates in a whole range of jobs of which teaching is only one (chosen by a mere 17%).[7] My informal discussions with careers advisers tend to confirm the impression that Modern Languages graduates are looked on favourably not only or even specially because they have language skills (in fact only 10% of graduates use their languages), but because they are a year older, have lived abroad and are generally more confident. They are perceived as adaptable and articulate. Those who have studied under the *POLISOX* seem to be particularly successful in getting jobs, since acquaintance with economics is seen by employers to be an advantage. There has then been quite a dramatic shift, from a situation where Modern Language departments train students to be Modern Language teachers to one where their graduates make careers predominantly in business and commerce.

As for transactions with the government, Modern Languages seems to appear to them as satisfyingly vocational. The idea of British salesmen needing to be as fluent in other languages as the Scandinavians and Germans has considerable appeal. However, I doubt whether it goes very deep. British firms are largely indifferent to foreign languages, and, while this may be deplorable, it has to be said that the status of English as an international language puts them in a very different situation from that of the French or the Germans. It must also be said that the quality and price of the product is more important than the polyglot capacities of the salesmen. Nevertheless, high level language skills do have a certain magical quality. The Modern Language graduate has a demonstrable something which a graduate in History or English or even Economics does not have, and that means that the sponsor (the government) can see and measure the result of the investment.

The subject is an Arts subject, and therefore theoretically subversive and suspect:

> English and Modern Languages represent a space in which subversion can take place. The very questioning of the subject makes it subversive. (29)

But in practice it is the cautious, pragmatic aspect of it which is perceived by governments. From this point of view Modern Languages is in a stronger position than, say, Philosophy, which has much greater coherence.

Linguistic skill is of ambiguous status – trivial in one sense, since when the interpreter is there he is a non-person and you can ignore him while getting on with the serious business, but fundamental in another sense, since if he is not there you are stuck. His status is that of an ignition key.

It seems to me however that the real vocationality of Modern Languages is at a higher level than the ability to interpret languages. It is at the level of interpreting people to people. The nature of the subject and of the people who go in for it means that graduates are likely to be flexible, empathic and free from insular thinking. This is the positive aspect of the uncertain identity or the permeable ego. *Paradoxically, the value of the subject for governments and employers may be the extent to which Modern Languages graduates have been incompletely socialized into the values of higher education.*

4 The future of modern languages

> I said to the patient: 'We don't know, do we!' I said this simply because it was true. (*Playing and Reality*, D. W. Winnicott (1974, p. 38))

This analysis of transactions with Sixth forms, employers and the government seems to be heartening for the future of the subject. What is required, it seems, is that these career facts should be known in schools, that the GCSE changes should have the desired effect of making languages more appealing, especially to boys, that University language courses should appear as the road to near-native foreign language proficiency and ambi-culturalism. If Modern Languages can change to meet these demands all will be well.

This scenario, which may appeal to many 17-year-olds and to 'society', does not appeal to University teachers (whatever their tribe). They see it as being appropriate for a language school but not for a University. They see the loss as unacceptable. As we saw when we discussed Salford, they feel that 'language alone is not enough'; and, when it is perceived by students as enough, that in itself is cause for concern:

> It doesn't matter what area people are taught to think in as long as they are taught to think . . . lots of language teaching doesn't do that. (36)

So the search is on for a University content which may serve as an alternative to literary studies. European Studies is, as we have seen, the obvious candidate, and the courses created under that broad heading demonstrate the ability of the subject (*POLISOX* working with *EFCOMS*) to adapt and find creative solutions. But there are difficulties and they are not confined to *PHILITS*.

First, for students. Students and staff complain of 'lots of descriptive courses involving mugging-up facts' (28). This is certainly a feature of undergraduate education in general; it is possible, as we saw, for literary studies to require nothing more than in- and re-gurgitation of fact and opinion. But, for linguists doing social science subjects, the likelihood of intellectual timidity is greater and the possibility of critical thought less, because the level of dependency is higher. As my language centre respondent pointed out (p. 105), it is hard for linguists to argue independently about social science matters, whereas literary texts are – potentially at least – open. The danger is that a set of major open-ended texts with the capacity to produce development and self-knowledge will be jettisoned in favour of trivial, ephemeral texts and information which from the student's point of view is 'inert knowledge'. The *PHILIT* position: 'What is important educationally – and even having in mind the possible changing of the world – is the exploration of the impact of big texts on people; criticizing texts helps to tell you who you are' (25), is a strong one and its abandonment difficult to contemplate. The fact that the pedagogy used in schools and universities has been inappropriate to it is a reason not for abandoning the aim but for improving the pedagogy.

'European Studies' also presents problems for staff. The degrees are run either in collaboration with social scientists or by *POLISOX* linguists. In the first case, the linguists are confined to the advanced language training; in the second they are 'amateurs' compared to the real *SOCSCIS*. Thus, 'European Studies' is no answer to the problem of the linguists' disciplinary and professional status. They may give undergraduate courses on the Fifth Republic, but they cannot direct theses or publish on it:

> In those areas [sociology etc.] we aren't doing anything that the other people aren't doing better. We are doing it because we happen to speak French, and we are deceiving ourselves if we think we can talk about these things as well as people who have had a proper training in that area. (24)

The undergraduate/postgraduate boundary is crucial (as is the School/University one). This is where new disciplines are created. An undergraduate who does a PhD in an aspect of European Studies and gets his first job in a department of European Studies is making a new discipline. But what actually happens is that the gatekeepers at this boundary are *PHILITS*. Even in Salford, for example, where very little literature is taught, the staff's *research* is literary.[8] The vast majority of current research in Modern languages is literary research directed by *PHILITS*.[9] Where a student does opt for social science research, the likelihood is that he or she will be socialized into an existing social science discipline and will get a job in a department of sociology or politics. This does nothing to solve the problem of the research-identity of the modern linguist (already labouring under the burden of having to compete with native scholars). This is not a problem for the language centre model, since research into methodology is not something that needs to be shared with the students (they simply reap the benefits); but for members of the university research community it *is* a problem: teaching needs research not so much – as is usually claimed – at the level of *content* ('keeping up') but at the meta-level of concepts and attitudes, specifically avoidance of reproduction.

The answer to this lies in 'reframing'[10] the discipline. Let me take two examples. Here is a member of the *POLISOX* tribe:

> I feel closer to sociologists and industrial relations people, possibly politics . . . but politics departments are not very interested in politics . . . my experience of these people is that their knowledge of foreign countries can never be adequate unless they have a good knowledge of the language. (10)

This linguist, far from seeing himself as an 'amateur' in another discipline, someone who 'couldn't direct a thesis' is challenging the social science discipline from his own perspective, challenging its bland political neutrality and its insularity (represented by mono-lingualism). Such challenges from 'outsiders' have a highly functional role in research communities, though the outsider's role is always an uncomfortable one.

My second example is linguistics. Of the various contents proposed as a substitute for literature, linguistics has a *prima facie* plausibility. But linguists have to fight for the territory:

> This distinction between linguist and linguistician is very insidious because you are soon shoved out of that central area, merely people who know certain foreign languages as opposed to people who know the principles behind language. (46)

'Linguistics', i.e. theoretical linguistics, is not particularly concerned with language learning, and its proponents (the *LINKSTICKS*) are monoglots:

> Most people who go in for linguistics start with no or with very little knowledge of other languages. They tend to base their theories of universals on English. They are not really immersed in other cultures. That is to do with the training of linguisticians, especially in the States. (34)

This is true even of applied linguistics:

> By definition they have been TEFL teachers. I've scarcely met an applied linguist who comes from a Modern Language background. The top of the profession did English. (34)

So, even in the field of language, the modern linguist is an amateur linguistician, an amateur applied linguist *unless the discipline itself is reframed so as to be less theoretical and less insular*. If modern linguists are to value themselves it seems then that they have little choice but to take up an *outsider* position with regard to existing disciplines (and to the native scholars of the country they study). This may not be easy, though a professor I interviewed did seem to have the requisite belligerence with regard to other disciplines and their 'tunnel vision compounded with blind spots':

> We don't make the news; we have got to go out and proclaim ourselves a bit more. We have got to say we are the people who can make more sense of the country now we are part of Europe. We have got to say that we are not narrow in the way that our colleagues in other disciplines are. We have got to rubbish other disciplines and we have got to show that you can combine technical subjects with something worth knowing about. That is a major challenge. We are the only practical Arts subject. We could label ourselves and make practical progress on public opinion and school opinion. (46)

A more radical way of expressing this is to say that the notion of discipline itself has to be challenged. Modern Languages can rate itself highly only to the extent that it questions rather than accepts the traditional British classification code. Indeed it can act as a leader in what is a necessary process towards integrative codes. One of my respondents saw this process as being exemplified in cultural studies:

> Cultural studies draws on approaches and methods from a range of disciplines. I would like to see the boundaries of disciplines redrawn and a different structure to higher education in Humanities. But because people are located within their assumptions they have an enormous investment in retaining them . . . The boundaries between disciplines are used to avoid looking at the assumptions. (17)

Esland writes (1972, p. 96) of the existence of 'summarising subjects' which are able to unify discrete zones: he mentions anthropology, communications, linguistics, design and technology, ecology, cybernetics.

Modern Languages, it seems to me, is part of an integrative summarizing subject whose principle of coherence (and label) is *communication*. This is the 'relational idea' (Bernstein) which is most likely to enable individuals to make sense of their experience in the profession.

The first step, already taken in many places, is for the differences in languages to be seen as a secondary level of classification. The suggestion, emanating from the UGC, that there should be 'integration' and 'new academic structures' is a valuable one and should indeed be acted upon in ways that are 'not purely cosmetic'.[11]

If the special contribution of the discipline of Modern languages is integration this should be enacted reflexively in the subject's organization.

If the special contribution is communication it should be reflected in the pedagogy. As regards language teaching, the dominance of translation, even in an institution like Salford, is a severe and debilitating tyrrany. Translation is only one small part of communication. Even in the domain of marketable, vocational skills there is a wide range of activities involving writing, reading, speaking, listening – in both inter- and intra-language forms. The skills of writing effective reports or summaries, of making presentations or chairing meetings are fundamental and manifestly in short supply in the world (including the world of the university). If Modern Languages meant in part acquiring these skills at a higher level, students' current aspirations would be met, the subject would be seen as satisfyingly instrumental, but at the same time the central activity would be 'humane', to do with human beings interacting via language. In fact, there is no reason to limit 'communication' in this vocational way. Writing could involve autobiography or fiction; speaking could involve a range of inter-personal situations even, *pace* Crossley and Wood, involving role-play and the exercise of the imagination. In general, 'communication' transcends the purely cognitive and encompasses affective aspects of interaction. Literature fits into this pattern as a particular form of communication, characterized by highly complex sender–receiver modes and by the preponderance of non-cognitive aspects. Most communication involves symbolic representation and fantasy: we never actually *know* enough and we always fill the gaps in our knowledge with our imagination. Understanding this process is crucial and one way is to study works of the imagination.

My respondents were right then to see language as the core, but not in the narrow language-school, translate-and-interpret sense. The strong case for communication as the principle of coherence is that language gives the discipline a meta-status *vis-à-vis* other disciplines all of which use language unreflectively.[12]

Kuhn, for example, points out that the men who called Copernicus mad because he said the earth moved had a language problem: 'Part of what they meant by "earth" was "fixed position"' (1970, p. 149). S. J. Evans says that a foreign language

> frees the mind from the tyranny of words. It is extremely difficult for a monoglot to dissociate thought from words but he who can express his ideas in two languages is emancipated.

Bilinguals, he says, have 'a more diversified structure of intellect' (quoted in Gardner, 1972, pp. 253, 271).

Diversification and emancipation may well be the specific offerings of the discipline. Communication takes place in language contexts and no exchange can be understood in isolation since each item refers to 'knowledge of the world'. Knowing *how* other groups construe or punctuate the world (which is the next step from knowing *that* this is what they do) is one specialized task of Modern Languages and their contribution to social science. This is the way in which European Studies can be integrated into the discipline without subservience to other specialisms and without students being reduced to dependency and 'fact-grubbing'.

The kind of reframing I have described means that language specialisms – linguistics, psycho-linguistics, socio-linguistics – are available as research areas in contact with teaching activities and provide appropriate fields for postgraduate research and socialization within the discipline. However, while specialized research is not excluded from this model, the logic of my argument is that research in Modern Languages is naturally of a different kind – integrative rather than fissiparous. As a research discipline it is more natural for it to build bridges than to dig wells.

In the same way, the teaching/research link is re-defined. The two dominant myths, 1) that teaching is ineffective unless the teacher is also a researcher 2) that a good researcher is *ipso facto* a good teacher, are replaced by a view which sees research as essentially *continuous learning by staff*. It now becomes possible to say that University teaching is ineffective where the teacher has ceased to be a learner and that, for Modern Languages, staff-learning is likely to involve making links between work with peers and work with students.

So far I have talked largely in terms of broad instrumentality, accepting the evidence of the interviews that Modern Languages students are, in comparison with students of English, instrumental, and applying the golden rule which is to be realistic and to start from real rather than fantasized students. But it is a dereliction of duty to respond passively to students' pragmatic demands while ignoring their developmental needs. Teaching is communication across an age gap and it is not enough for people on either side of the chasm to pretend there is a wonderful aerial edifice already in existence, nor is it enough to journey back to a place where there is no chasm and have picnics and party games there. Between pragmatic students concerned with speaking better French and German and getting a good job and staff who believe in 'horizons of value' there has to be a dialogue, though the dialogue is very difficult and, since traditional pedagogic forms prevent our learning, no-one is very good at it. Nevertheless, to educate means to meet someone in the place where they are and, with their consent, lead them somewhere else; Bess is surely right to say that what he charmingly calls 'generative contact with naive persons' (1981, p. 46) can be deeply satisfying. It may be that Modern Languages, which has diluted but never abandoned the liberal university's attachment to pedagogy, will, more than other disciplines, be able to modify its pedagogical practice away from monologue and towards dialogues. I deliberately use the plural because, as the first part of this book demonstrated, students are extremely varied in their developmental needs. While I take it as axiomatic that the University's role is developmental and that its province is the whole range of life tasks listed in Chapter 3, nevertheless I do not believe that the path for any individual can be prescribed. As we saw, Modern Languages students are searching, and the teacher's role is to offer not a succession of hoops and hurdles but opportunity for discovery. It follows that pluralism and flexibility are positive virtues.

While literature is a privileged route to self-knowledge and the later developmental stages, not all students are ready for those stages or able to use literature to reach them, though the readiness may, as we saw, increase as they get older. Teachers and systems need to be ready for the readiness. The evidence of the student interviews points clearly to their moving away from an instrumental view of their chosen discipline or, rather, moving towards a personal balance between vocation and development.

As Raymond Williams pointed out in *The Long Revolution* (1961, p. 161), the idea that real learning was undertaken without thought of practical advantage was 'an absurd defensive reaction' on the part of humanists to the new scientific knowledge of the 19th century. Classics had always been vocational. In other words, it is not a matter of choosing between vocationality and personal development but of striking a balance. The perceived advantage of a discipline is not to be narrowly defined in terms of adult work. This is especially true at a time when the future of work as we know it is problematic so that the capacity to creatively enjoy the world and to develop one's human potential is at least as important as the capacity to earn one's living. The reader may care to guess the author of the following statement:

> Opportunities for higher education are not . . . to be determined primarily by reference to broad estimates of the country's future needs for highly qualified people . . . The government consider higher education valuable for its contribution to the personal development of those who pursue it; at the same time, they value its continued expansion as an investment in the

> nation's human talent in a time of rapid social change and technological development.[13]

How we deal with this requirement to balance personal development and investment in the nation is crucially important. Raymond Williams offers a useful historical analysis. He sees three groups in the 19th century: the 'public educators' who believed in democracy and education as a right for all; the 'industrial trainers' who believed industrial success depended on an educated workforce; and the 'liberal humanists' who were opposed to both because they believed that mass education would vulgarize liberal education and that industrial training would destroy it. The public educators used the arguments of the liberal humanists but, says Williams, sweepingly perhaps, 'the industrial trainers won in the end because of the inertia and stupidity of the old humanists'. He praises Huxley, one of the few to see that the new learning had to become part of a general education and liberal culture desired by the public educators and that the professional training desired by the industrial trainers could follow.

In these terms, we could say that University Modern Languages could go over to the industrial trainers (and vanish) if the old humanists (whom I have called the *PHILITS*) do not successfully transform themselves into public educators and thus enable the 'new knowledge' (in this case areas like linguistics, psychology and sociology) to be incorporated into a liberal (literary) culture and thence into an individual's personal development. But the whole system needs to rediscover a liberal pedagogy based on dialogue, in order to meet the needs of both trainers and humanists.

The future depends very much on the quality of the leadership. Some of my *EFCOM* respondents expressed the pessimistic view:

> As long as you have the current academic hierarchy in the language you will have the same problem in some shape or form. It is a self-perpetuating thing. The people in power appoint people like themselves. (34)

John Trim of CILT seemed to be expressing the same view in his contribution to the NCML conference in 1984. There is clearly a danger that leadership by *PHILITS* will be succeeded by leadership by no-one. And yet, recent senior appointments tend, it seems to me, not to bear this out. It does look as if the leaders are capable of selecting new leaders who may, to be sure, not be totally different from themselves, but who are nevertheless sufficiently different to manage loss and change.

It also depends on the way that University as a whole responds to outside pressure. Crisis is both threat and opportunity:

> When Modern Languages were going through lean times and we were getting fewer students it was a good period; it woke a lot of people up and they started making up new courses and dropping dodos. I have always maintained that students must come back to Modern Languages because it is something of our time and that is what is happening. And it will get

better because the courses on offer are so much more attractive now and correspond to the needs of the undergraduates. (18)

Bess (1982, pp. 194–5) describes the different possible responses:

> Faculty themselves are ready for change . . . Used imaginatively and constructively, such emotions can be employed in service of change and growth both for individuals and organisations. Mismanaged, Faculty efforts will be channelled into increased collective bargaining, retreatism, self-protectionism, and regression.

It is very much a matter of confidence and morale. I believe that the discipline has the capacity to be singularly in touch with future British society. My earlier analysis of the anomalous position of the discipline, and the consequent sense of insecurity, was based partly on assumptions about British society which may be ceasing to be true. Britain's identity crisis seems to be resolving itself in the direction of the Channel rather than the Atlantic. The European Community is no longer a novelty; neither is wine, lager or the continental quilt. Burgess's (1966) view, in his novel *Tremor of Intent*, may no longer be true:

> For that matter, my own ability to speak French and Russian quite well, and Polish moderately well was seized on with no eagerness. I even had difficulty in transferring to the Intelligence Corps when it was formed in July 1940. My officers spoke French with public school accents. The British have always been suspicious of linguistic ability, associating it with spies, impresarios, waiters, and Jewish refugees: the polyglot can never be a gentleman. (p. 20)

There are implications for Modern Languages in this shift but they are to be found not so much in a re-assessment of purely linguistic demands (though the status accruing from knowing foreign languages will increase as will the stigma of not knowing them) but in the shift to ways of thinking which I have described as being specific to Modern Languages. I am suggesting that the move towards Europe represents for Britain a move towards post-imperial modesty, an acceptance of pluralism, of a more diffuse identity, of ambiguity and of the need for negotiation and collaboration – what Marris (1974) calls 'a pervasive and insistent process of confrontation and negotiation' (p. 161).

To say that the future of Modern Languages is linked to the revival of the values of the liberal university, to the reduction of disciplinary cell-splitting, to an educational switch from collective codes to integrative codes, from a pedagogy of monologue to one of dialogue, to a rethinking of the notion of vocationality and to the Europeanization of post-imperial Britain is to say that the discipline's future is very uncertain indeed. There is no way of telling whether the experience of language people in the future will be that of a beleaguered and rather eccentric minority group, plaintively re-living the history of classics, or that of a community whose unique history and identity enables its members to perform a specific task on behalf of society. In Chapter 4, I described this task as maintaining the hope of resolution, the belief that the dialectic of same and different, of distintegration and integration, of past and present, can be worked out peacefully. To say that the principle of coherence of the discipline is communication and that the method is acceptance of pluralism and ambivalence is to put the same idea into more operational terms. At one stage, I thought of calling this book 'Before Pentecost'.

No individual person, no single group or discipline has control over the system. But the system is nothing but the total set of relations between individuals, groups and disciplines. To understand these relations better is to lessen to some degree the extent to which the experience of a group is beyond the control of the group and to increase to some degree the extent to which the group itself, through self-knowledge, may determine the nature of its own experience, now and in the future.

Notes

Chapter 1

1 Source: Universities Statistical Record. As at 31 December 1983, Tab 9 15182.

2 A rare example of research is Eardley's survey of sixth formers in North Wales (1984). The usefulness of the research is restricted by the fact that the questionnaire used is not reproduced (so that one cannot easily dismiss one's suspicions that – with regard to literary study for example – the author got the answers he wanted) and by the usual limitations of such surveys. What emerges is that lack of career relevance is the main reason for *not* choosing modern languages, especially with boys and that 'always was a favourite subject' is the main reason for choosing it for A-level. See also Bardell (1982).

3 Liam Hudson describes a Cambridge experiment to select students according to the criterion of creativity, using projective tests (Hudson, 1968, p. 76).

4 I am referring to some research I conducted at the University of London Schools Examination Board. The aim was to compare, over the last four years, the proportion of A-level entries which paired a modern language with English with the proportion of A-level entries which paired a modern language with a social science subject (defined as Economics, Sociology, Geography or History). Pairings with other subjects (Art, Mathematics, etc.) were assumed to be constant over the period. While I make no great claims for this exercise, the results do show a clear trend:

A = modern language + Social Science subject
B = modern language + English

A as a percentage of A + B

June 1982 26.72%
June 1983 37.13%
June 1984 39.30%
June 1985 41.60%

Chapter 2

1 The survey of Bradford University students conducted by Frank Willis and his colleagues (Willis *et al.*, 1977) offers a complementary source of information on

students' experience of the year abroad since it relies on questionnaires rather than interviews. It is concerned with improvement in language performance and distinguishes the various ways of spending the year – student, work placement, assistant. The conclusions of the chapter 'Residence abroad and personal development' are very much in line with my own: students becomes more 'happy-go-lucky', more open-minded.

Chapter 3

1 See Stern (1983) pp. 373–390 for a useful summary of research on what he calls (p. 390) the 'largely unexplored area' of the relationship between personality and language learning.
2 See Hudson (1966 and 1968) for 'yielding' and convergence/divergence.
3 Hudson himself (1968, p. 91) says that he used the converger/diverger distinction as a principle of classification in *Contrary Imaginations* but claims he was not 'pigeonholing'. Convergers and divergers, he says, are 'ideal types' and furthermore individuals change over time or even in different circumstances.
4 Oddly, economists seem to have had identical results to linguists throughout.
5 Based on a conversation with Alasdair Mant, but Roizen and Jepson make a similar point: 'the very concept of maximization of profit may be one which is in fact far from the minds of those in the organisation actually responsible . . . for recruitment' (p. 162). They also show that these 'university' values may be those of a very limited number of institutions – Oxbridge in particular.
6 A questionnaire I distributed to a group of ECS students in Cardiff contained questions about newspaper-reading. Of the 44 students, 11 read a British newspaper 'rarely', 3 'two or three times a week', 13 'every week' and 17 (39%) 'every day'. The papers read every day were: *Daily Mirror* (5), *Guardian* (4), *Daily Mail* (4), *Times* (3), *Daily Telegraph* (1), *Sun* (1).
7 The same questionnaire asked for their response to the following statement: 'I don't like being asked to choose my own subject to write about. I don't have all that many strong views or things I want to say'. Results were: Agree 29%, Uncertain 13%, Disagree 57%.
8 Hudson (1973) attempts to link the converger/diverger distinction with subject choice and development via the notion of 'crystallisation'. I find his argument confused but the basic idea is attractive. Science subjects are chosen earlier (at latency) at a time when the important life task is to control impulse with reason; arts subjects are chosen later with impulses uppermost (at adolescence). 'Crystallisation' would seem to be a way of describing the fixing of an identity via subject choice. In this sense (though Hudson does not say so) arts subjects are means of avoiding crystallization rather than achieving it.
9 Hudson's method entails comparing scores on an IQ test with scores on open-ended 'creative' tests and measuring the *difference*. 'All-rounders' are equally good (or bad) at both. (1968, p. 97).
10 'The fox knows many things but the hedgehog knows one big thing', Isiah Berlin's epigraph to his *The Hedgehog and the Fox* (1957).
11 Loveday's book (1982) deals with the issue with a broad sweep (the assumption I had always made on the basis of French – that the native speaker appreciates a foreigner speaking well – turns out not to be universal; the Japanese, apparently, are suspicious). See also Hatch (1978).

Chapter 4

1 A striking example of this is the Duras/Resnais film *Hiroshima mon amour* where the French heroine whose German lover was shot and died in her arms has repressed this experience ('c'est la chose au monde à laquelle je pense le moins et dont je rêve le plus'). Many years later, after an experience with a Japanese lover (with a foreign accent) she is able to relive the past ('J'ai raconté notre histoire') and thus 'reconcile the past with the present'. The accent seems to be an example of the 'magic of speech', creating an association with the past which is not cognitive.

2 In order not to confuse the exposition I have omitted the homosexual aspect: when in difficulty these clients frequently developed relationships with people of the same sex *and* the same nationality, a complete reversal and presumably another denial of the tension of sameness and difference. I have also omitted Cohen's observation that all the individuals had failed to make an identification with a same-sex parent and Morley's hypothesis that exogamy is a means of avoiding incest, i.e. by choosing a partner as different as possible from the parent.

3 Precise statistics on staff mobility are difficult to obtain. However the Universities Statistical Record (USR) was able to review for me all those members of academic staff from French, German, Italian, Spanish, Portuguese, Latin American Studies and Russian who entered university service in 1972 (the first year in which usable records were kept) and who are still in university service as full-time academics (as at December 31st 1984). *80% of this cohort are still in the university to which they were recruited.*

Chapter 6

1 'Bruce Truscot' does discuss both staff and students in *Red Brick University* (1945). However, only a few pages actually deal with the relationship. Scott's book, *Dons and Students* (1973), also deals with the two groups, but separately rather than in relationship. Ian Lewis, *The Student Experience of Higher Education* (1984) in spite of the title, does take the staff–student relatedness seriously and comes to similar conclusions to my own. 'The onus for breaking the spiral of confusion must rest with the faculty staff. It is their messages which are being misconstrued, and it is they who provide evaluative judgements which, when mediated to the students, are taken to reinforce the prior misconceptions' (p. 152).

2 The underlying assumption is that relations between groups are determined not by 'objective fact' but by the sets or schemata which are used to interpret (or create) facts. See M. L. J. Abercrombie, *The Anatomy of Judgement* (1960). The inter-group event is a feature of group relations conferences in the Tavistock tradition.

3 See James Gustafson 'The pseudomutual small group or institution' in *Exploring individual and organizational boundaries*, W. G. Lawrence (ed.) 1979. Pseudomutuality is described as a defence against individuation, change and growth which depends for its effect on the blurring of boundaries (p. 70). 'People will seem to share identical developmental interests, when they do not in fact, the problem of pseudo-mutuality' (Gustafson, J. P. and Cooper, L. C. in Pines, M. (1985), Chapter 8).

4 See above, Chapter 1, p. 13 for the statistics.

5 Hamon and Rotman in their study of French Secondary-school teachers (1984) make a similar comment: 'Nous entrons ici dans le maquis du non-dit . . . cette dimension érotique est niée, occultée . . . c'est la dimension ô combine souterraine de la relation pédagogique' (p. 106).

Chapter 7

1

Subject	*Men*	*Women*	*% women*
French	426	175	29
French/German	24	8	25
German	284	71	25
Hispanic	166	47	22
Total	900	301	25

SOURCE: USR Tab S14739, as at 31 December 1983.
Staff.

2 Acker and Piper (1984), p. 28 (13.9%).

3 A comment made by one of my respondents at a workshop on Gender in Higher Education (Gregynog 86: 24–26 March, 1986).

4 I have discussed this value system with specific reference to language-learning in an article 'On comprehension' (Evans, 1984).

Part 4

1 My understanding of systems thinking comes from a) Gregory Bateson, *Steps to an Ecology of Mind*, and *Mind and Nature: a Necessary Unity*; b) Anthony Wilden, *System and Structure*; c) the work of the Grubb Institute (see *Practice and Theory in the Work of the Grubb Institute, 1974–1981*) and of the Tavistock Institute of Human Relations (see Gordon Lawrence, (ed.), *Exploring Individual and Organisational Boundaries: A Tavistock Open Systems Approach*). The basic insight – there are no things, only relations – is, of course, structuralist.

2 'A *metalogue* is a conversation about some problematic subject. This conversation should be such that not only do the participants discuss the problem, but the structure of the conversation as a whole is also relevant to the same subject . . . the history of evolutionary theory is inevitably a metalogue . . . in which the creation and interaction of ideas must necessarily exemplify evolutionary process', G. Bateson, *Steps to an Ecology of Mind*, New York, Balantine Books, 1972 (this passage is not in the British edition – Bateson, 1973).

Chapter 8

1 Details of works by these authors are in the Bibliography. See especially Glock, 1971.

2 This distinction – discipline/subject – is not in Young: it is my way of making what seemed a necessary distinction. Musgrove (quoted in Stenhouse, 1975, p. 10), puts it well: 'subjects are communities of people, competing and collaborating with one another, defining and defending their boundaries, demanding allegiance from their members and conferring a sense of identity upon them'.

3 It would be interesting to trace this cell-splitting in one particular field via the creation of new journals. I am thinking particularly of psychology, social psychology

and the social psychology of language and of a journal, *Language and Social Psychology*. Peacocke and his colleagues (1985) have studied the phenomenon under the title of 'Reductionism'. My impression is that new journals often set out with the express intention of integrating fragmented worlds, but end up by being part of the fragmentation.

4 See L. Coser, *The functions of social conflict*, Chicago, 1956, for an account of the way that competing sub-groups within a system ensure the system's capacity to adapt to the environment.

5 This is based on Goode, W. J. (1969), 'The theoretical limits of professionalism'. See also Bess (1981), pp. 28–31. Bess's analysis is similar to mine: 'There is some considerable doubt that what is now known as the academic profession has enough of the characteristics of a "profession" technically to justify that appellation . . . Splintering of the fields of knowledge . . . has virtually eliminated what is probably the *sine qua non* of any profession – a common core of technical knowledge in codified form . . . The faculty member as a teacher cannot be described as a professional, and the faculty member as a researcher cannot be called a professional. The label is attached to the occupation because it appears to have the *benefits* of a profession, namely a very great amount of individual autonomy . . . The benefits seem to have arisen out of the mystique of the tasks'.

Chapter 9

1 I investigated, some years ago, the way in which IBM dealt with its language problem when the company took the decision to work through English in European countries (Evans, 1978).

2 See the NUT response to the government's consultative document on Modern Languages (1983).

3 See Firth, 1929, p. 54 for an account of the role of Philology at Oxford.

4 The following account is closely based on a conversation with Christopher Bettinson.

5 Hagboldt, 1940; Hawkins, 1981 (Chapter 4); Howatt, 1984.

6 An exception is Sullivan's history of the French department at Cardiff (Sullivan, 1983).

7 See Thomas and King (1986) for a rare case study of modern languages graduate destinations. They follow the careers of 31 students of the 1977 cohort. The authors also provide general statistics: 61% of graduates have as their 'first destination' 'Industry and commerce'.

8 See the Annual Report of the University of Salford, 1985, 'Publications'.

9 John Trim, Director of CILT, 'Language Needs and Social Policy' (in *Second language learning*, CILT, 1985). 'All but some six of the 84 pages of the 1982 guide to research in progress in French are literary . . . It is difficult to see why the present system should not be almost indefinitely self-perpetuating'.

10 For the concept of re-framing see Watzlawick *et al.*, *Change: Principles of Problem Formation and Problem Resolution* ('The gentle art of re-framing', p. 98).

11 *French Studies Bulletin*, 15 (1985), p. 13, report of a meeting of the Association of University Professors of French.

12 There will always be competition for this disciplinary high-ground. Capra, in *The Turning Point* (Fontana 1982), claims it for Physics.

13 Margaret Thatcher, 1972 (CMND 5174, para. 18) quoted by Kogan (1983), p. 23.

Appendix

Details of respondents: Staff

REFERENCE	Professor	Senior Lecturer	Lecturer	Male	Female	French	German	Italian	Hispanic	Non-European Language	Non-Modern Language	Administrative Staff	Native Speaker	Tape Interview
1			X		X	X								X
2			X	X		X								X
3			X	X		X								X
4			X	X		X								X
5		X		X			X							X
6	X			X			X							X
7			X		X			X						X
8			X		X	X								X
9		X		X		X								X
10			X	X				X						X
11			X	X		X							X	X
12		X		X					X				X	X
13			X	X		X							X	X
14		X		X							X			X
15	X			X							X			X
16	X			X			X							X
17			X		X		X							X
18			X	X				X						X
19			X		X	X								X
20		X		X		X								X
21				X								X		X
22			X	X		X								X
23		X			X	X								X
24			X	X		X								X
25		X		X		X								X
26		X		X		X								X
27		X		X							X			X
28			X	X		X								X
29			X	X		X								X
30			X		X	X								X
31	X			X		X								X
32	X			X		X								X
33			X	X		X							X	X
34			X	X						X				X
35		X			X	X								X
36			X	X		X								X

REFERENCE	Professor	Senior Lecturer	Lecturer	Male	Female	French	German	Italian	Hispanic	Non-European Language	Non-Modern Language	Administrative Staff	Native Speaker	Tape Interview
37			X		X	X								
38			X		X	X								X
39			X	X		X							X	X
40			X		X				X					X
41			X		X			X						X
42	X			X			X							
43				X								X		
44			X	X			X							
45		X		X					X					
46	X			X		X								X

Details of respondents: Students

REFERENCE	Female	Male	1st Year	2nd Year	3rd Year	4th Year	Postgraduate	In Employment	Mature Undergraduate	French	German	Italian	Hispanic	Language + Literature	Language + Non-Literature	Non-Modern Language	Taped Interview
50		X				X				X				X			X
51		X				X				X			X	X			X
52	X					X				X				X			X
53	X			X						X				X			X
54	X			X					X	X				X			X
55	X				X					X				X		X	X
56	X			X						X		X		X			X
57	X					X				X				X			X
58		X		X						X			X	X			X
59		X				X				X				X			X
60	X					X				X	X			X			X
61		X				X				X			X	X			X
62	X					X				X				X			X
63	X					X				X				X			X
64	X					X				X		X		X		X	X
65	X					X				X				X			X
66		X	X							X				X			X
67	X		X							X			X	X			X
68	X			X						X				X			X
69	X			X						X				X			X
70	X							X		X				X			X
71		X				X				X				X		X	X
72		X		X						X				X			
80	X			X						X	X				X		X
81	X			X						X	X				X		X
82		X		X						X	X				X		X
83		X				X				X	X				X		X
84	X					X				X		X			X		X
85	X					X				X		X			X		X
86	X					X				X		X			X		X
87	X					X				X		X			X		X
88	X					X				X			X		X		X
89	X					X				X		X			X		X
90	X				X					X			X		X		X
91		X			X					X	X				X		X

REFERENCE	Female	Male	1st Year	2nd Year	3rd Year	4th Year	Postgraduate	In Employment	Mature Undergraduate	French	German	Italian	Hispanic	Language + Literature	Language + Non-Literature	Non-Modern Language	Taped Interview
92	1	4	4		1		GROUP INTERVIEW								X		X
93		X			X					X			X		X		X
94	X				X				X	X			X		X		X
95	X				X						X		X		X		X
96	X				X					X	X				X		X
97	X		X		PAIR INTERVIEW					X			X		X		X
97	X				X					X	X				X		X
98		X								X	X		X		X		X
100	X				X											X	X
101		X			X											X	X
102		X			X											X	X
103	X				X											X	X

Bibliography

Abercrombie, M. L. J. (1960: 1969). *The Anatomy of Judgement*. London, Penguin.

Acker, S. and Piper, P. W. (eds) (1984). *Is Higher Education fair to women?* Guildford, SRHE/Nelson.

Adelson, J. (1962). 'The Teacher as a model', in Sanford, 1962: 396–417.

Adorno, T. W. *et al.* (1950). *The authoritarian personality*. New York, Harper and Row.

Alatis, J. E. *et al.* (1981). *The second language classroom. Directions for the 1980s*. New York, Oxford, Oxford Univ. Press.

Astin, A. W. (1977). *Four critical years*. San Francisco, Jossey-Bass.

Atton, R. B. (1983). *'Seven years after': Summary report of a follow-up survey of the early careers of graduates of 1974 of the university of Reading in pure and applied sciences* (mimeo).

Axelrod, J. (1973). *The University teacher as artist*. San Francisco, Jossey-Bass.

Bailey, F. G. (1977). *Morality and expediency: The Folklore of academic politics*. Oxford, Blackwell.

Bardell, G. (1982). *Options for the fourth: the report of an exploratory study in the schools*. London, School Council.

Barnett, R. A. (1985). 'Higher Education: legitimation crisis', *Studies in Higher Education*, 10, 3, 241–255.

Bateson, G. (1973). *Steps to an ecology of mind*. St Albans, Paladin.

Bateson, G. (1979). *Mind and nature: a necessary unity*. New York, Bantam Books.

Baxbaum, E. (1949). 'The role of a second language in the formation of ego and superego', *Psychoanalytic Quarterly*, 18: 279–289.

Becher, T. and Kogan, M. (1980). *Process and structure in Higher Education*. London, Heinemann.

Becher, T. (1981). 'Towards a definition of disciplinary cultures', *Studies in Higher Education*, 6, 2:109–122.

Becker, H. S. *et al.* (1961). *The Boys in White*. Chicago University Press.

Becker, H. S. *et al.* (1968). *Making the grade: the academic side of College life*. New York, Wiley.

Bell, R. E. and Youngson, A. J. (eds) (1973). *Present and future in Higher Education*. London, Tavistock.

Bereiter, C. and Freedman, M. B. (1962). 'Fields of study and the people in them', in Sanford, 1962: 563–596.

Berger, J. (1979). *Pig Earth*. London, Writers and Readers Cooperative.

Bernstein, B. (1972). 'On the classification and framing of educational knowledge', in Young, 1972: 47–69.

Bertaux, D. (ed.) (1981). *Biography and Society: the Life History Approach in the Social Sciences*. Beverly Hills, California, Sage.

Bess, J. L. (1973). 'Integrating student and faculty life cycles', *Review of Educational Research*, Fall, 1973, 43, 4.

Bess, J. L. (1977). 'The academic profession in transition', *Higher Education Review*, Fall, 1977, 1, 1.

Bess, J. L. (1981). *University organization: a matrix analysis of the Academic Professions*. New York, Human Science Press.

Bettinson, C. (1986). *European Studies and related degree courses in UK universities, polytechnics and colleges*. London, University Association for Contemporary European Studies.

Birkmaier, E. (1971). 'The meaning of creativity in Foreign Language teaching'. *Modern Language Journal*, Madison, 55: 345–52.

Blair, R. W. (ed.) (1982). *Innovative approaches to language teaching*. Rowley Mass., Newbury House.

Bloom, B. S. (1956). *A Taxonomy of Educational Objectives*. New York, David McKay.

Blum, A. F. 'The Corpus of Knowledge as a normative order', in Young, 1972: 117–132.

Bok, D. (1982). *Beyond the Ivory Tower: Social responsibilities of the modern University*. Harvard University Press.

Bourdieu, P. and Passeron, J. P. (1979). *The Inheritors: French students and their relation to culture*. Trans. R. Nice. Chicago and London, University of Chicago Press.

Brachfeld, O. (1936). 'Individual psychology in the learning of languages', *International journal of individual psychology*, 2, 77–83.

Brown, H. D. (1973). 'Affective variables in second language acquisition', *Language Learning*, 23: 231–246.

Brown, R. (ed.) (1982). *Knowledge, education and cultural change: papers in the sociology of education*. London, Tavistock.

Bruner, J. S. (1966). *Towards a theory of instruction*. Harvard, Harvard University Press.

Bulmer, M. (1979). 'Concepts in the analysis of qualitative data', *Sociological Review*, 27: 4.

Burgess, A. (1966). *Tremor of intent*. London, Penguin.

Burgess, R. G. (1983). *Experiencing Comprehensive Education: A study of Bishop McGregor School, London*. London, Methuen.

Burgess, R. G. (1984). *In the Field*. London, George Allen and Unwin.

Burstall, C. *et al*. (1974). *Primary French in the balance*. Windsor, NFER.

Campbell, D. T. (1969). 'Ethnocentrism of disciplines and the fish-scale model of omniscience', in Sherif and Sherif (eds) 1969: 328–348.

Caplow, T. and McGee, R. J. (1958). *The academic marketplace*. New York, Basic Books.

Carter, R. (1985). 'A Taxonomy of Objectives for Professional Education', *Studies in Higher Education*, 10, 2, 135–150.

Case, T. (1887). 'An appeal to the University of Oxford against the proposed Final School of Modern Languages'. Oxford, 1887.

Charlton, K. (1965). *Education in Renaissance England*. London, RKP.

Chastain, K. (1975). 'Affective and ability factors in second-language acquisition', *Language learning*, 25, 1: 153–161.

Chickering, A. W. and associates (1981). *The Modern American College*. San Francisco and London, Jossey-Bass.

CILT (1975). *Less commonly taught languages: resources and problems*. CILT reports and papers 12, London, CILT.

CILT (1986). *Sex differences in foreign language learning: a reading list to supplement the bibliography in CILT information guide 24*. London, CILT.

Clark, B. R. (1962). *Faculty Culture*. Berkeley, California, Centre for the Study of Higher Education.

Clark, B. R. (1983a). 'Governing the higher education system', in Shattock, 1983.

Clark, B. R. (1983b). *The Higher Education System: academic organization in a cross-national perspective*. Berkeley, California and London, University of California Press.

Claxton, C. S. and Murrell, P. H. (1984). 'Developmental theory as a guide for maintaining the vitality of College Faculty', in Mehrotra, 1984: 29–44.

Cohen, B. (1985). 'Skills, Professional Education and the Disabling University', *Studies in Higher Education*, 10, 2, 175–186.

Cohen, D. (1977). Interview with Liam Hudson, in *Psychologists on psychology*. London, RKP.

Cohen, N. (1982). 'Same or different? A problem of identity in cross-cultural marriages', *Journal of family therapy*, 4: 177–199.

Coleman, D. (1985). 'Ethnic intermarriage in Great Britain', *Population Trends*, 40: 4–10.

Crane, D. (1969). 'The invisible college: social structure in a group of scientists', *American Sociological Review*, 34, 3: 335–351.

Crossley, C. and Wood, D. (1984). 'The Northern Drift: untimely reflections', *French Studies Bulletin*, 11: 6–8.

Cullen, J. B. (1978). *The structure of professionalism: a quantitative study of occupational group stratification*. Princeton, N. J., Petrocelli Books.

Czikszentmihalyi, M. (1975). *Beyond boredom and anxiety*. San Francisco, Jossey-Bass.

Daniell, D. (1985). 'Love and work: complementary aspects of personal identity', *International Journal of Social Economics*, 12, 2: 48–55.

Dartington, T., Miller, E. and Gwynne, G. (1981). *A life together: the distribution of attitudes around the disabled*. London, Tavistock.

Dawkins, R. (1978). *The Selfish Gene*. London, Paladin.

De Board, R. (1978). *The Psychoanalysis of organisations*. London, Tavistock.

Delamont, S. (1976). *Interaction in the classroom*. London, Methuen.

Dewey, J. (1974). *John Dewey on Education*. University of Chicago Press.

Dineen, F. P. (1969). 'Linguistics and the social sciences', in Sherif and Sherif, 1969.

Eardley, M. (1984). 'Language Study in the sixth form: or attitude survey', *British Journal of Language Teaching*, 22, 1:3–7.

Eiduson, B. T. (1962). *Scientists: their psychological world*, New York, Basic Books.

Eisner, E. W. and Vallance, E. (eds) (1974a). *Conflicting conceptions of the curriculum*. Berkeley, California, McCutchon Publishing Co.

Eisner, E. W. and Vallance, E. (1974b). 'Five conceptions of curriculum: their roots and implications for curriculum planning', in Eisner and Vallance, 1974a: 1–18.

Elton, L. (1981). 'Can Universities change?', *Studies in Higher Education*, 6, 1.

Erikson, E. (1950: 1963). *Childhood and Society*. London, Penguin.

Esland, G. M. (1972). 'Teaching and learning as the organization of knowledge', in Young, 1972: 70–16.

Etzioni, A. (1969). *The semi-professions and their organisation*, New York, The Free press.

Etzioni, A. and Lehman, E. W. (3rd edn) (1980). *A sociological reader on complex organisations*. New York, Holt, Rinehart and Wilson.

Evans, C. (1978). 'Language Teaching: the IBM solution', *Audio-visual Language Journal*, 16, 1, 40–44.

Evans, C. (1981). 'Taine: note retrospective', *Romantisme*, 32.

Evans, C. (1984). 'On comprehension', *British Journal of Language Teaching*, 22, 23–27.

Evans, R. I. (1967). *Resistance to innovation in Higher Education*. San Francisco, Jossey-Bass.

Firth, C. (1929). *Modern languages at Oxford 1724–1929*. Oxford University Press.

Fulton, O. (ed.) (1981). *Access to Higher Education.* Guildford, Society for Research into Higher Education.

Fulton, O. (1983). *University entry: the candidates' view.* UCCA.

Gagne, R. M. (1970). *The Conditions of Learning*, 2nd ed. New York, Holt, Rinehart and Wilson.

Ganguley, S. R. and Ormond, M. B. (1981). 'Ego attitudes in second language learning: an analysis of sex-related differences', *British Educational Research Journal*, 7, 2, 155–165.

Gardner, R. C. and Lambert, W. F. (1972). *Attitudes and motivation in Second Language learning.* Rowley, Mass., Newbury House.

Gardner, R. C. (1979). 'Social psychological aspects of second language acquisition', in Giles and St Clair, 1979.

Gardner, R. C. (1985). *Social psychology and second language learning, the role of attitudes and motivation.* London, Arnold.

Gerstl, J. E. and Hutton, S. P. (1966). *Engineers: the anatomy of a profession.* London, Tavistock.

Giles, H. and St Clair, R. (1979). *Language and Social Psychology.* Oxford, Blackwell.

Gilligan, C. (1982). *In a different voice: psychological theory and women's development.* London and Cambridge Mass., Harvard University Press.

Ginzberg, E. *et al.* (1951) (1966 repr.). *Occupational choice: an approach to a general theory.* New York, London, Columbia University Press.

Giroux, H. A. (1983). *Theory and Resistance in Education: a pedagogy for the opposition.* London, Heinemann.

Glock, M. E. (ed.) (1971). *Guiding learning: readings in educational psychology.* London, Wiley.

Goetz, J. P. and Le Compte, M. D. (1984). *Ethnography and qualitative design in education research.* New York, Academic Press.

Goffman, E. (1959). *The Presentation of Self in Everyday Life.* London, Penguin.

Golby, M. (ed.) (1975). *Curriculum design.* Milton Keynes, Open University.

Goode, W. J. (1969). 'The theoretical limits of professionalism', in Etzioni, 1969: 266–313.

Gordon, A. (1981). 'The Educational choices of young people', in Fulton, 1981.

Greenson, R. R. (1950). 'The mother tongue and the mother', *International Journal of Psychoanalysis*, 21: 18–23.

Gross, N. *et al.* (1966). *Explorations in role analysis.* New York, John Wiley.

Grubb Institute (1978), *Freedom to Study* by Bruce Reed, Jean Hutton, John Bazalgette, London Overseas Students Trust.

Guiora, A. Z. (1972). 'Construct validity and transpositional research: towards an empirical study of psychoanalytic concepts', *Comprehensive Psychiatry*, 13, 2: 139–150.

Guiora, A. Z. *et al.* (1975). 'Language and person. Studies in language behaviour', *Language learning*, 25, 1: 43–61.

Guiora, A. Z. *et al.* (1972). 'The effects of experimentally induced changes in ego states on pronunciation ability in a second language: an exploratory study', *Comprehensive Psychiatry*, 13, 5: 421–428.

Hagboldt, P. (1940). *The Teaching of German.* Boston, Heath.

Halsey, A. H. and Trow, M. A. (1971). *The British Academics.* London, Faber and Faber.

Hammersley, M. and Atkinson, P. (1983). *Ethnography: Principles in Practice.* London, Tavistock.

Hamon, H. and Rotman, P. (1984). *Tant qui'il y aura des profs.* Paris, Seuil.

Harder, P. (1980). 'Discourse as self-expression – on the reduced personality of the second-language learner', *Applied Linguistics* I, 3: 262–272.

Hatch, E. (1978). 'Discourse analysis and second language learning', in *Second Language Acquisition: a book of readings*, ed. E. Hatch. Rowley, Mass., Newbury House.

Hawkins, E. (1981). *Modern Languages in the curriculum*. Cambridge University Press.

Hawkins, E. (1984). *Awareness of Language: An Introduction*. Cambridge University Press.

Healey, F. G. (1966). *Foreign Language Teaching in the Universities*. Manchester University Press.

HMI (1975). *Curricular differences for girls and boys*. Education Survey No. 21. London, HMSO.

HMI (1985). *Boys and Modern Languages*. Inspection Report. London, DES.

Hietsch, U. and Larcher, D. (1984). *Fremdsprachenlernen an Universitäten*, (Zeitschrift für Hochschuldidaktik, 8, 1).

Hoey, M. (1983). 'A tentative map of discourse studies and their place in linguistics', *Analysis*, I, 1: 7–26.

Hoey, M. (1983). 'Three metaphors for examining the semantic organisation of monologue', *Analysis*, I, 1, 27–53.

Hoey, M. (1983). *On the Surface of Discourse*. London, Allen and Unwin.

Holt, S. (1981). 'Purposes and problems in European Studies', *Journal of Area Studies*, 4 (Supplement).

Howatt, A. P. R. (1984). *A History of English Language Teaching*. Oxford University Press.

Hudson, L. (1966). *Contrary Imaginations*. London, Methuen.

Hudson, L. (1968). *Frames of Mind*. London, Methuen.

Hudson, L. (ed.) (1970). *The Ecology of Human Intelligence* (selected readings). London, Penguin.

Hudson, L. (1972: 1976). *The Cult of the Fact*. London, Cape.

Hudson, L. (1973). 'The Psychological basis of subject choice', in Bell and Youngson, 1973.

Hurman, A. (1978). *A charter for Choice. A study of option schemes*. London, NFFR.

Hutchings, D. (1974). 'Curriculum structure: the subject choice syndrome', *Journal of Applied Education Studies*, 3, 1, 22–28.

Illich, I. (1970: 1973). *Deschooling Society*. London, Penguin.

Jackson, J. A. (ed.) (1978). *Professions and professionalization*. Cambridge University Press.

Jackson, P. W. (1968). *Life in classrooms*. New York, Holt, Rinehart and Wilson.

Jacobson, H. (1984). *Coming from Behind*. London, St Martin.

Jaffe, J. (1960). 'Formal language patterns as defensive operations', in Barbara, D. A. (ed.), *Psychological and Psychiatric aspects of Speech and Learning*. Springfield, Ill, Charles C. Thomas, and Oxford, Blackwell.

Jaques, E. (1965). 'Death and the mid-life crisis', *International Journal of Psychoanalysis*, 46, 4, 502–514.

Jeanson, F. (1960). *Sartre par lui-même*. Paris, Seuil.

Johnson, K. (1982). *Communicative Syllabus Design and Methodology*. Oxford University Press.

Jung, C. G. (1983). *Jung: Selected writings introduced by Anthony Storr*. London, Fontana Paperbacks.

Katz, J. and Sanford, N. (1962). 'The curriculum in the perspective of the theory of development', in Sanford, 1962: 418–440.

Kelly, A. (ed.) (1981). *The missing half: girls and science education*. Manchester University Press.

Kelly, L. G. (1969). *Twenty-five centuries of Language Teaching*. Rowley, Mass., Newbury House.

Kerr, C. (1963). *The Uses of the University*. Cambridge, Mass., Harvard University Press.

Keys, W. and Ormerod, M. B. (1976). 'Some factors affecting pupils' subject preferences', Durham Research Review, 3, 36, 1109–1115.

Kogan, D. and Kogan, M. (1983). *The Attack on Higher Education*, London, Kogan Page.

Kolb, D. A. (1981). 'Learning styles and disciplinary differences', in Chickering, 1981: 232–255.

Krapf, E. E. (1955). 'The choice of language in polyglot analysis', *Psychonalytic Quarterly*, 24, 343–357.

Krashen, S. and Terrell, T. (1983). *The Natural Approach: language acquisition in the class-room*. Oxford, Pergamon-Alemany.

Krishnamurti (1970). *The Penguin Krishnamurti reader*. London, Penguin.

Kuhn, T. S. (2nd edn, enlarged) (1970). *The Structure of Scientific Revolutions*. University of Chicago Press.

Lacey, C. *et al.* (1973). Tutorial schools research project. Vol. 1, Teacher Socialization: The Post-graduate training year. University of Sussex, unpublished.

Lacey, C. (1977). *The Socialization of teachers*. London, Methuen.

Laing, R. D. (1961: 1971). *Self and Others*. London, Penguin.

Lawrence, G. (ed.) (1979). *Exploring individual and organizational boundaries: a Tavistock open-systems approach*. Chichester, Wiley.

Lawrence, G. and Robinson, P. (1975). *An innovation and its interpretation being a study of the development of syndicate methods in six Colleges of Education*. Tavistock Institute of Human Relations.

Lazarsfeld, P. F. and Theilens, W. Jr. (with a field report by Riesman, D.) (1977). *The academic mind. Social scientists in a time of crisis*. New York, Arno Press.

Lejeune, P. (1971). *L'autobiographie en France*. Paris, Armand Colin.

Lewin, K. (1961). 'Quasi-stationary social equilibria and the problem of permanent change', in Bennin, W. G. *et al.* (eds), *The Planning of Change*. New York, Holt, Rhinehart and Winston.

Lewis, D. G. (1972). 'Subject choice in the Sixth Form: a critical review of research', *Educational Research*, 15, 1: 21–27.

Lewis, I. (1984). *The Student Experience of Higher Education*. London, Croom Helm.

Littlewood, W. (1984). *Foreign and Second Language Learning*. Cambridge University Press.

Loveday, C. (1982). *The Sociolinguistics of learning and using a non-native language*. Oxford, Pergamon.

Lowe, W. (1971) Structuring the learning task', in Glock, 1971.

Ludwig, J. (1983). 'Attitudes and expectations: a profile of female and male students of College French, German and Spanish', *Modern Languages Journal*, 67, 3: 216–227.

McDonough, S. H. (1981). *Psychology in Foreign Language Teaching*. London, George Allen and Unwin.

McLaughlin, B. (1978). *Second Language Acquisition in Childhood*. Hillsdale, N.J., Lawrence Erlbaum Associates.

Mant, A. (1977). *The Rise and Fall of the British Manager*. London, Macmillan.

Marris, P. (1964). *The Experience of Higher Education*. London, RKP.

Marris, P. (1974: 1988). *Loss and Change*. London, RKP.

Marton, F., Hounsell, D. and Entwistle, N. (eds) (1984). *The Experience of Learning*. Edinburgh, Scottish Academic Press.

Mattinson, J. (1988), *Work, Love and Marriage; the impact of unemployment*. London, Duckworth.

Mattinson, J. and Sinclair, I. (1979). *Mate and Stalemate*. Oxford, Blackwell.
Matulis, A. (1977). *Language – a hope: an introduction to metaglossotherapy*. Detroit, National Research Institute for Psychoanalysis and Psychology.
Mead, G. H. (1934). *Mind, Self and Society*. Chicago University Press.
Meara, P. (1978). 'Schizophrenic symptoms in foreign language learners'. UEA Papers in Linguistics 7.
Medgyes, P. (1983). 'The schizophrenic teacher', *ELT Journal*, 37: January, 2–6.
Mehrotra, C. M. N. (ed.) (1984). *Teaching and Aging*. San Francisco, Jossey-Bass.
Miller, E. (1973). *Authority, leadership and organization in the Universities*. London, Tavistock Institute of Human Relations.
Miller, E. (1982). *Psychotherapists and the process of Profession Building*. London, OPUS.
Mills, C. W. (1959: 1983). *The Sociological Imagination*. London, Penguin.
Morley, R. (1975). 'Some observations and reflections upon cross-cultural marriages'. Unpublished IMS document, No. M 66.
Murphy, J. J. (1974). *Rhetoric in the Middle Ages*. Berkeley, University of California Press.
Naiman, N. *et al.* (1976). *The Good Language Learner*. Ontario, Ontario Institute for Studies in Education.
National Council for Modern Languages (1984). *Research and development needs in modern language teaching in higher education, special conference issue*. NCML Newsletter.
Norman, R. D. and Redlo, M. (1952). 'MMPI personality patterns for various college major groups', *Journal of Applied Psychology*, 36: 404–409.
Palmer, D. J. (1965). *The Rise of English Studies*. Oxford University Press.
Parlett, M. R. (1970). 'The Syllabus Bound Student', in Hudson, 1970.
Parlett, M. R. and Dearden, G. (eds) (1977). *Introduction to illuminative evaluation*. Cardiff by the sea, California, Pacific Soundings Press.
Parsons, T. (1971). 'The strange case of academic organization', *Journal of Higher Education*, 42, 6.
Peacocke, A. (1985). *Reductionism in Academic Disciplines*. London, SRHE.
Perkins, J. A. (1973). *The University as an Organization*. New York, McGraw-Hill.
Perry, W. G. Jr. (1981). 'Cognitive and ethical growth: the making of meaning', in Chickering, 1981: 76–116.
Petersen, A. D. C. (1960). 'The myth of subject-mindedness', *Universities Quarterly*, 14, 3.
Pines, M. (ed.) (1985). *Bion and group psychotherapy*. London, RKP.
Platt, J. (1981). 'On interviewing one's peers', *British Journal of Sociology*, 32: 75–91.
Powell, B. (1986). *Boys, girls and languages in school*, London, Centre for information on language teaching and research.
Pratt, J., Bloomfield, J. and Seale, C. (1984). *Option choice: a question of Equal Opportunity*. London, NFER-Nelson.
Printon, V. (ed.) (1986). *Facts and figures: Languages in Education*. London, CILT.
Reason, P. and Rowan, J. (1981). *Human enquiry, a sourcebook of new paradigm research*. Chichester, John Wiley and Sons.
Reinharz, S. (1979). *On becoming a social scientist*. San Francisco, Jossey-Bass.
Rice, A. K. (1970). *The Modern University: a model organization*. London, Tavistock.
Rivers, W. M. (1983). *Communicating naturally in a second language*. Cambridge University Press.
Roach, J. (1971). *Public Examinations in England, 1850–1900*. Cambridge University Press.
Roe, A. (1951). *A Psychological Study of Physical Scientists*. Genetic psychology monographs, 43, 2.
Roe, A. (1953). *A psychological study of eminent psychologists and anthropologists and a comparison*

with biological and physical scientists. Genetic psychology monographs, Vol. 63, No. 352.

Roizen, J. and Jepson, M. (1985). *Degrees for jobs: Employer expectations of higher education*. London, Nelson-SRHE.

Roszak, T. (ed.) (1969). *The Dissenting Academy*. London, Chatto and Windus.

Ryrie, A. C. *et al.* (1979). *Choices and chances: a study of pupils' subject choices and future career intentions*. London, Hodder and Stoughton.

Sanford, N. (ed.) (1956). 'Personality development during the College Years', *Journal of Social Issues*, 12, 4.

Sanford, N. (ed.) (1962). *The American College, a psychological and social interpretation of the higher learning*. New York, Wiley.

Sanford, N. (1982). 'Social psychology, its place in personology', *American Psychologist* 37, 8: 896–902.

Sartre, J.-P. (1957). *Being and Nothingness*. Trans. Hazel Barnes. London, Methuen.

Sartre, J.-P. (1964). *The problem of method*. Trans. Hazel Barnes. London, Methuen.

Schatzman, L. and Strauss, A. L. (1966). 'A Sociology of Psychiatry', *Social Problems*, 14, 1: 3–16.

Schumann, J. H. (1975). 'Affective factors and the problem of age in second language acquisition', *Language Learning*, 25: 2, 209–235.

Schwab, J. (1964). 'Structure of the disciplines: meanings and significances', in Golby, 1975.

Scott, J. M. (1973). *Dons and Students, British Universities Today*. London, Plume Press/Ward Lock.

Scott, P. (1984). *The Crisis of the University*. London, Croom Helm.

Shattock, M. (ed.) (1983). *The Structure and Governance of Higher Education*. Guildford, SRHE.

Sherif, M. and Sherif, C. W. (eds) (1969). *Interdisciplinary relationships in the Social Sciences*. Chicago, Aldine.

Sherwood, R. (1980). *The Psychodynamics of Race: Vicious and Benign Spirals*. Brighton, Harvester Press.

Skynner, R. (1976). *One Flesh: Separate Persons*. London, Constable.

Smalley, W. A. (1963). 'Culture Shock, Language Shock, and the Shock of Self-Discovery', *Practical Anthropology*, 10, 49–56.

Snyder, B. R. (1971). *The Hidden Curriculum*. Cambridge, Mass., MIT Press.

Spradley, J. (1980). *Participant Observation*. New York, Holt Rhinehart and Wilson.

Spradley, J. (1979). *The ethnographic interview*. New York, Holt, Rinehard and Wilson.

Stengel, E. (1939). 'On learning a new language', *International Journal of Psychoanalysis*, 20, 471–479.

Stenhouse, C. (1975). *An introduction to curriculum research and development*, London, Heinemann.

Stern, H. H. (1964a). 'Modern Languages in the Universities', *Modern Languages*, XLV, 3: 87–97.

Stern, H. H. (1964b). 'The future of modern languages in the Universities', *Modern Languages*, XLV, 3: 87–97.

Stern, H. H. (1983). *Fundamentals of Language Teaching*. Oxford University Press.

Sternberg, C. (1955). 'Personality trait patterns of College students majoring in different fields', *Psychological Monographs*, 69, 18.

Stevick, E. (1976). *Memory, Meaning, Method. Some psychological perspectives on language learning*. Rowley, Mass., Newbury House.

Stubbs, M. (1976: 1983). *Language Schools and Classrooms*. London, Methuen.

Sullivan, H. S. (1955). *The interpersonal theory of psychiatry, edited by Helen Smith Perry and Mary Ladd Gawel*. London, Tavistock.

Sullivan, W. A., (1983) in: Chrimes, S., *University College, Cardiff: a centenary history, 1883–1983*, 'French', 232–236.

Super, D. E. (1980) 'A theory of vocational development', *American psychologist*, 8, 185–190.

Swallow, T. (1986). 'Modern Languages in post-16 Education: a Midlands Survey of preferences and expectations of students', *British Journal of Language Teaching*, 24, 1: 5–25.

Taylor, J. (1986). 'The employability of graduates: differences between Universities', *Studies in Higher Education*, 11, 1: 17–27.

Teevan, R. C. (1954). 'Personality correlates of undergraduate field of specialization', *Journal Consult. Psychology* 18: 212–214.

Thomas, G. and King, A. (1986). 'Modern Languages in higher education', in Printon, 1986: 62–72.

Trim, J. (1985). 'Language needs and social policy', in *Second Language Learning: research problems and perspectives*. London, CILT.

Truscot, B. (1945: 1951). *Red Brick University*. London, Penguin.

Tucker, G. R., Hamayan, E. and Geresee, F. H. (1976). 'Affective, cognitive and social factors in second language acquisition', *Canadian Modern Languages Review*, 32, 3: 214–226.

Turquet, P. M. (1975). 'Threats to identity in the large group', in L. Kreeger (ed.), *The Large Group*. London, Constable, 87–144.

Vickers, B. (ed.) (1982). *Rhetoric revalued*. New York, Center for Medieval and Early Renaissance Studies.

Watson, F. W. (1909). *The beginning of the teaching of modern subjects in England*. London, Pitman.

Watzlawick, P. *et al.* (1974). *Change: Principles of problem formation and problem resolution*. New York, Norton.

Weathersby, R. P. (1981). 'Ego development', in Chickering, 1981: 41–75.

Weinreich-Haste, H. (1981). 'The image of Science', in Kelly, 1981: 216–229.

Weinreich-Haste, H. (1984). 'The values and aspirations of English women undergraduates', in Acker and Piper, 1984.

Wenger, M. G. (1976). 'The case of academia: Demythologization of a non-profession', in Gerstl, J. and Jacobs, G. (eds), *Professions for the people, the politics of skill*, Cambridge, Mass., Shenckman.

Wilden, A. (1972: 1977). *System and structure: Essays in communication and exchange*. London, Tavistock.

Williams, R. (1961: 1965). *The Long Revolution*. London, Penguin.

Willis, F., Doble, G., Sankaraya, U. and Smithers, A. (1977). *Residence abroad and the student of modern languages*. Bradford, University of Bradford.

Winnicott, O. W. (1974) *Playing and Reality*. London, Penguin.

Woods, P. (1986). *Inside Schools: Ethnography in schools*. London, Routledge.

Young, MFD (1971). *Knowledge and control: New directions for the sociology of education*. London, Collier Macmillian.

and last but not least,

Zeldner, M. (1963). 'The bewildered Modern Language Teacher', *Modern Language Journal* (USA), XLVII, 6: 245–253.

Index

The Society for Research into Higher Education

The Society exists both to encourage and co-ordinate research and development into all aspects of Higher Education, including academic, organizational and policy issues; and also to provide a forum for debate, verbal and printed. Through its activities, it draws attention to the significance of research into, and development in, Higher Education and to the needs of scholars in this field. (It is not concerned with research generally, except, for instance, as a subject of study.)

The Society's income derives from subscriptions, book sales, conferences and specific grants. It is wholly independent. Its corporate members are institutions of higher education, research institutions and professional, industrial, and governmental bodies. Its individual members include teachers and researchers, administrators and students. Members are found in all parts of the world and the Society regards its international work as amongst its most important activities.

The Society discusses and comments on policy, organizes conferences and encourages research. Under the Imprint SRHE & OPEN UNIVERSITY PRESS, it is a specialist publisher, having some 40 titles in print. It also publishes *Studies in Higher Education* (three times a year) which is mainly concerned with academic issues, *Higher Education Quarterly* (formerly *Universities Quarterly*) which will be mainly concerned with policy issues, *Research into Higher Education Abstracts* (three times a year), and a *Bulletin* (six times a year).

The Society's committees, study groups and branches are run by members (with help from a small staff at Guildford), and aim to provide a form for discussion. The groups at present include a Teacher Education Study Group, a Staff Development Group, a Women in Higher Education Group and a Continuing Education Group which may have had their own organization, subscriptions or publications; (eg the *Staff Development Newsletter*). The Governing Council, elected by members, comments on current issues; and discusses policies with leading figures, notably at its evening Forums. The Society organizes seminars on current research for officials of DES and other ministries, an Anglo-American series on standards, and is in touch with bodies in the UK such as the NAB, CVCP, UGC, CNAA and the British Council, and with sister-bodies overseas. Its current research projects include one on the relationship between entry qualifications and degree results, directed by Prof. W. D. Furneaux (Brunel) and one on questions of quality directed by Prof. G. C. Moodie (York). A project on the evaluation of the research standing of university departments is in preparation. The Society's conferences are often held jointly. Annual Conferences have considered 'Professional Education' (1984), 'Continuing Education' (1985, with Goldsmiths' College) 'Standards and Citeria in Higher Education' (1986, with Bulmershe CHE), 'Restructuring' (1987, with the City of Birmingham Polytechnic) and 'Academic Freedom' (1988, the University of Surrey). Other conferences have considered the DES 'Green Paper' (1985, with the Times Higher Education Supplement), and 'The First-Year Experience' (1986, with the University of South Carolina and Newcastle Polytechnic). For some of the Society's conferences, special studies are commissioned in advance, as 'Precedings'.

Members receive free of charge the Society's *Abstracts*, annual conference Proceedings (or 'Precedings'), *Bulletin and International Newsletter* and may buy SRHE & OPEN UNIVERSITY PRESS books at booksellers' discount. Corporate members also receive the Society's journal *Studies in Higher Education* free (individuals at a heavy discount). They may also obtain *Evaluation Newsletter* and certain other journals at a discount, including the NFER *Register of Educational Research*. There is a substantial discount to members, and to staff of corporate members, on annual and some other conference fees.